Wildlife

in

Persimmon Paradise

ISBN-13: 978-0-9994538-6-5

ISBN-10: 0-9994538-6-6

First Printing, December, 2018

Published by:

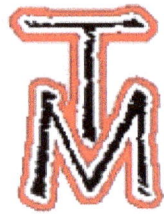

ThomasMax Publishing
P.O. Box 250054
Atlanta, GA 30325
thomasmax.com

Wildlife in Persimmon Paradise

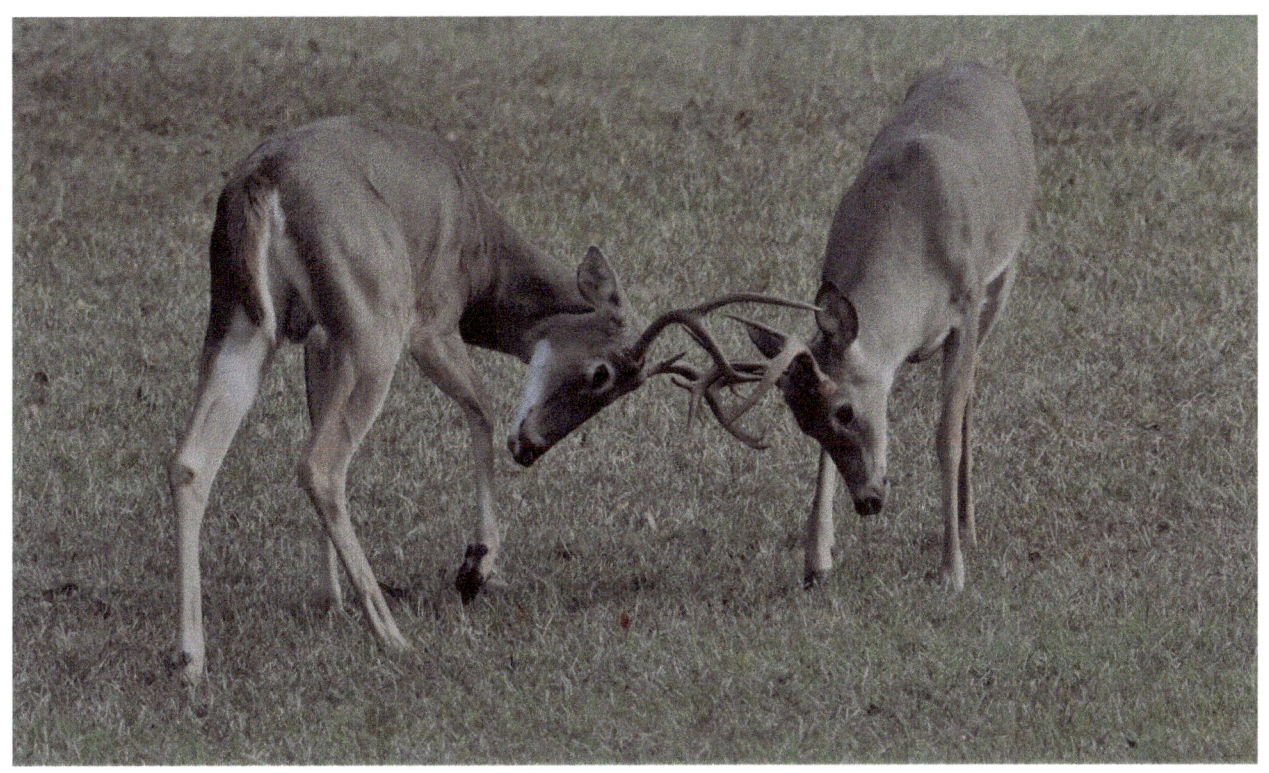

Susan Lindsley

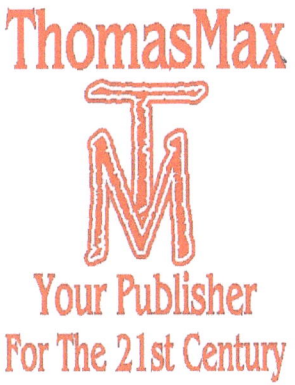

ThomasMax

Your Publisher
For The 21st Century

Praise for *Wildlife in Persimmon Paradise*

"There is no better way of understanding wildlife than living with it and that is what Susan Lindsley has done." -- Dr. Leonard Lee Rue III, Naturalist, Wildlife Photographer, Author www.ruewildlifephotos.com.

"If you enjoy watching wildlife, you'll love this outstanding array of Susan Lindsley's photos. As a wildlife photographer myself, I can tell you that finding a special place to get good pictures of deer, turkeys and other wild critters in good light is always a challenge. Susan has found that unique one-in-a-million-spot under her magical persimmon trees." -- Duncan Dobie, Wildlife photographer and first-place award winning author from the Georgia Outdoor Writers Association

"In the spirit of the greatest outdoor writer and photographer of our time, Leonard Lee Rue III, Susan shares a part of her life through the lens of her camera capturing some of the most incredible wildlife photographs taken right outside her back door. Susan is also one of the finest outdoor scribes to ever set the pen to parchment! Her experience as a hunter and knowledge of the outdoors allows her to share her outdoor wisdom and prowess in her own genuine and unique way. Anyone who loves the outdoors will fall in love with Susan and all of her books. Especially this one!" -- H. J. Thiel - Mossy Oak Pro-Staff, Award Winning Freelance Outdoor Writer, Photographer and Outdoor Television Personality

"Many wildlife photographers travel the globe to do what Susan Lindsley did literally in her own backyard, that is, combine food and water for the animals with bright lights and a good camera. The result? A rollicking exhibition of Georgia wildlife at its finest. These animals, from the smallest of birds to *Big Ten*, a specimen ten-point buck, are full of surprises, whimsy, and merriment. An educational, close-up taste of what most of us never have the privilege to observe in our backyards." -- Jameson Gregg, Georgia Author of the Year, Author of *Luck Be A Chicken*

"Susan Lindsley's love and years of devotion to preservation are shared with us through these unique images of autumn wildlife. A book you will enjoy again and again." -- Doug Dahlgren, Author, radio talk-show host

For Wayne Barnes

Chuck Beaty,

who turned on the lights,

and Norman Simpson,

my first hunting buddy

Other Books by Susan Lindsley

Novels, Southern historical
    The Bottom Rail
    When Darkness Fell

Memoirs
    Blue Jeans and Pantaloons in YESTERPLACE
    Possum Cops, Poachers and the Counterfeit Game Warden

Biography
    Susan Myrick of Gone With the Wind
    The Lindsleys of Westover

Collections of others' works edited
    Myrick Memories
    Margaret Mitchell: A Scarlett or a Melanie?
    Luther Lindsley: His Literary Works

Poetry
    O Yesterplace and other poems (out of print)
    Christmas Gift

Short Story collections
    Emperor of the United American States (out of print)
    Whitetails and Tall Tales

TABLE OF CONTENTS

Acknowledgments

First and foremost I would like to thank Lee Clevenger and Preston Ward for accepting this manuscript as the fourth book of mine to be published by ThomasMax Publishing that is not a self-published book. The fifth such book is due out the summer of 2019 and will my fifteenth book with ThomasMax Publishing.

I also thank the photographers and authors who reviewed and praised my book. They advised me on a variety of matters and provided unlimited moral support.

Thanks are also due Pat Blanks, my buddy from childhood, who is my first reader and tough critic.

And of course I thank Gail Cabisius, my life partner, for her constant and unconditional support.

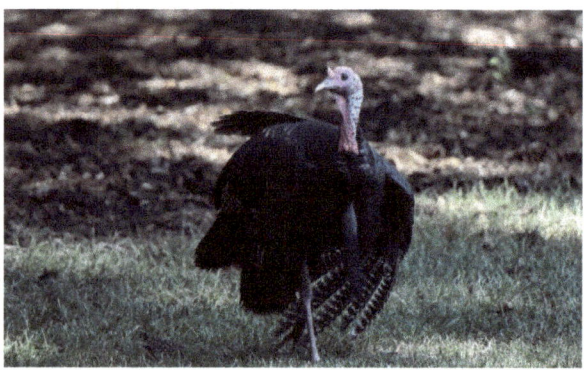 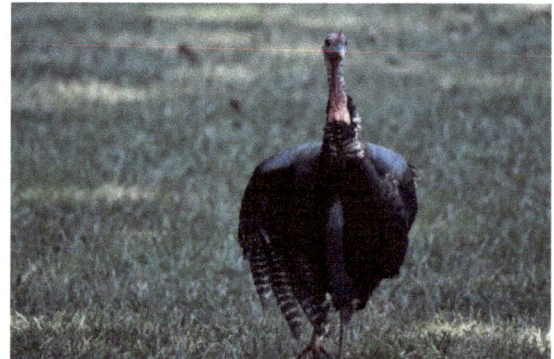

INTRODUCTION

I was reared in the country but spent several years gadding about in big cities. It wasn't long, however, before I returned to the country, where I had hunted raccoons and possums in my youth. One deer hunt and an acute case of buck fever turned me into an avid lover of deer and only increased my already deep love of the farmland.

After I retired, I built a second residence on my land, in the midst of oaks and persimmon trees. I could look out my kitchen window and see deer browse on honeysuckle and muscadine vines, seek acorns under the various varieties of oaks, and race each other to the persimmon trees.

I planted daffodils every fall, and scattered azaleas under the dogwoods that whitened the hardwoods every spring. Deer quickly did in the azaleas, but ignored the daffodils. Spider lilies also survived.

But I took a chance on a pool because I wanted water lilies, which we had had in my childhood in the family farm pond. I had no idea what would result from that decision.

I had a hole dug in the yard, and lined it with a waterproofing sheet that I spread outside the hole to prevent unwanted weeds and grass from encroaching. I pushed in the plastic landscaping pool, had a pipe run to it and filled it with water. I lined the edge of the waterproofing with brick from my old high school building just torn down. Inside the circle, I weighted the sheeting with pea stones.

Off I went for the water lilies. One of the four already bore a bud. When I arose the next morning, however, the blossom was gone and so were the plants. The whitetail deer love them.

I did not replant the lilies. The pool became a watering hole for every critter in the neighborhood, from chipmunks to the deer.

I had two 1000-watt lights placed on the north end of the house and would often scatter corn on the ground. If the lights were on, the deer know they could come into the yard for a snack. One evening, we had the lights on for an outside project and one of the men said, "Look." About twenty pairs of eyes glowed as the deer waited for us to get out of the way. So we fed them as soon as we finished our project. Thereafter, I obtained an automatic feeder and programmed it to dispense about a quart of corn twice a day.

The lights *broke down* after a few years, and in 2018, two friends and hunters, Chuck and Wayne, repaired the wiring and replaced burned-out bulbs—and danced to the tune of the 220-volt system.

That same summer, I planned a trip to "hunt" elk with my camera and purchased a new Nikon D7200 24.5-megapixel camera and an 80-to-400 mm vibration-stabilizing lens. I needed to try both out before going after the elk. So I tried out the camera and lens on an old tripod at my farm.

This book is the result of three August days and sixteen September days of shooting wildlife through the kitchen window. I have not edited or enhanced any of the pictures except to crop them to fit the pages. Sunlight, night shadows and colors are as I saw them.

When I hunted for meat, I usually could manage about three hours in a blind or stand. I surprised myself with my unending patience with the camera. But I was sitting inside, in A/C comfort rather than the unusual heat of autumn or freezing cold of deer season. I could make a pit stop or have a snack. So I sat by the kitchen window daily, from 6:30 a.m. until 10:00 or so each morning and again in the afternoon from 3:30 until nearly or even after midnight. Those 1000-watt lights illuminated the back yard for about one-hundred yards.

I soon learned I had to be ready if I were to capture some special memory, and had to keep my trigger finger on the shutter release constantly. I have been amazed at how contrast and color vary under the various lighting conditions: Sunlight, cloud cover, and artificial light in daylight and at night. Exposure in *RAW* format (a Nikon format) might have made a difference.

I took more than ten thousand pictures and culled these from the best and the most interesting. Some of the most interesting, however, are strange or maybe a bit blurry because the speed of action at times was too fast for the camera to freeze the image.

THE PERSIMMON TREES

In the fall, raccoons, possums (yes, us country folk leave off the "o") and fox enter the yard from the direction of one of the persimmon trees. The deer might stop to browse under the oaks, but if they are not alone they race their traveling companions for the persimmons. Nothing in the wild can compare with the flavor of a ripe persimmon. Nor can any sweet wine compete with homemade persimmon wine. I've never seen a tipsy deer, but then the persimmons don't stay on the ground long enough to ferment.

Some of the trees are close enough for photographs, some were shrouded in shadows and others were either too far away or hidden by other growth for photographs.

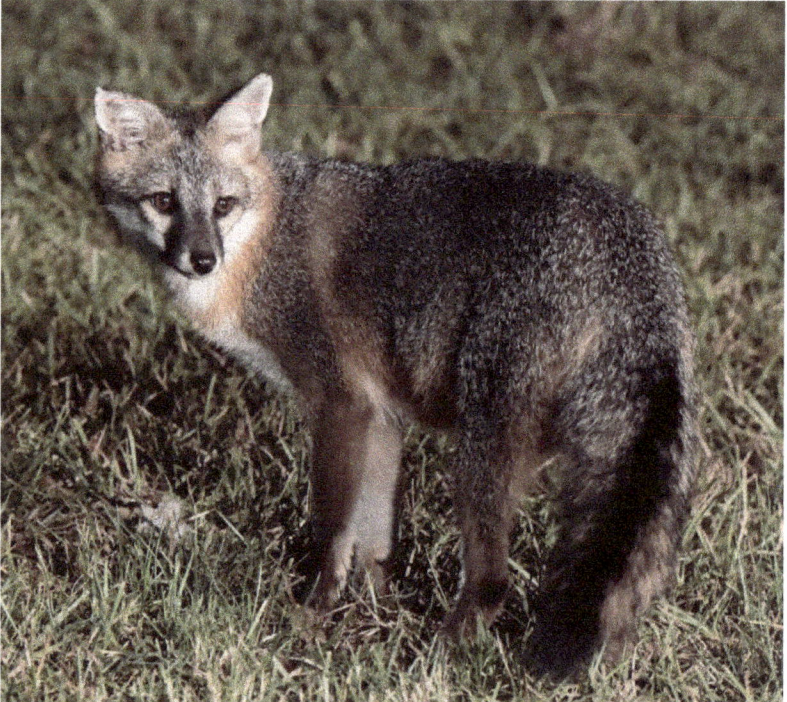

**The vixen seldom came far into the yard from the western persimmon tree.
She usually fed under one and headed for another.**

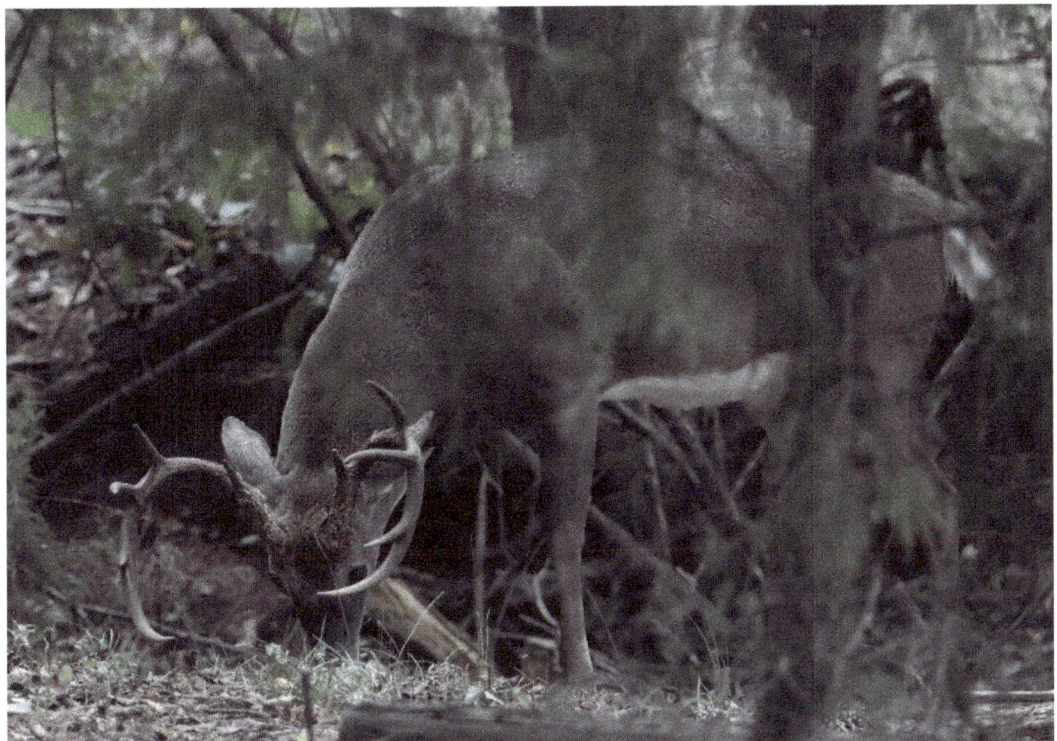

This buck, which I named *Big Ten*, is feeding on persimmons.

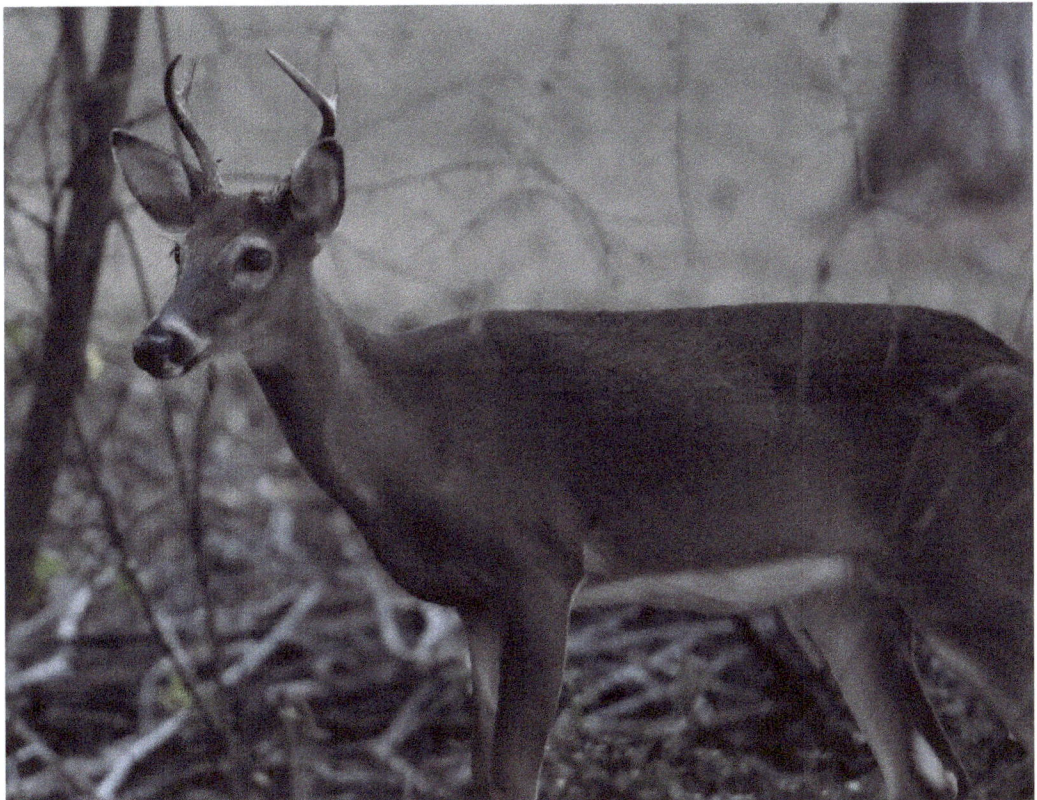

This youngster spotted something that pulled his attention away from the persimmons.

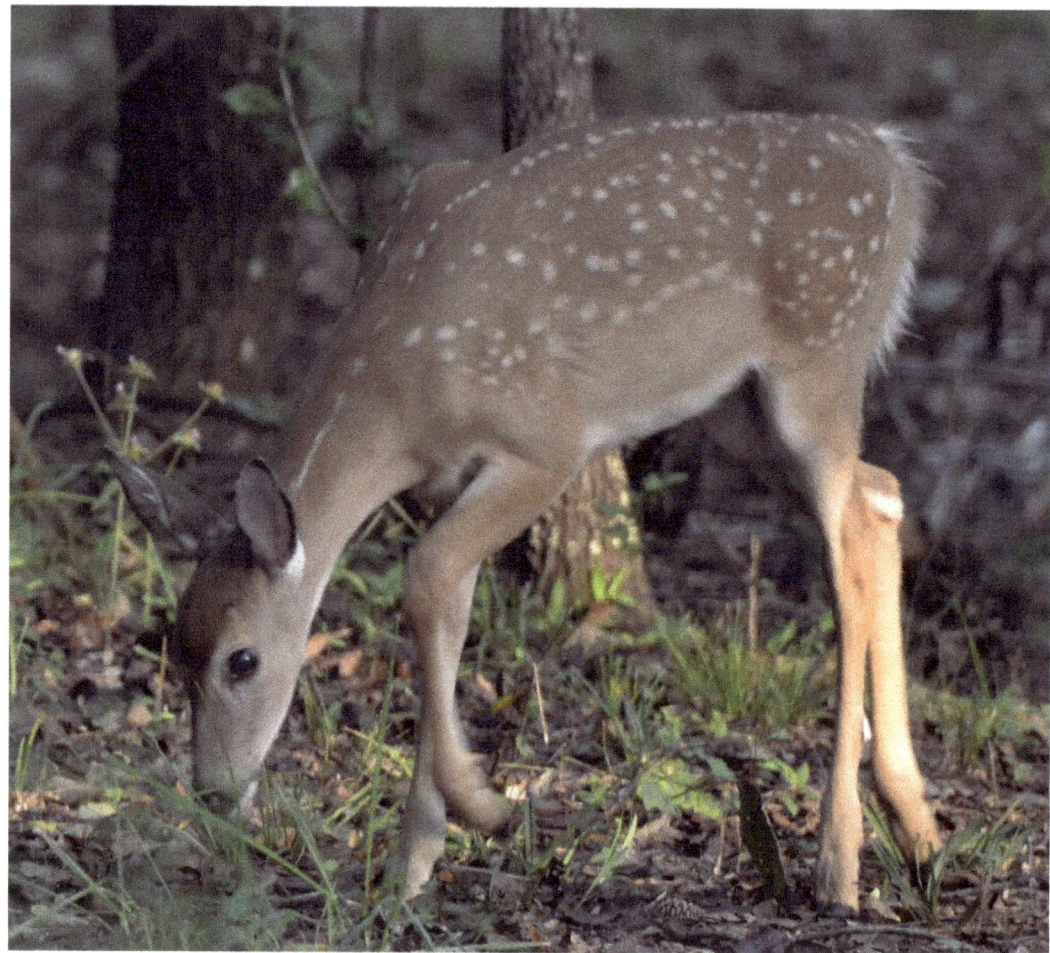

The button buck is searching for persimmons. They learn early on to love the taste.

The persimmon seed is said to predict the coming winter if it is split. If the image is a spoon, expect a lot of snow. If a fork, expect a mild winter, maybe light snow. A knife means the winter will be cold with cutting winds.

Whatever the weather, all critters love the persimmons and it is an autumn staple for many, especially deer, raccoon, fox and coyotes.

Hunters, if you come upon raccoon, coyote or fox scat, poke around for persimmon seeds and scatter them about in the woods you hunt and love. You will feed animals for generations to come. Just take a small plastic Ziplock bag and paper towels with you on your hunt. The seeds must be striated to germinate, and the gut of these critters will do the job.

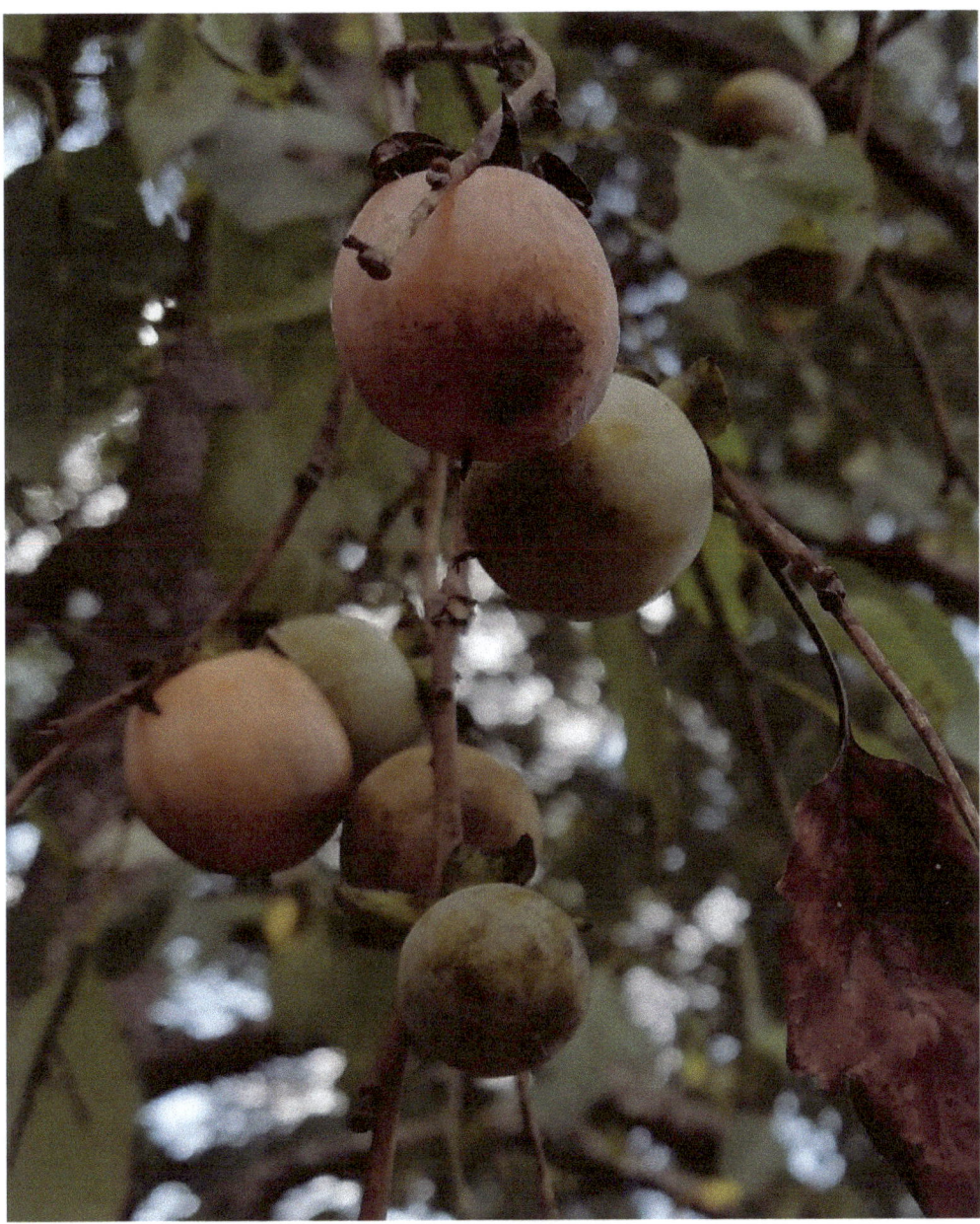

Persimmons at various stages of ripeness in late September in middle Georgia. Although animals eat them half-ripe, if you should eat one before frost (or before it is soft and ripe), you will feel that your mouth has turned inside out.

THE POOL

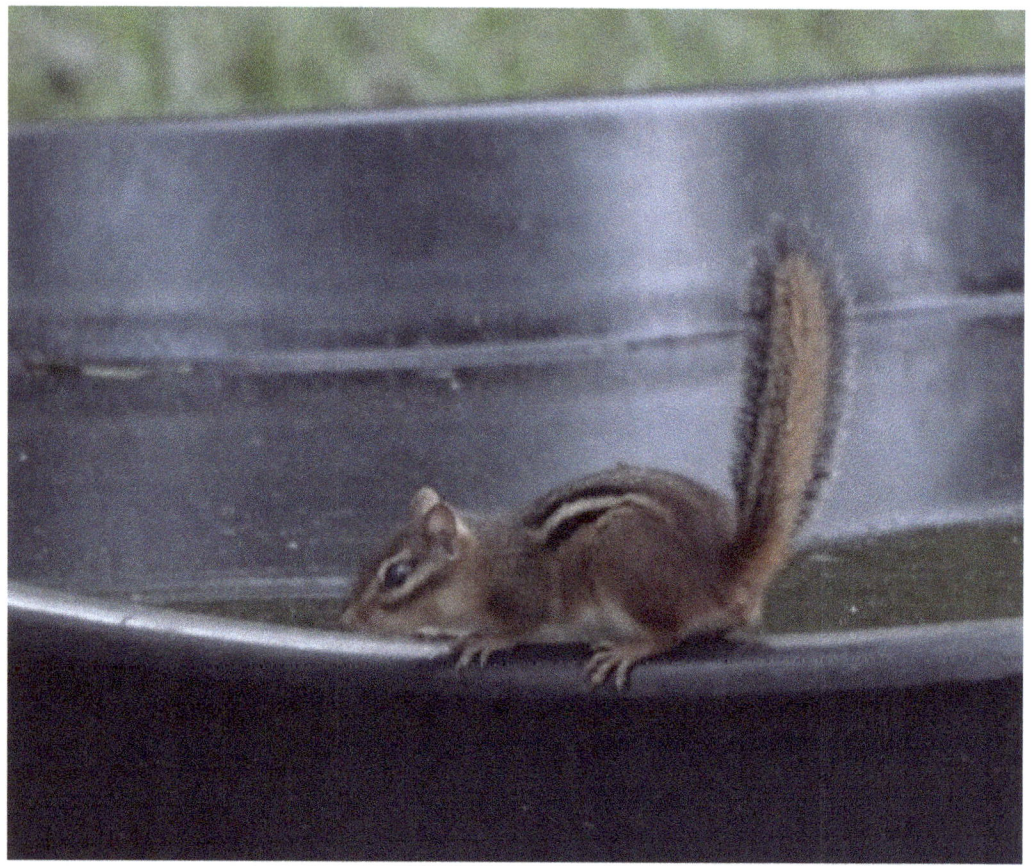

The chipmunk had a tough time getting up on the edge to reach the water, so after a few days, I pulled up some of the brick I had used as a border around the pool—the deer had already scattered a number of them—and made a brick staircase at one end.

Deer didn't like the stepping stones. Something looked different, and the something must have smelled like my human hands. Those who approached from that side would extend their noses, sniff, nod their frustration, and back away.

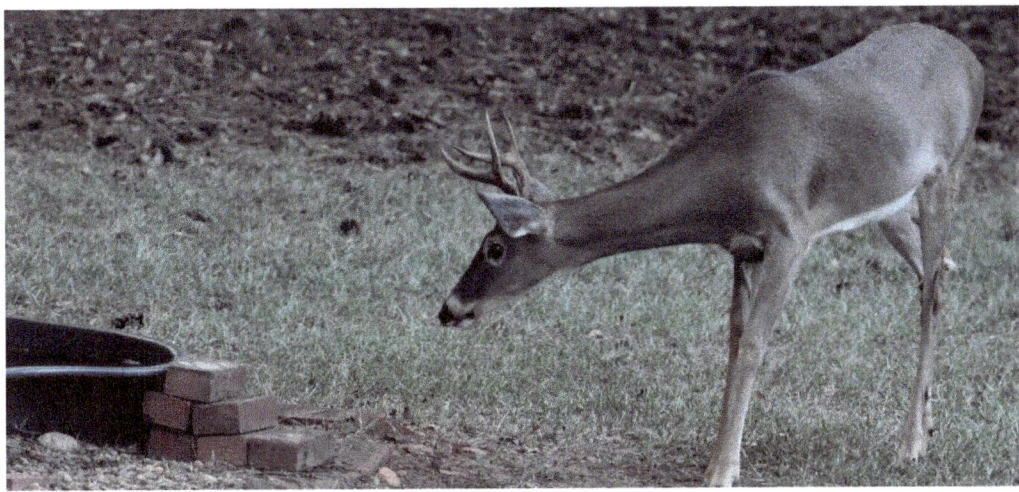

The doves didn't care whether or not they had a staircase. They perched on the edge, enjoyed their refreshments and cooled down before they took off to other lands.

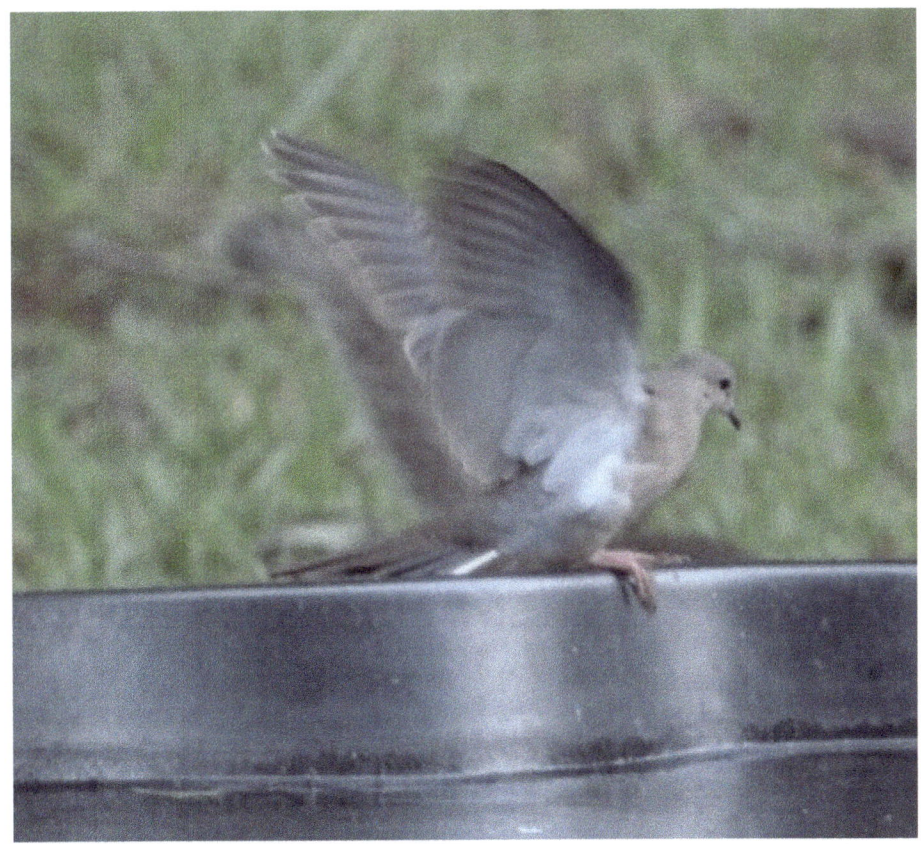

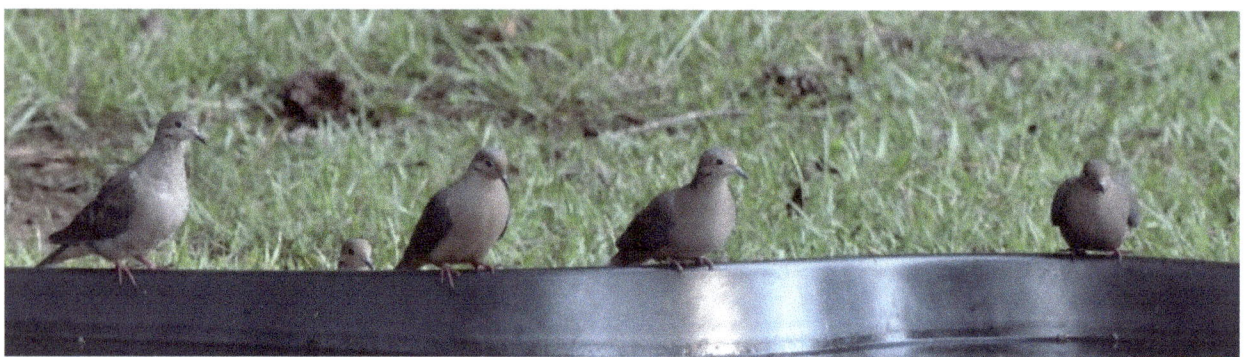

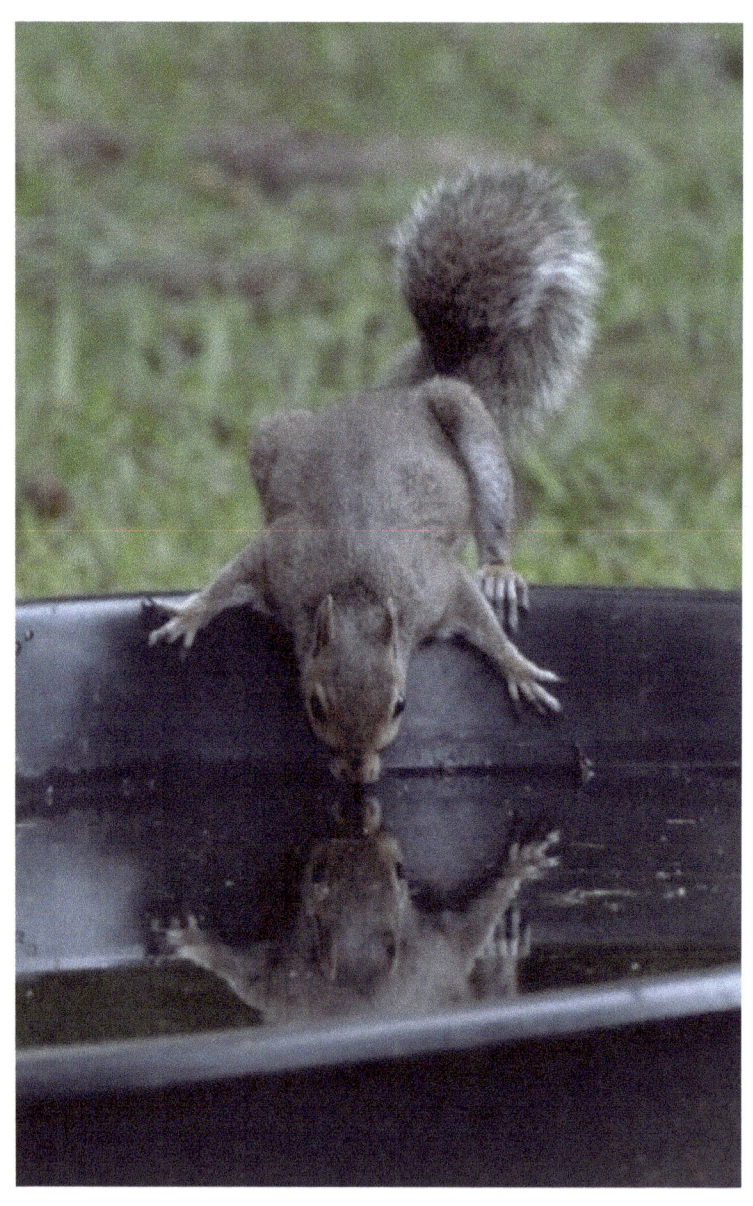

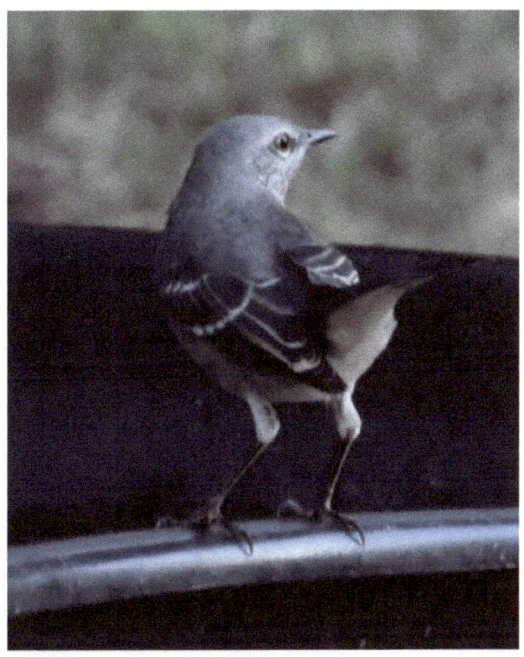

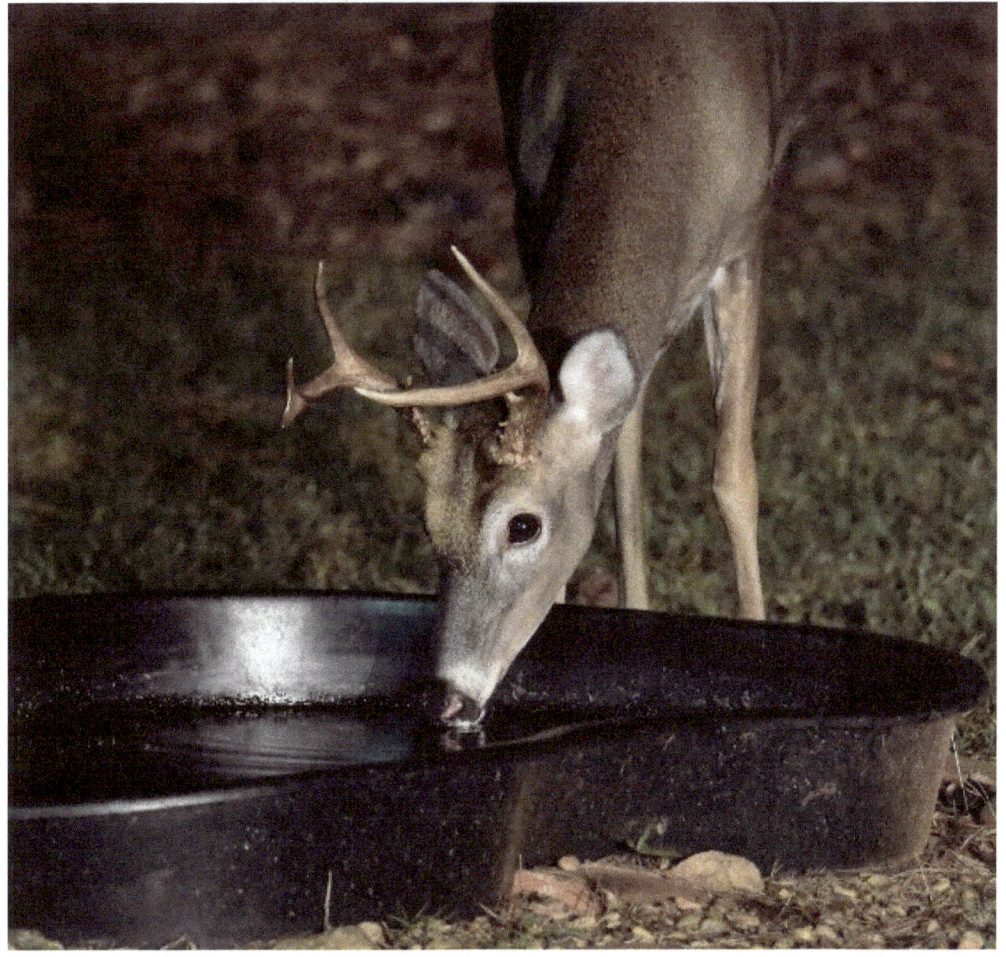

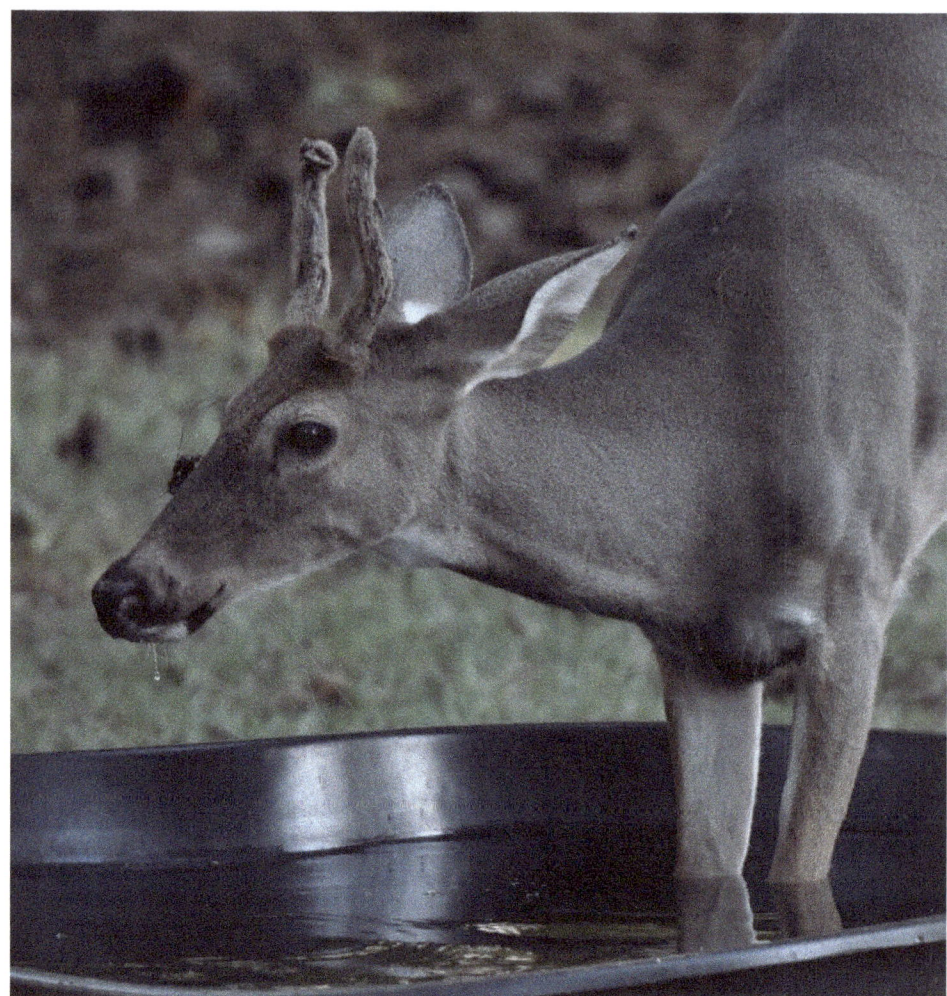

He should have ducked his head to get rid of his visitor.

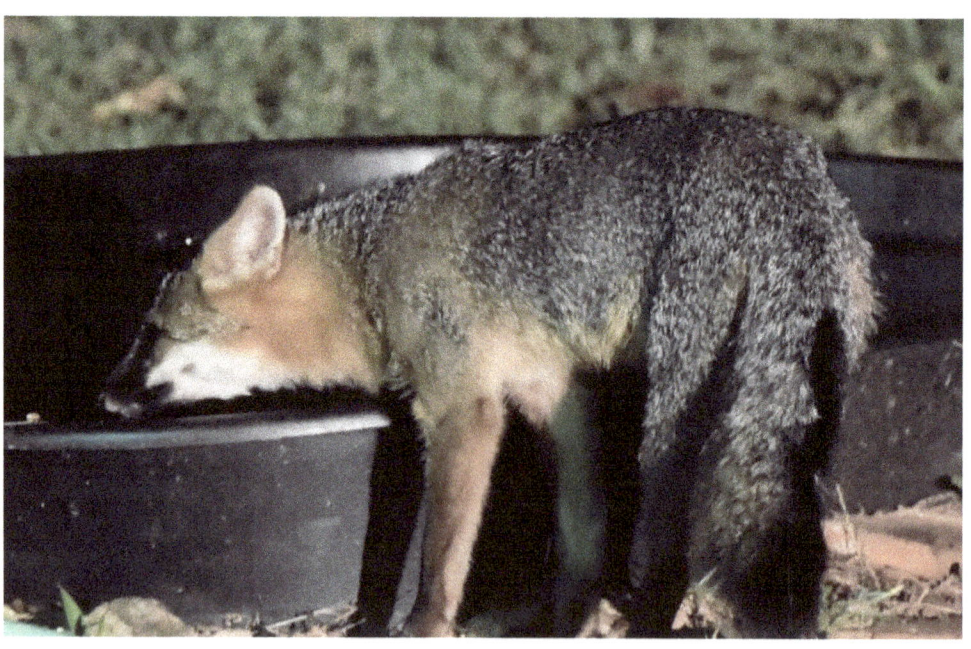

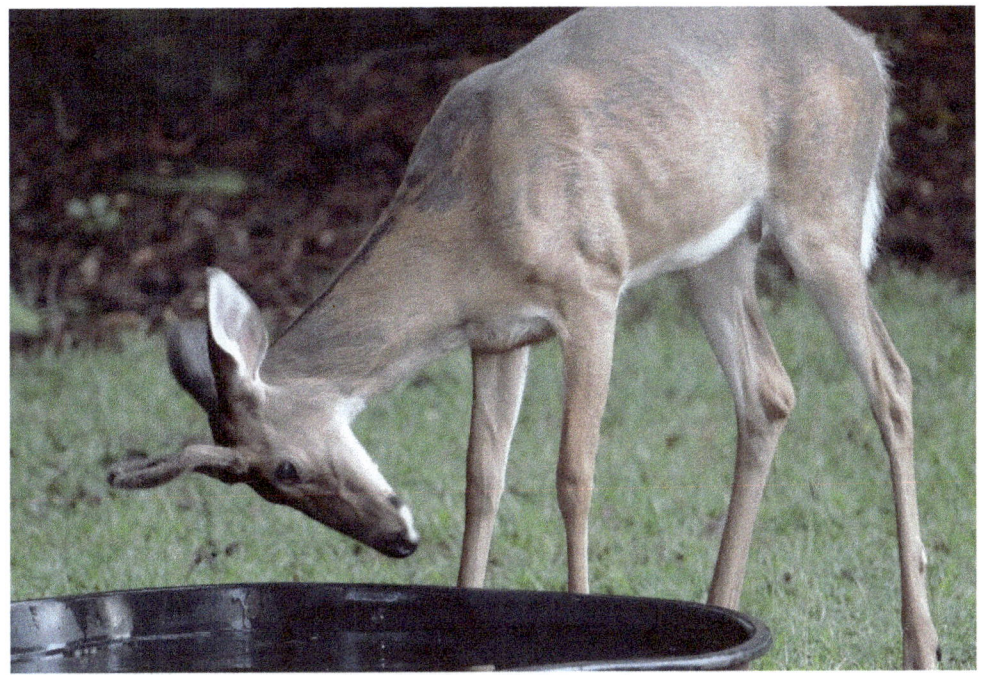

I wonder if this fella was seeing his reflection.

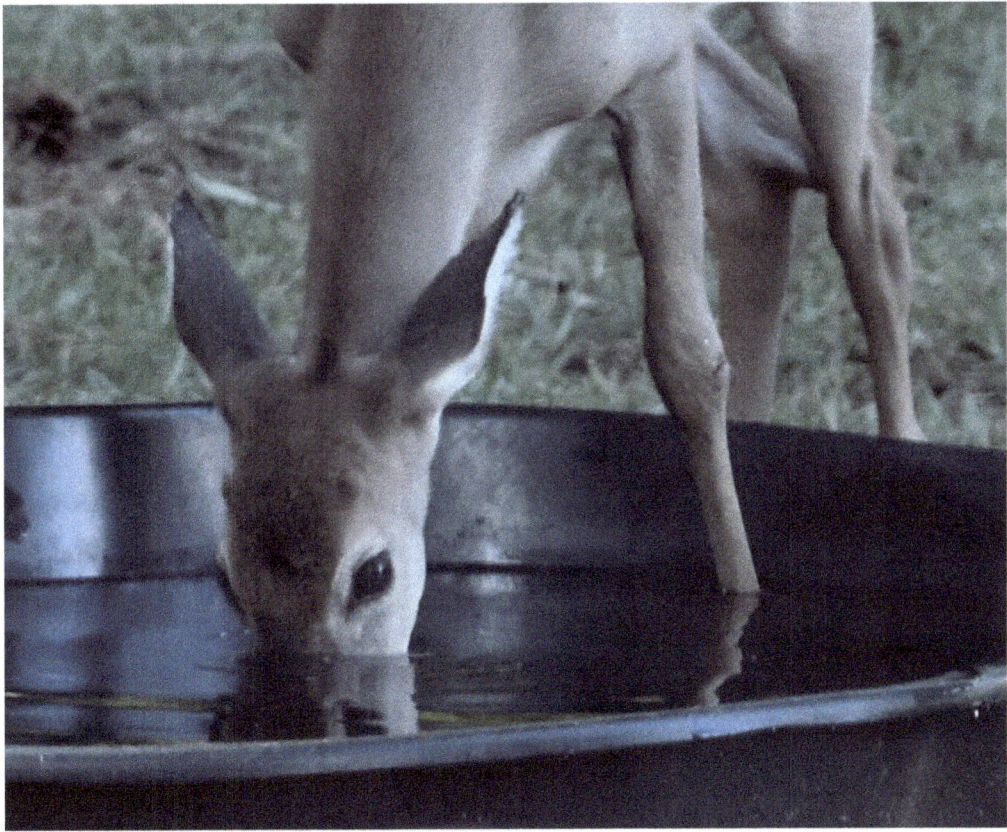

This button buck played moose and pulled up yucky stuff from underwater.

RACCOONS

Raccoons are always fun to watch. This mama and twins visited the pool and then set about to scratch around for corn.

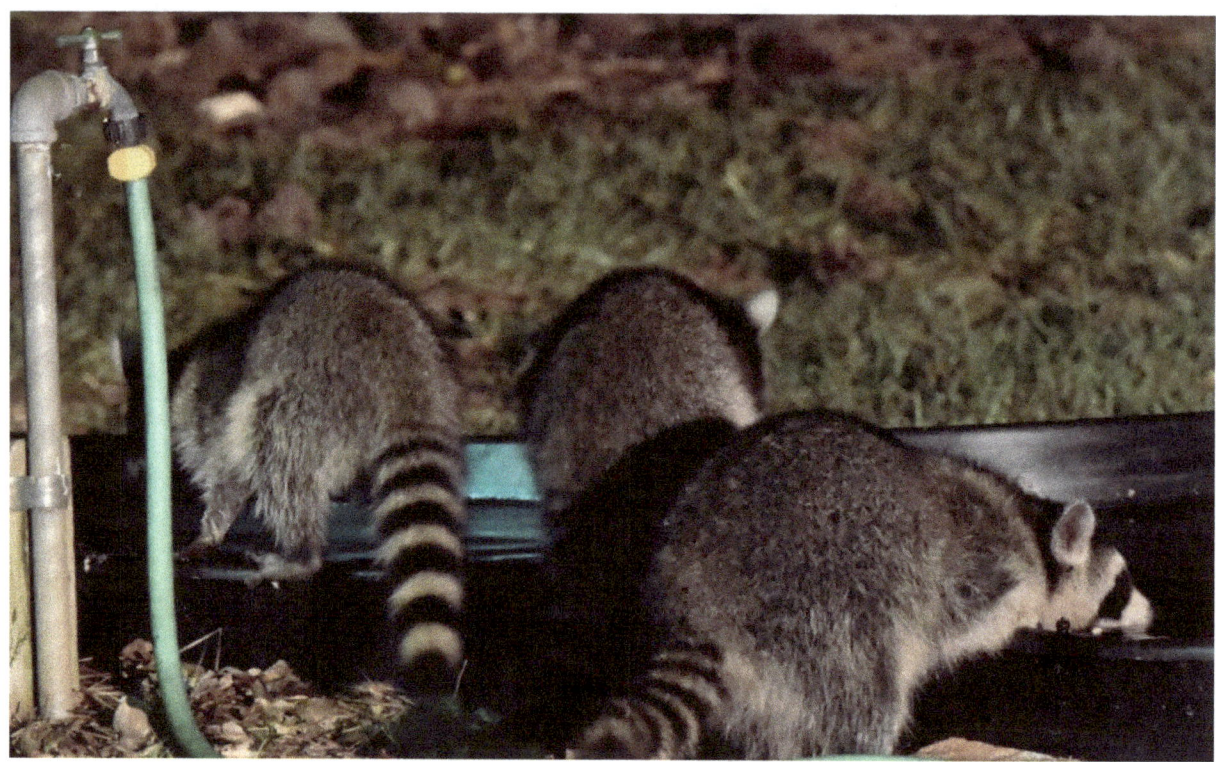

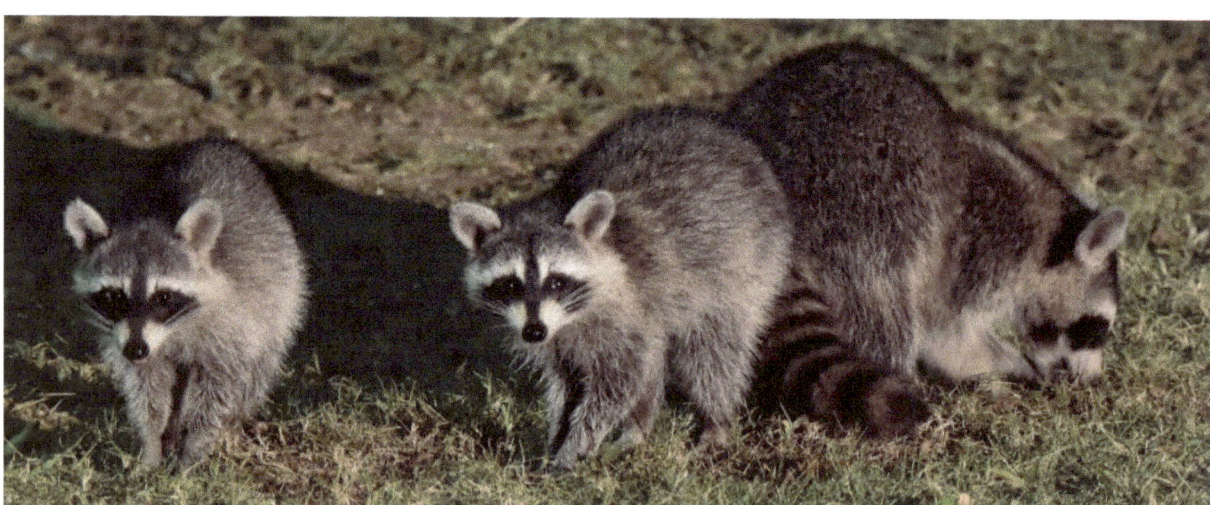

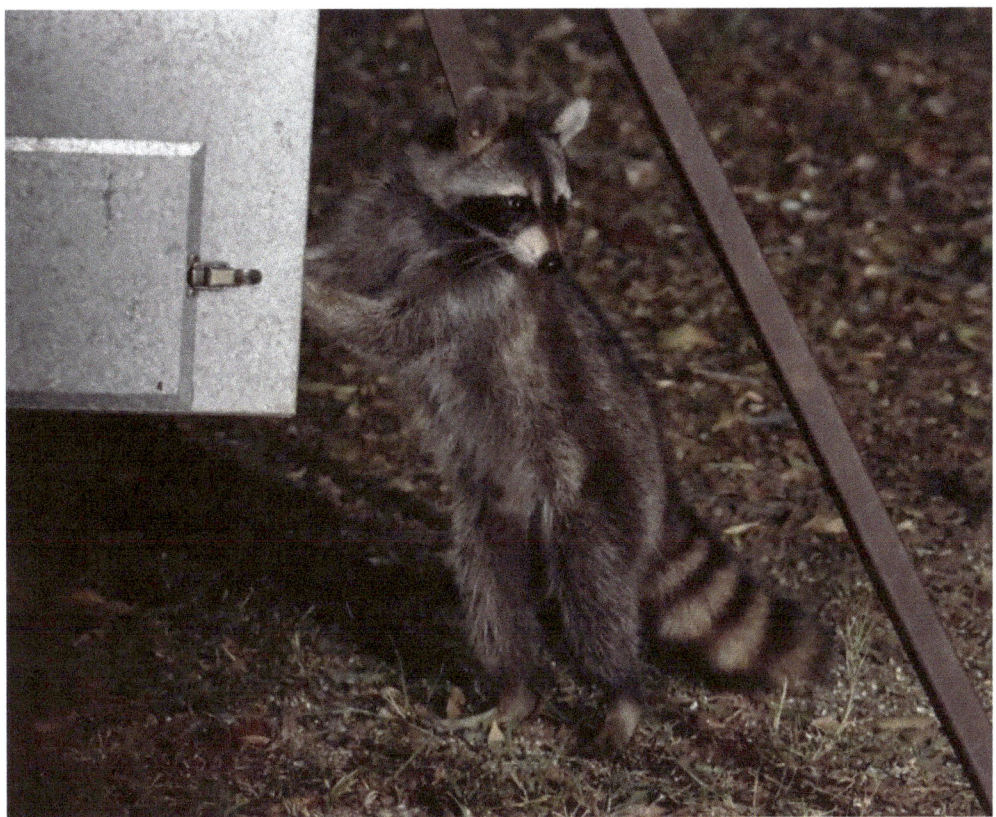

The big boy swept some corn from the feeder before he began to
scrounge around for what the deer and birds left behind.

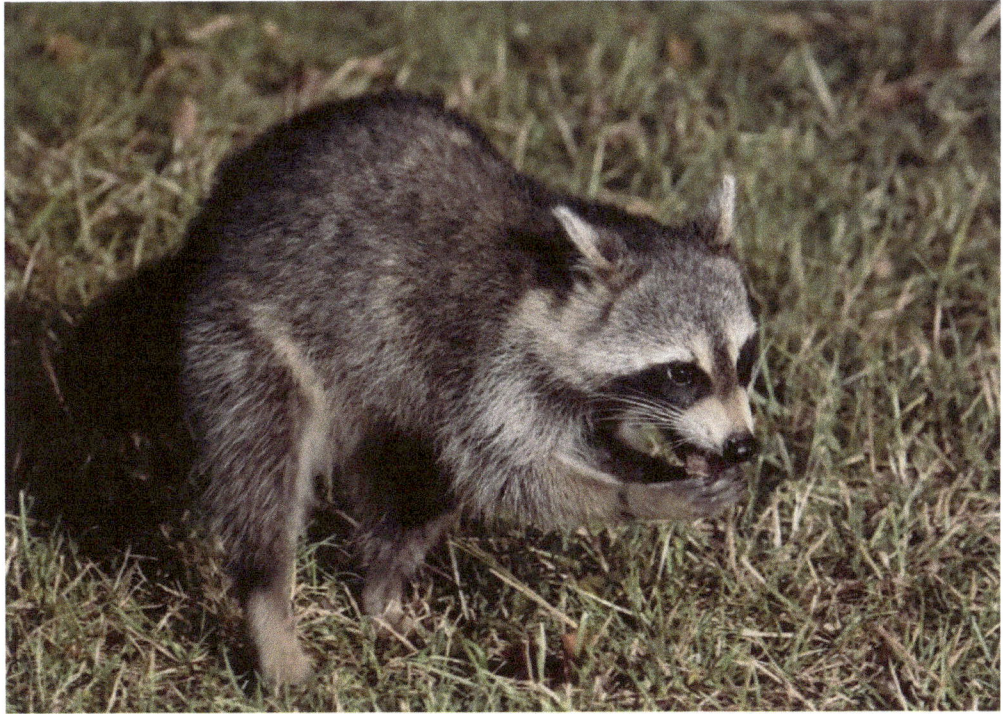

He raided the foxes' food and snacked on a piece of dry, cooked bacon.

GRAY FOXES
Elusive, Sly and Beautiful

Years ago, a fox trotted through the yard and I lured it back with a bowl of dry cat food. The first night, the fox ate the food, but the next night, he struggled and managed to lift the bowl.

Unfortunately for him, he tilted the bowl and left a trail of food across the yard; he left the bowl in the woods and I found it three years later. Cat food tempted him again the September of this camera shoot.

One night he and the vixen trotted around the yard among the deer as if trying to get to the food. Every time a deer lifted its head, the pair ran off. They did not slow down enough for the camera to stop movement, but the evening was exciting with the foxes spooking the fawns and the older deer spooking the foxes. Morning found the food untouched.

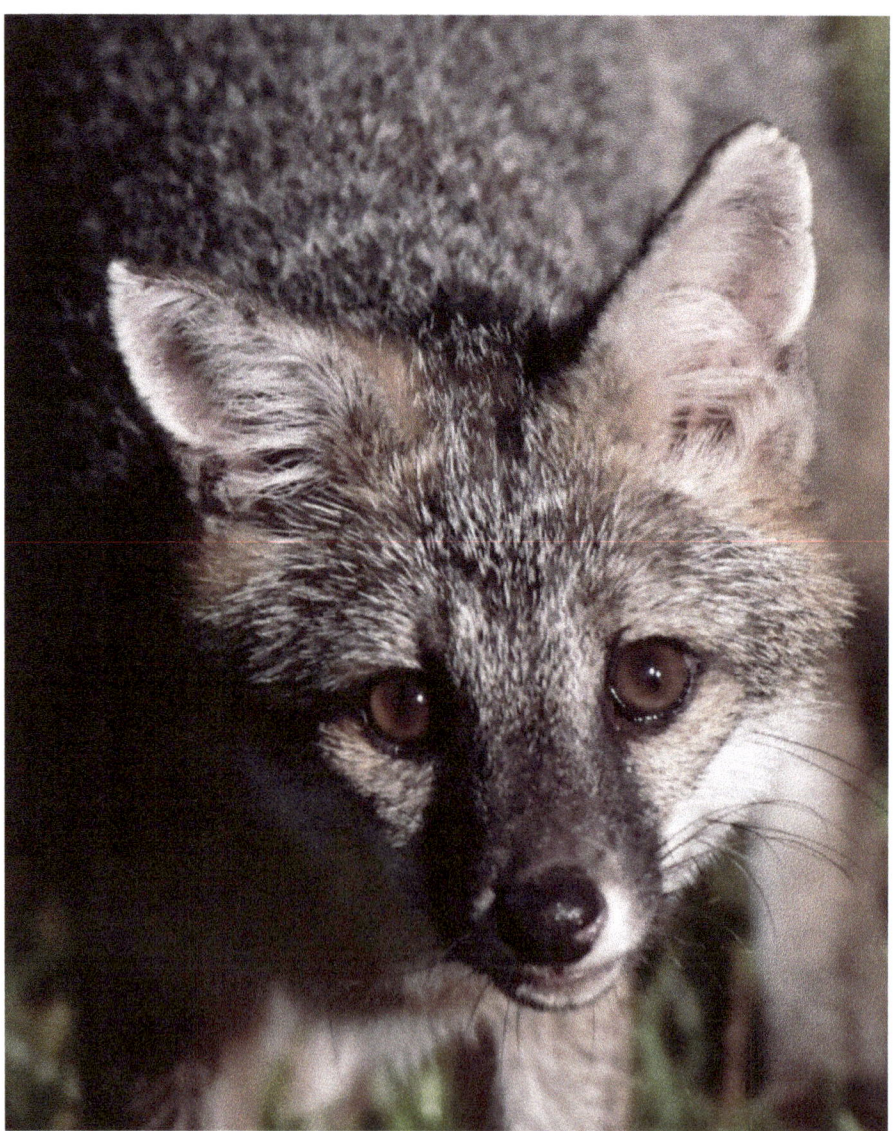

The male caught a glimpse of my camera lens and stared at the window.

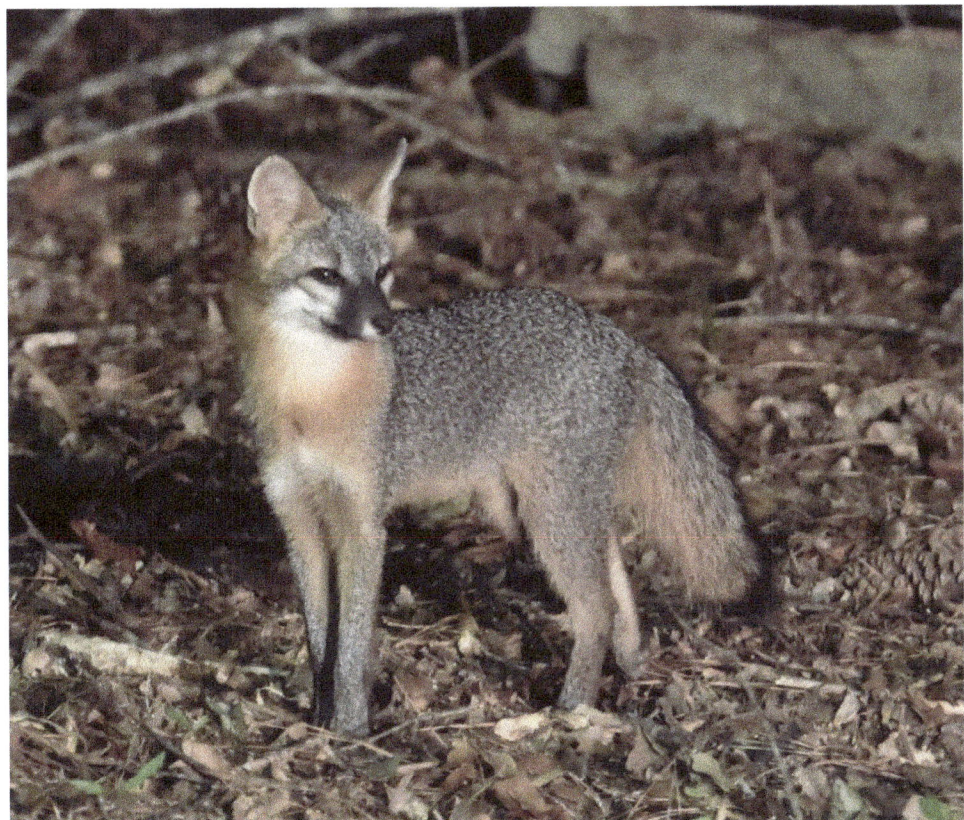

The vixen

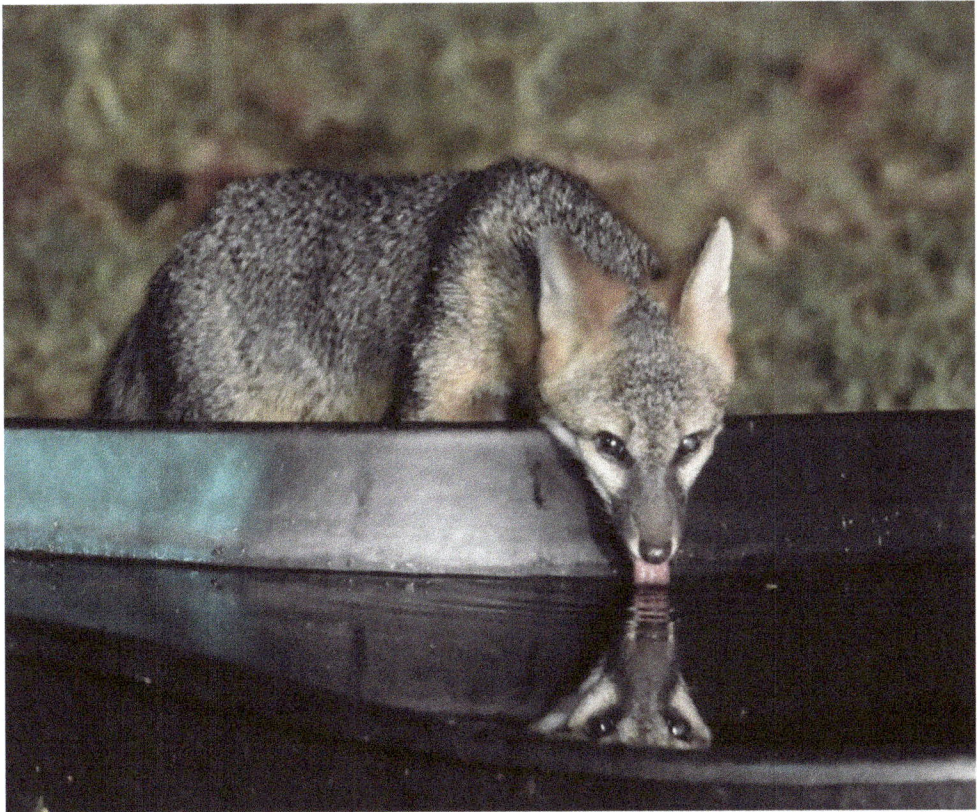

The vixen stopped in for a drink one night and reflected in the water.

A fox, I thought the vixen, urinated in the yard, and the next night the male smelled the urine and wallowed in it. I wondered what he would do if he thought an unknown fox invaded his territory. So I poured a couple of drops of red fox urine onto a bare spot near the food bowl. (I had a bottle I bought in the 1970s which I used as a human-odor cover while hunting. It stinks!). Mister Fox trotted a few circles around the pee and the bowl and then went to the spot, sniffed, and began to slide and roll on the site.

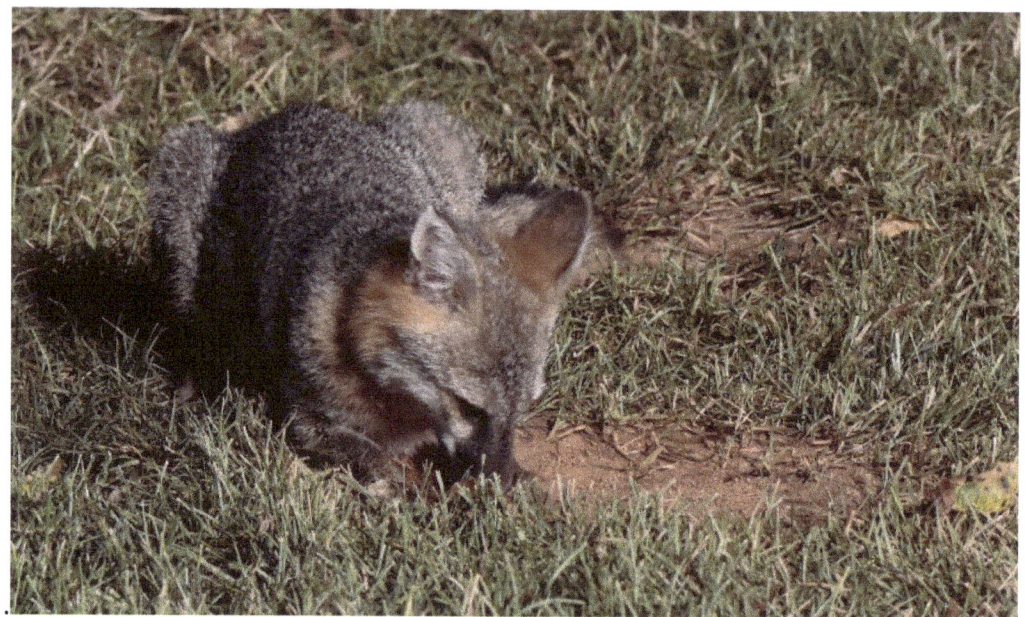

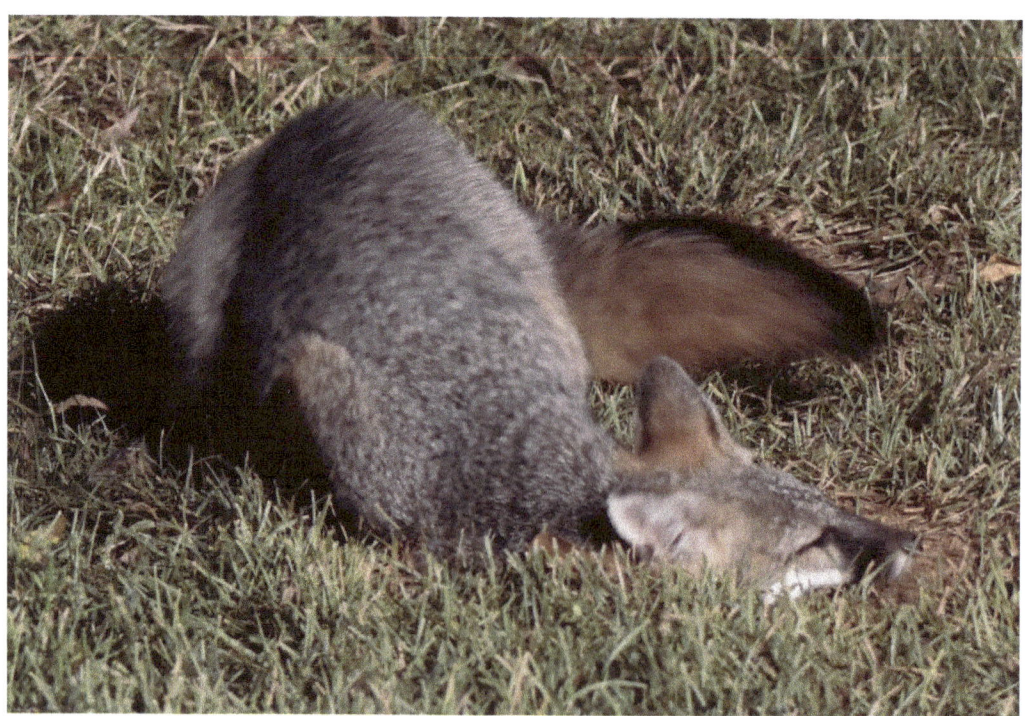

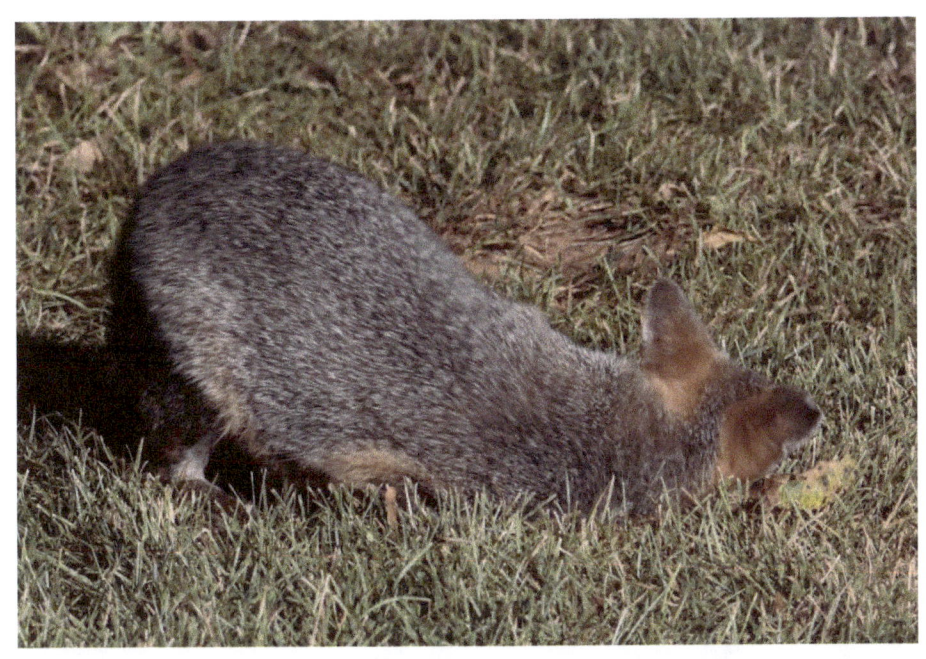

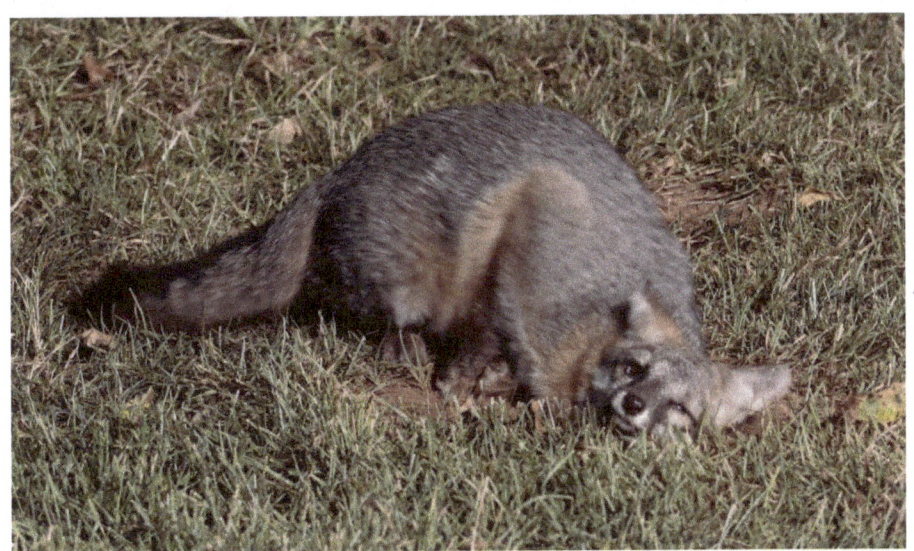

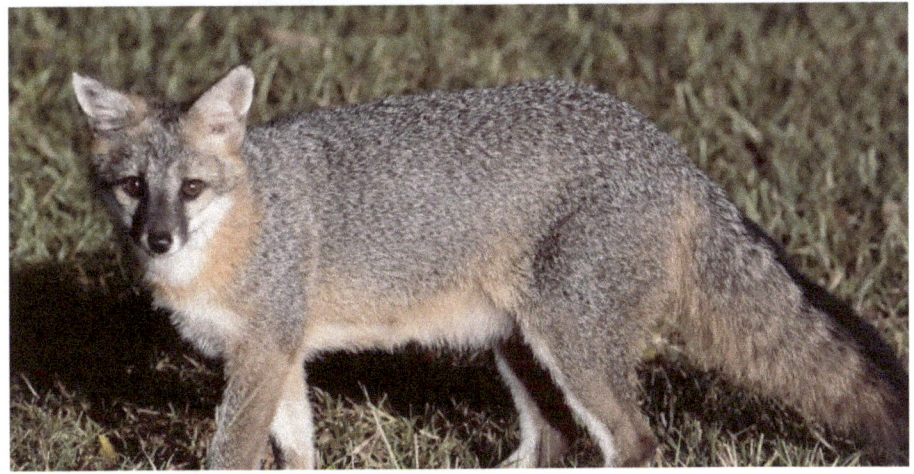

SMALL BIRDS

I added bird seed/grain to the lure of corn. Crows, blue jays, cardinals and doves were happy with the corn. A few smaller birds enjoyed the small seeds.

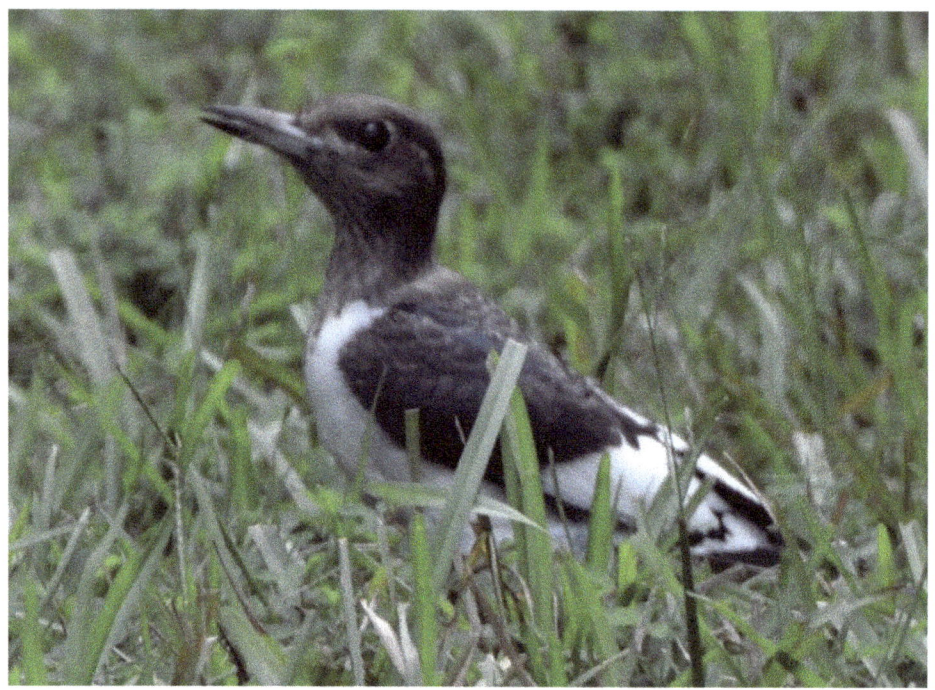

Juvenile red-headed woodpecker.

Doves visited daily, not only for food but for water. September was dry in spite of Hurricane Florence, for it gave us only a little more than a mist.

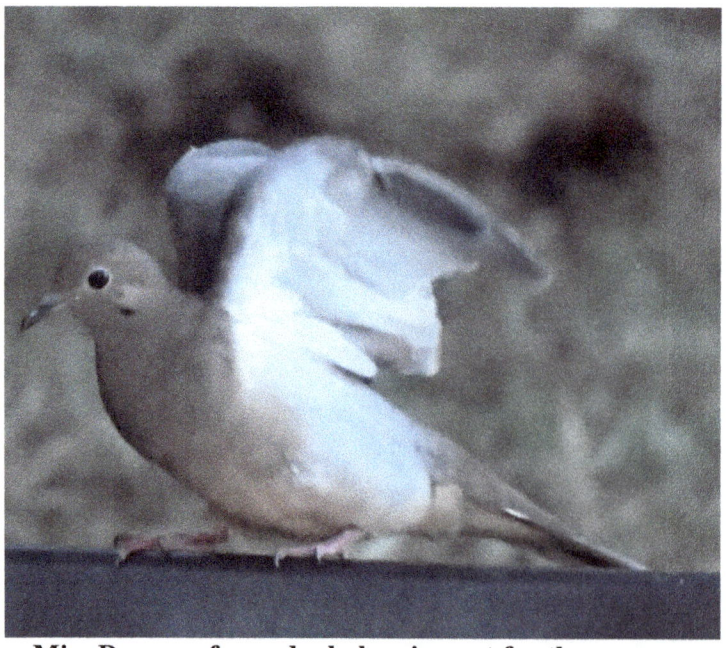

Miss Dove performed a balancing act for the camera.

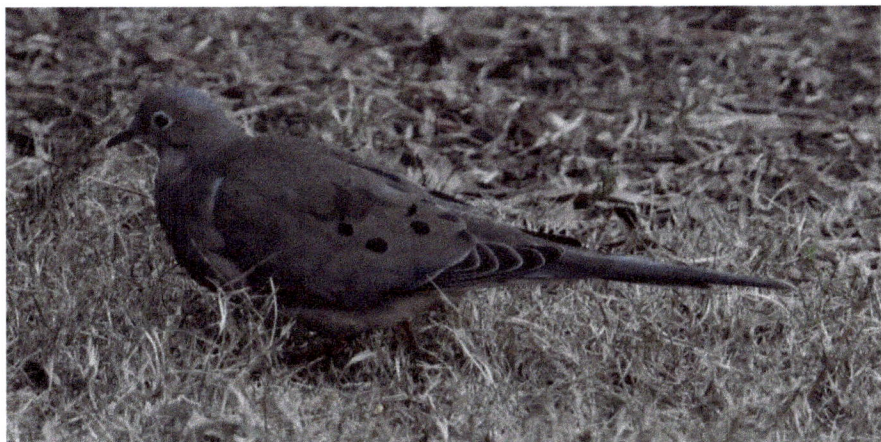

Visiting doves came in a variety of colors. This was the darkest.

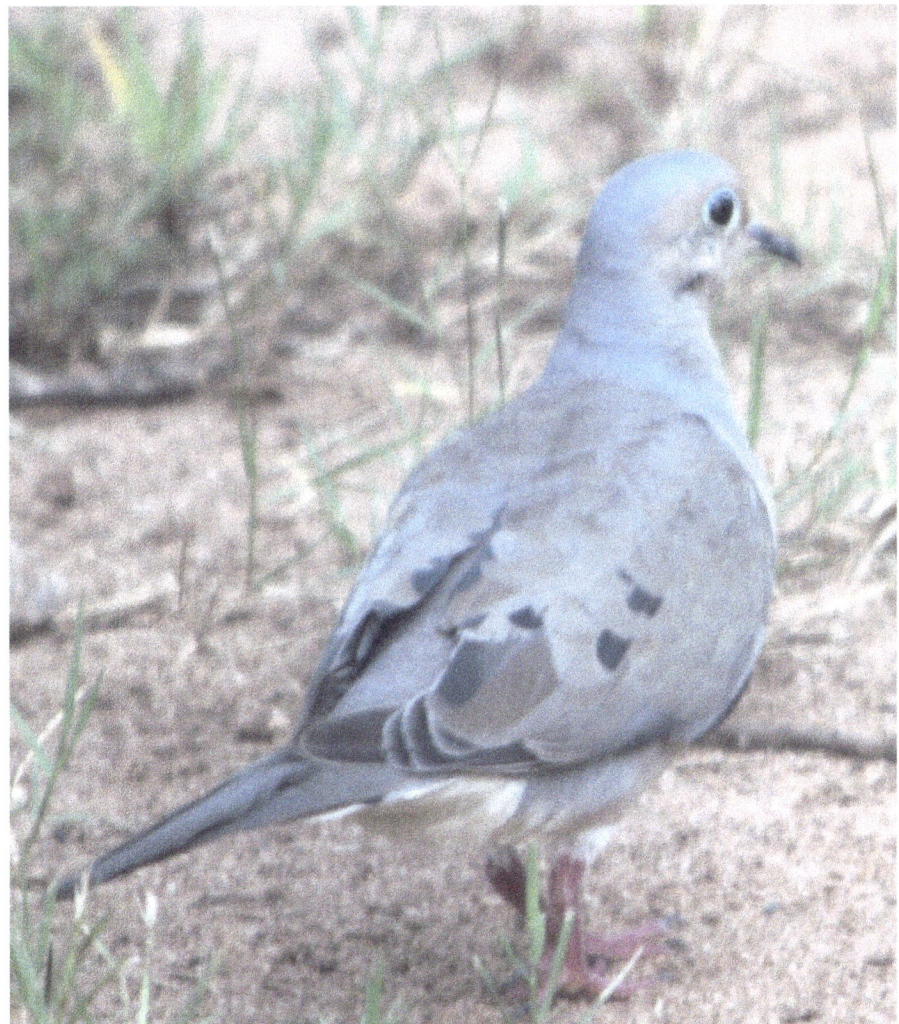

Mr. Blue was the lightest. This picture was taken in "RAW" and converted to JPG, which apparently is the cause of it being so bright. I did not enhance it. It is the only picture I managed to get of this dove.

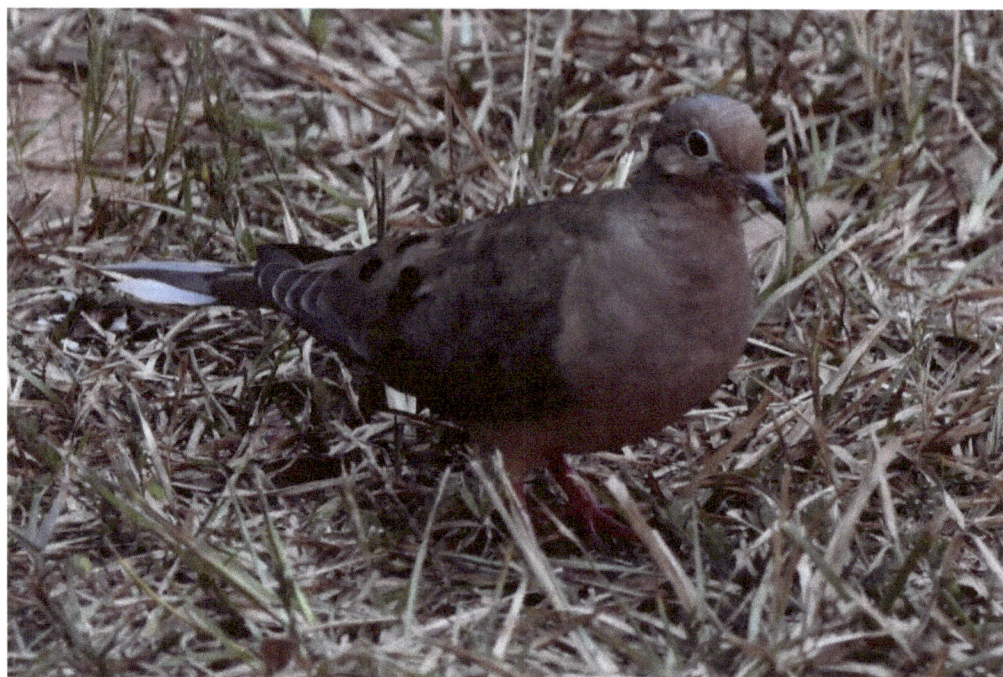

This one or a look-alike visited morning and evening several days.

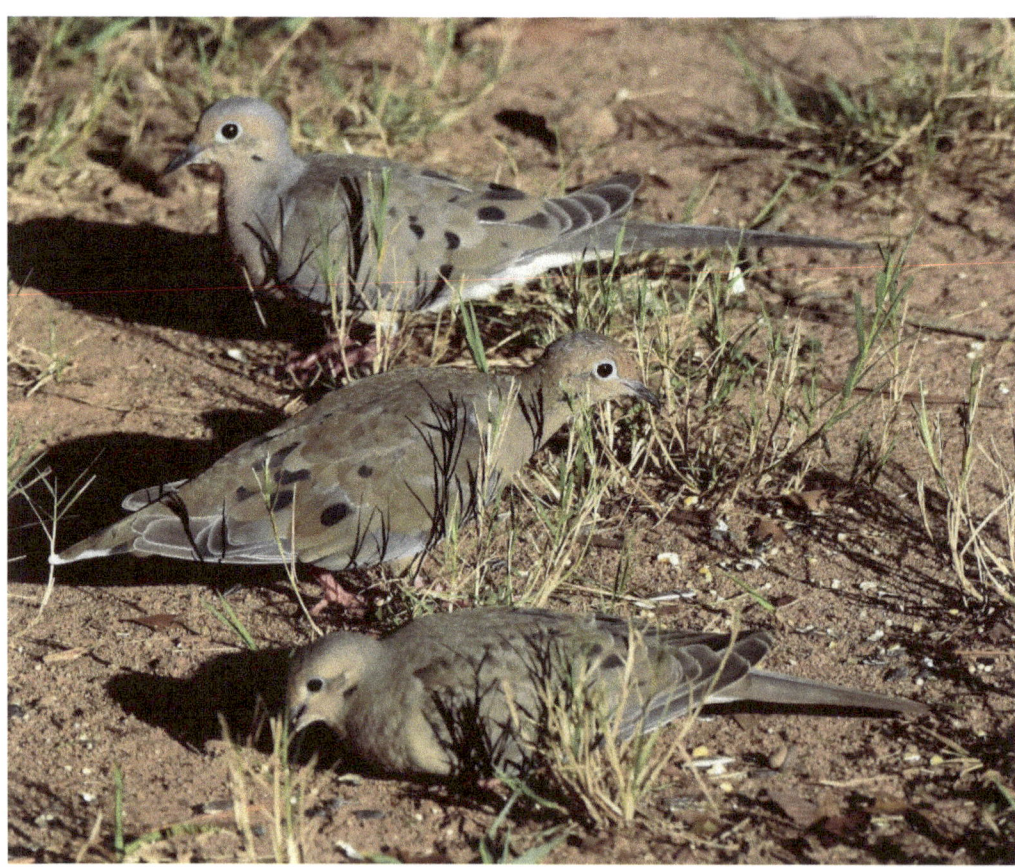

These three lined up to be the most typical.

Just as the deer scrambled over food, a pair of doves got into a spat. The argument lasted about five seconds and one took to the air.

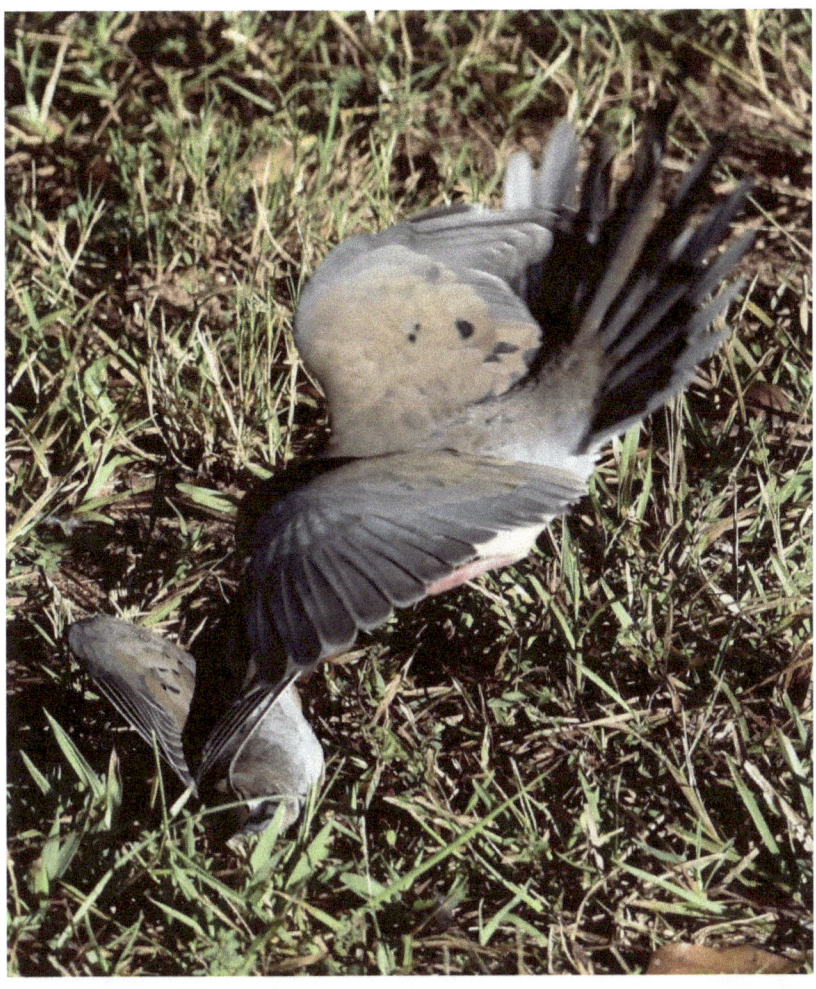

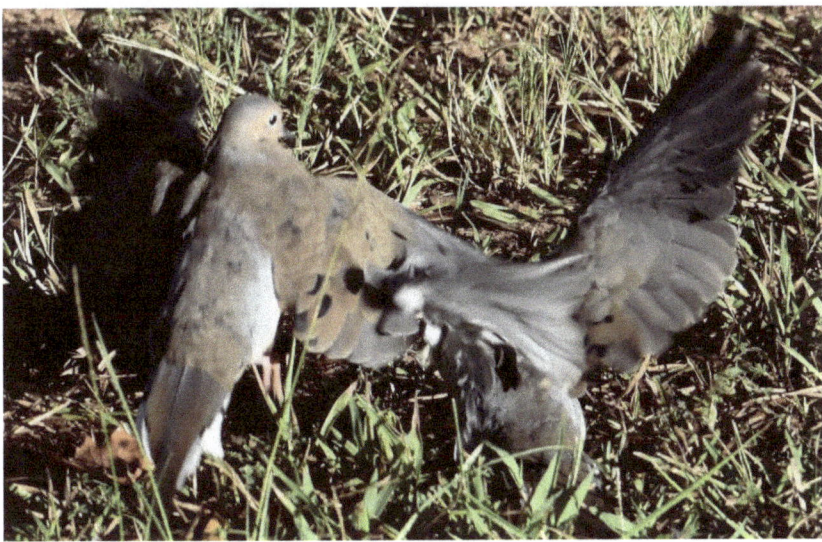

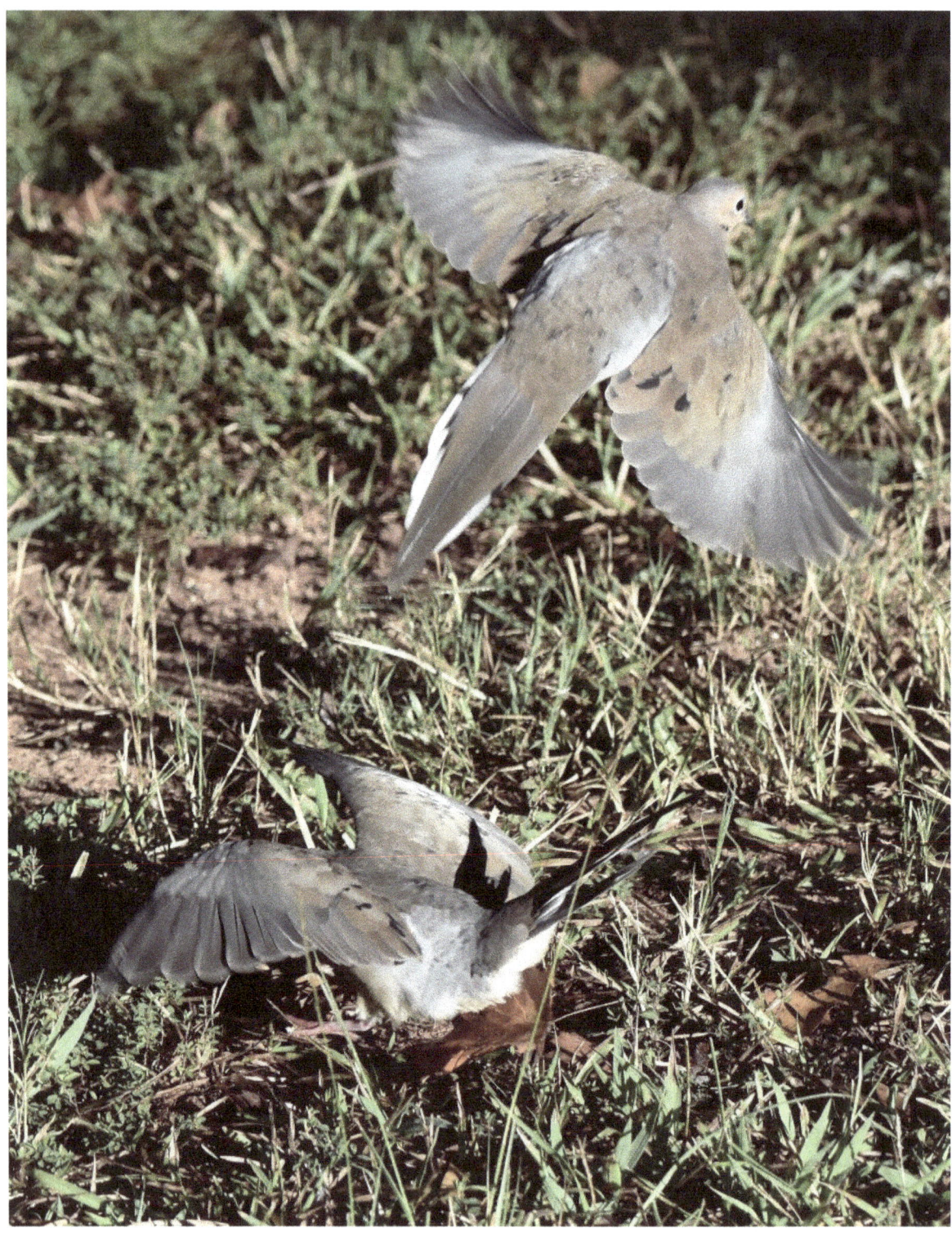

Cardinals and jays added color every morning and afternoon.

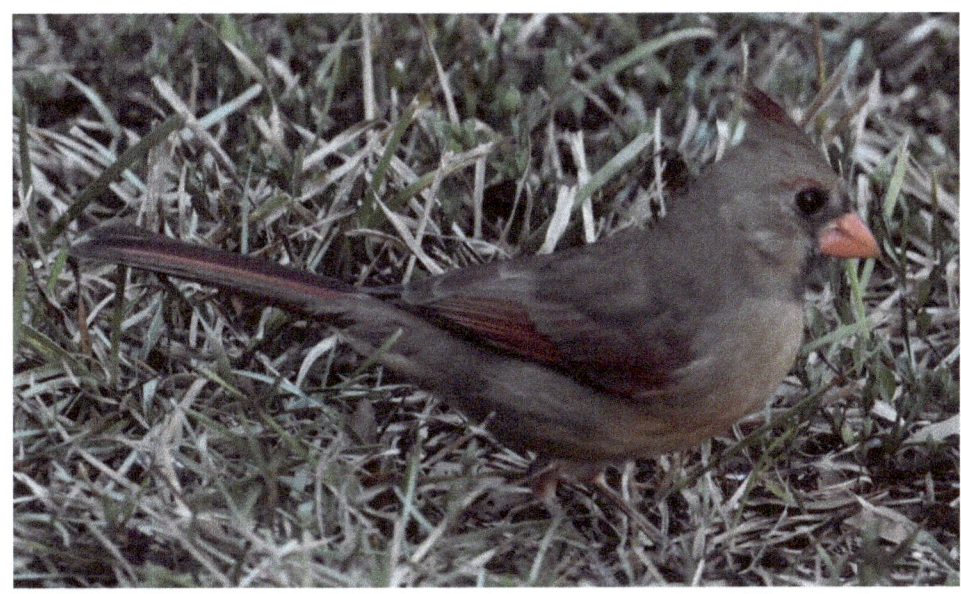

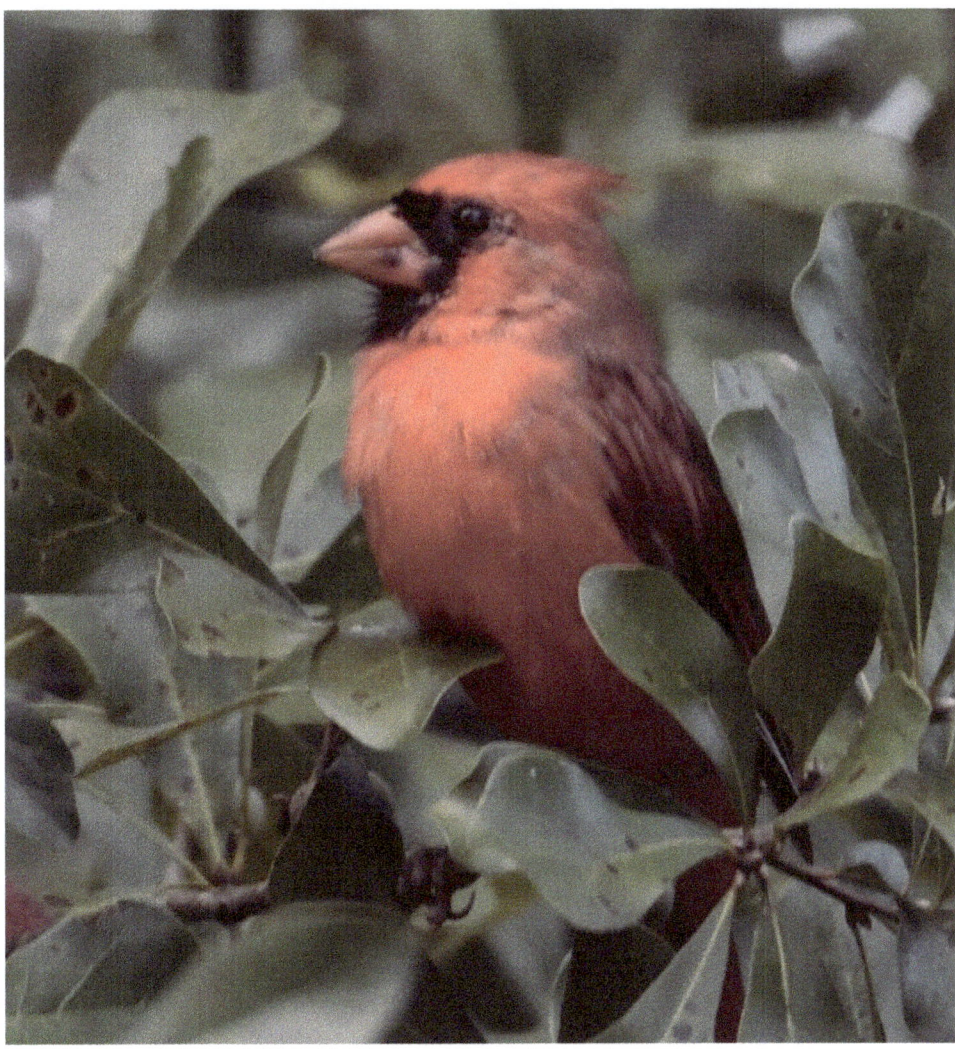

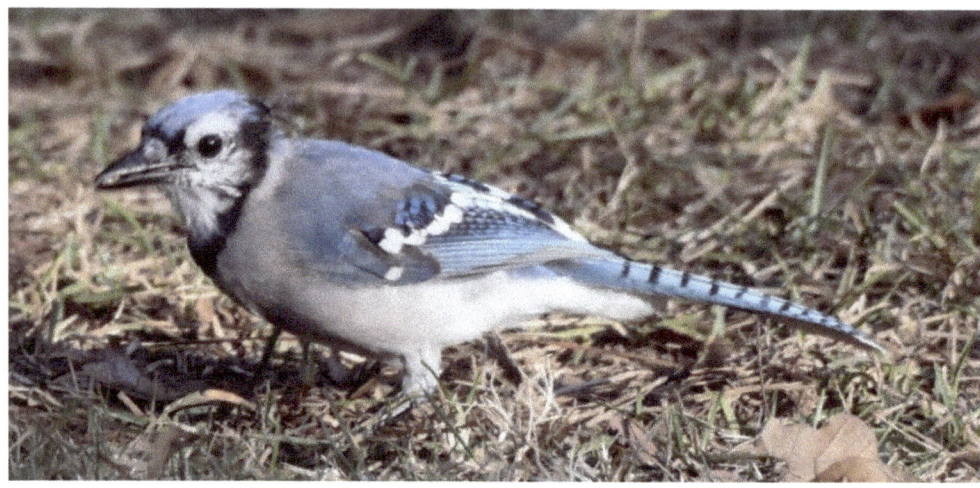

Crows just added squawks. For the first time, I saw them as blue and not just black.

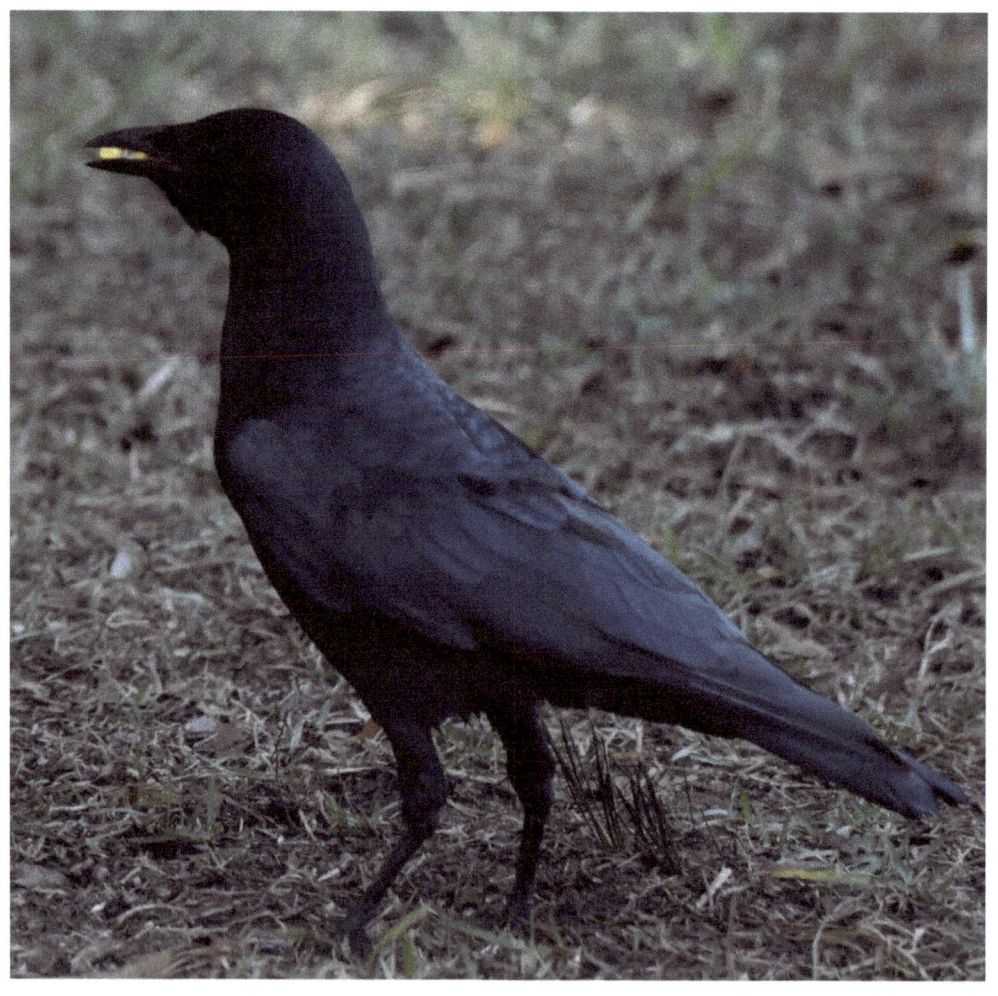

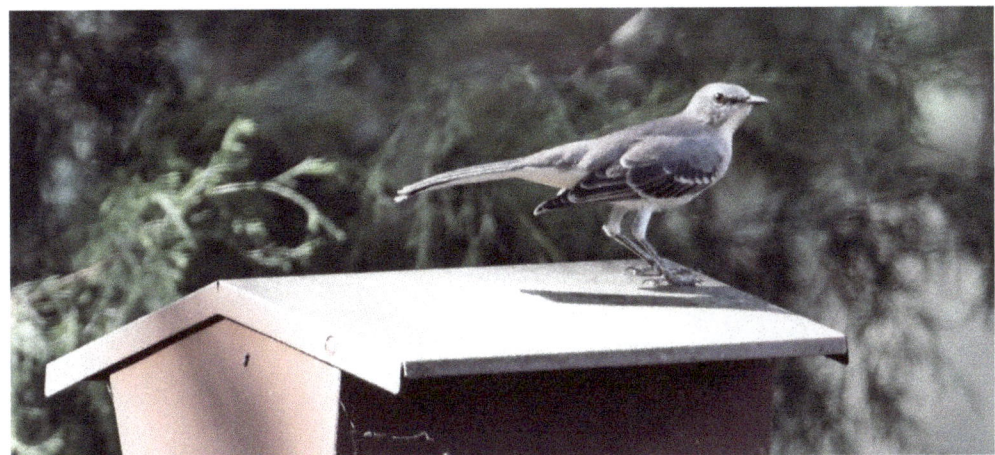

The mockingbird visited daily.

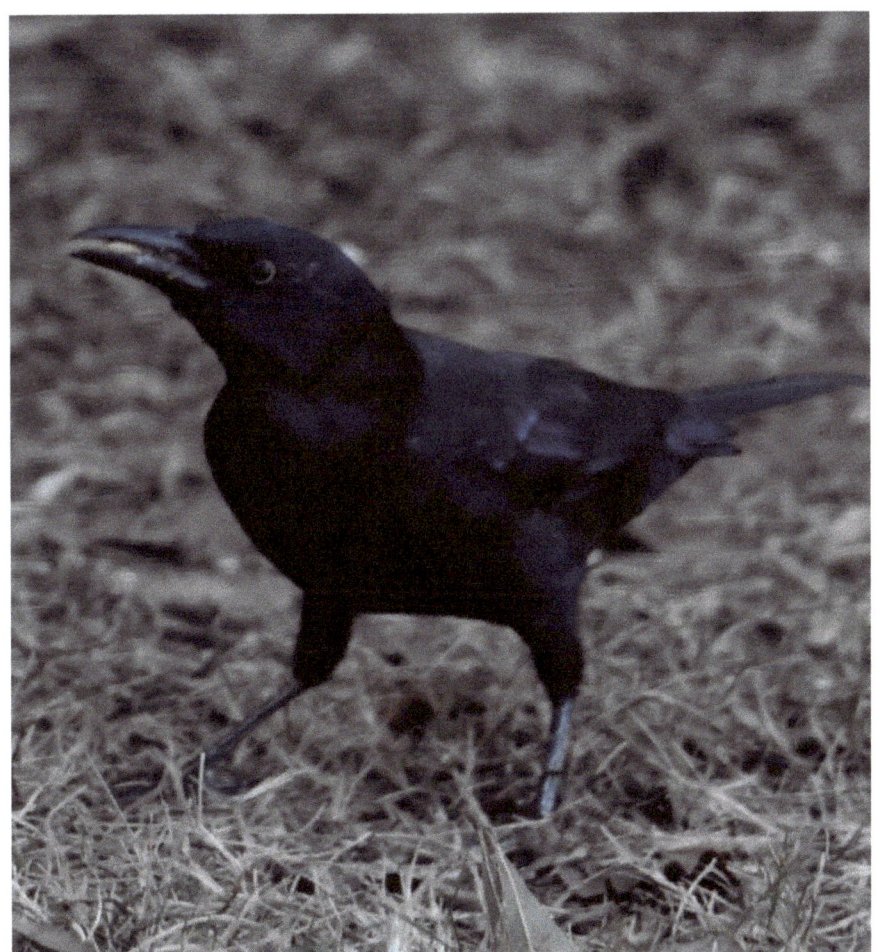

I didn't know until this one showed up to be photographed that we have the common grackle in my neighborhood.

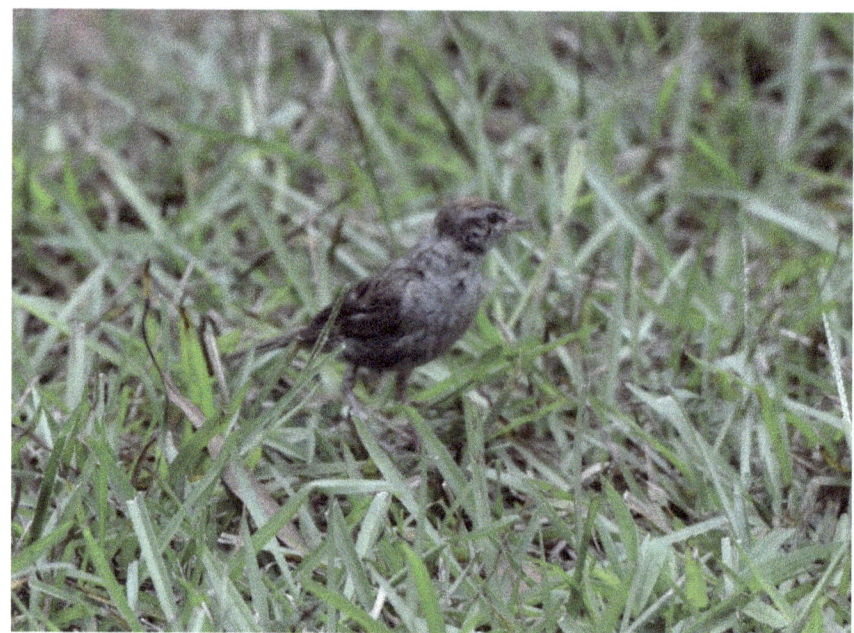

Juvenile chipping sparrow.

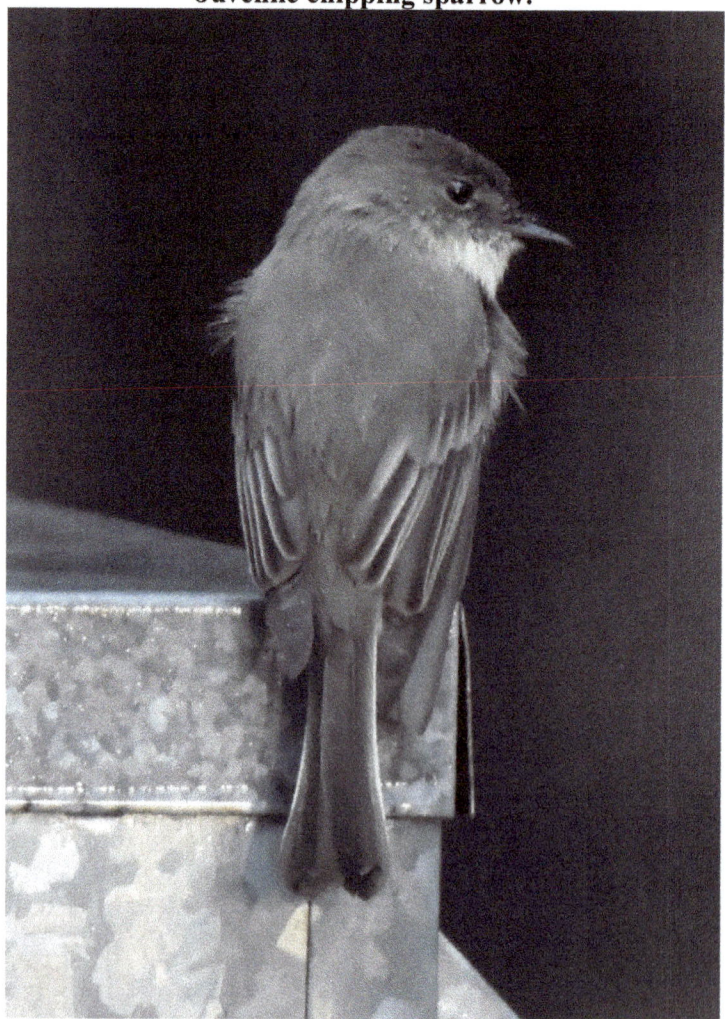

The eastern phoebe flitted in and out often.

THE WHITETAILS
Meet the Boys and Girls

The deer consumed most of the food and also most of my time with the camera. Only when I looked at the pictures did I realize how many different characters visited me from one day/evening to the next.

Two spikes look alike through the camera. And two large-framed eight pointers may seem to be the same buck. Close-ups with a camera or with a telescopic sight show the difference. My 400-mm lens was a big help.

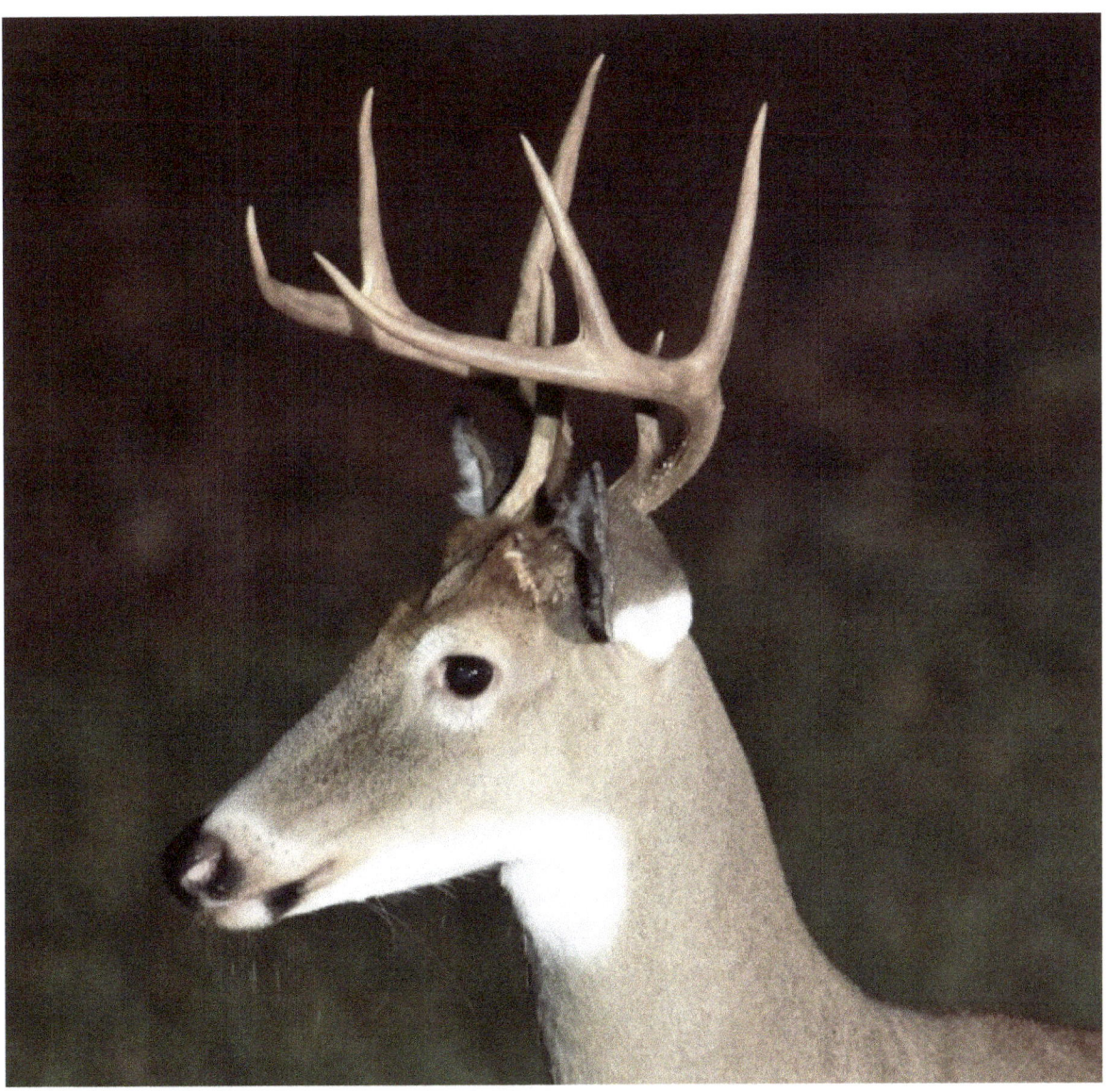

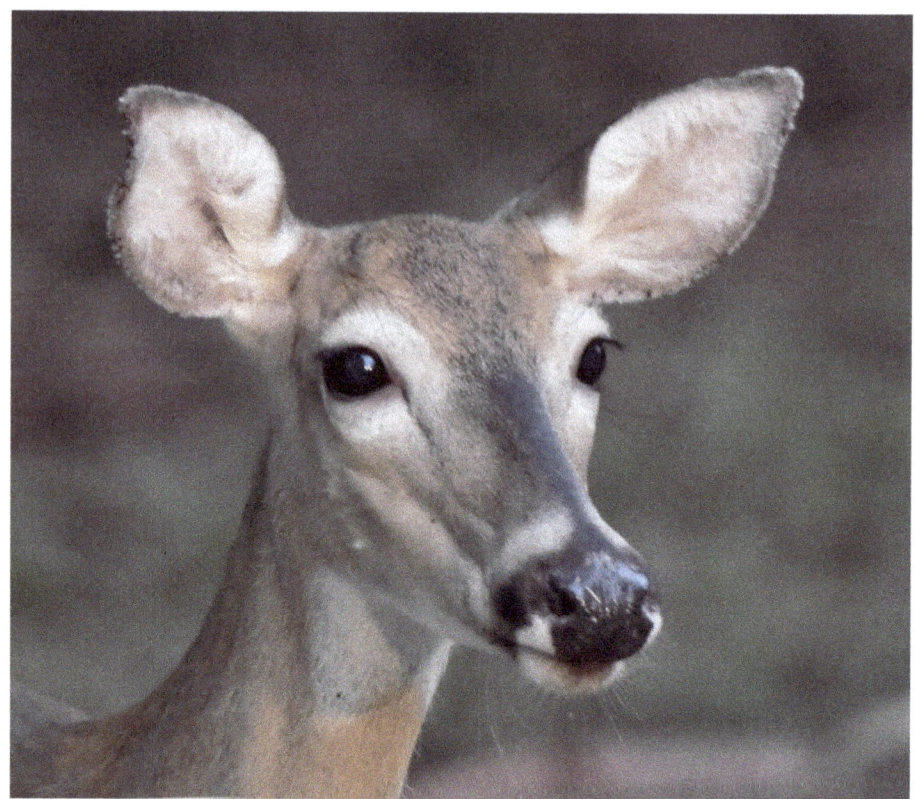

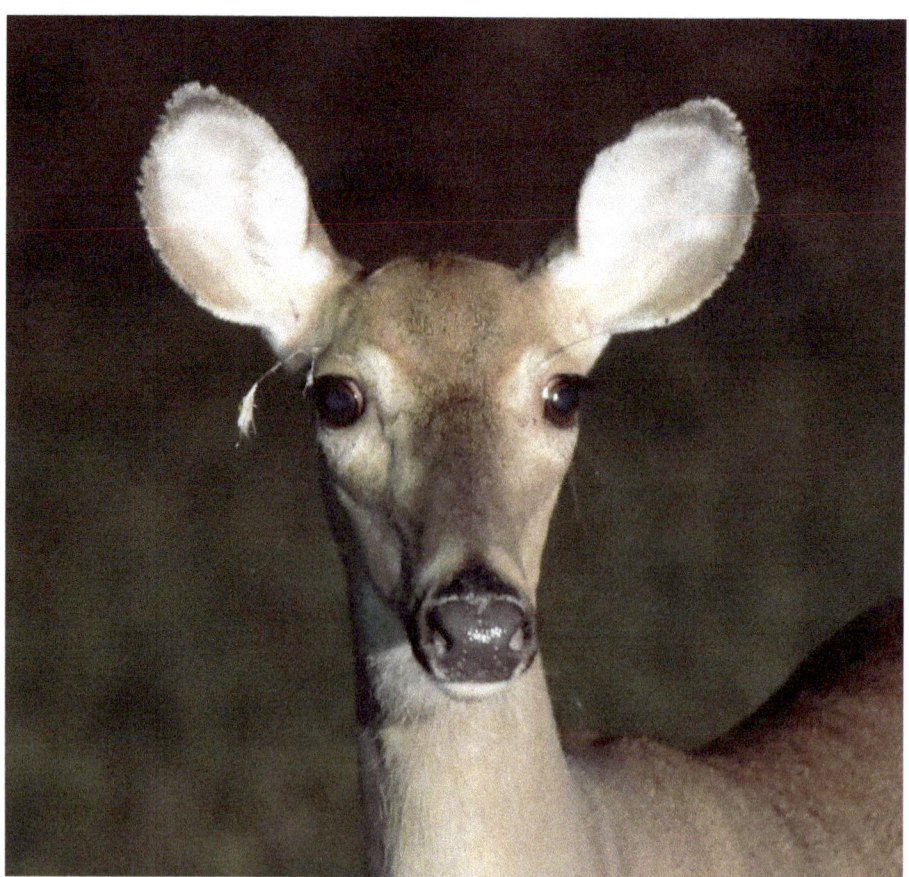

Looks like a flying seed stuck to her eyebrow.

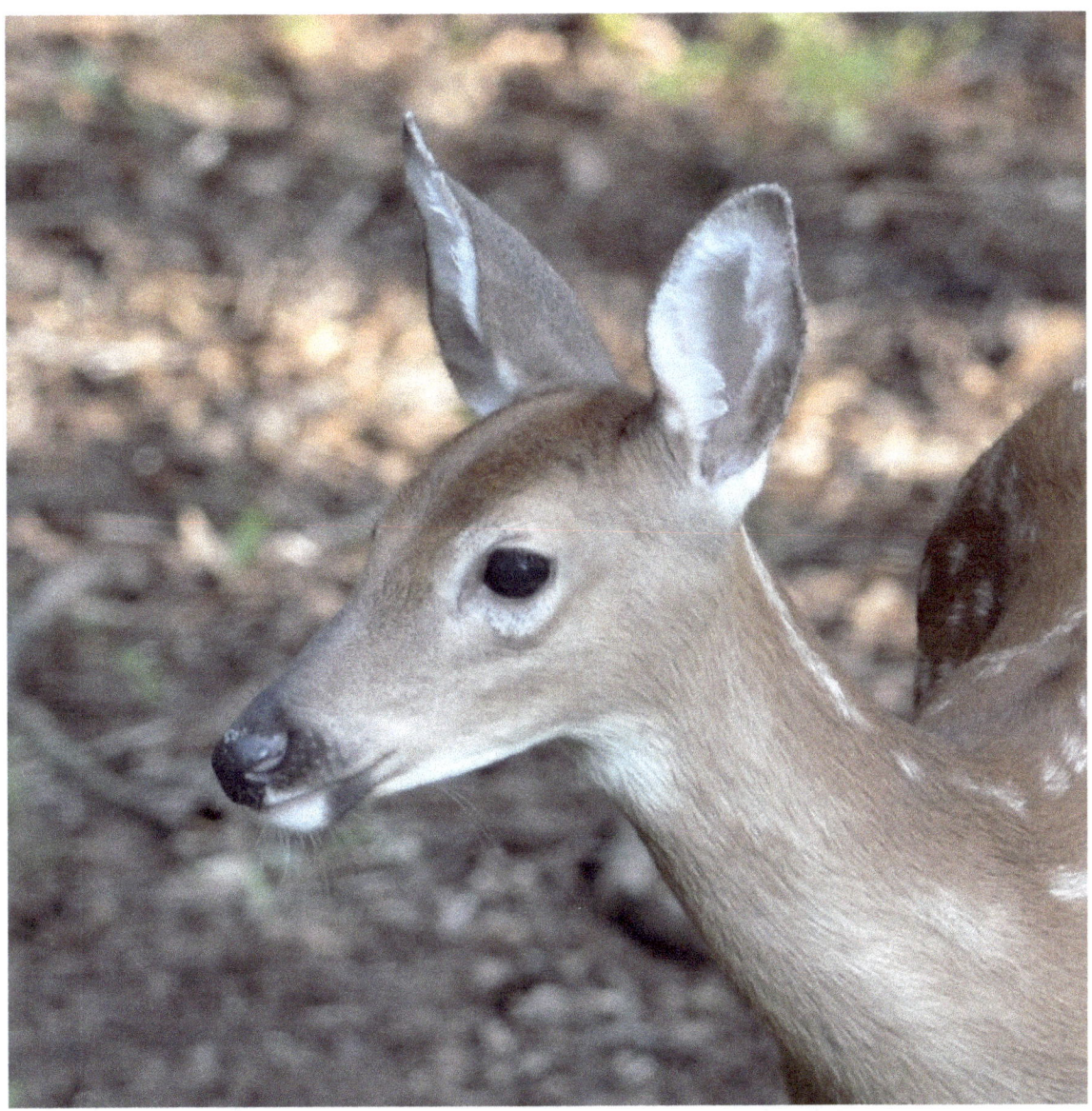

I called this fawn *Little Miss* since she was smaller than the other fawns in the yard. By the end of September, the others had lost their spots. She still had hers.

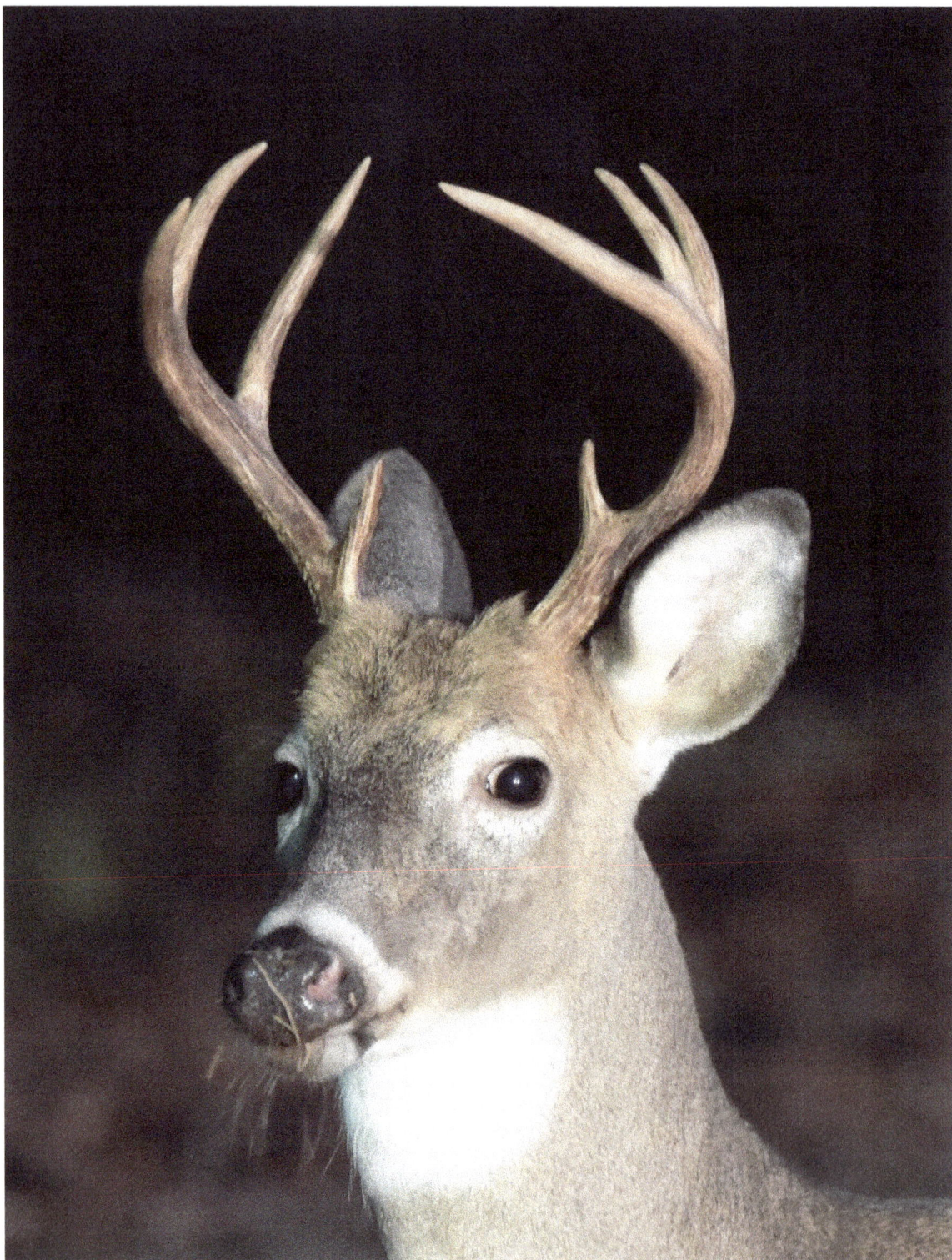

This fella needed to wash the dirt and twigs from his face before I took his picture.

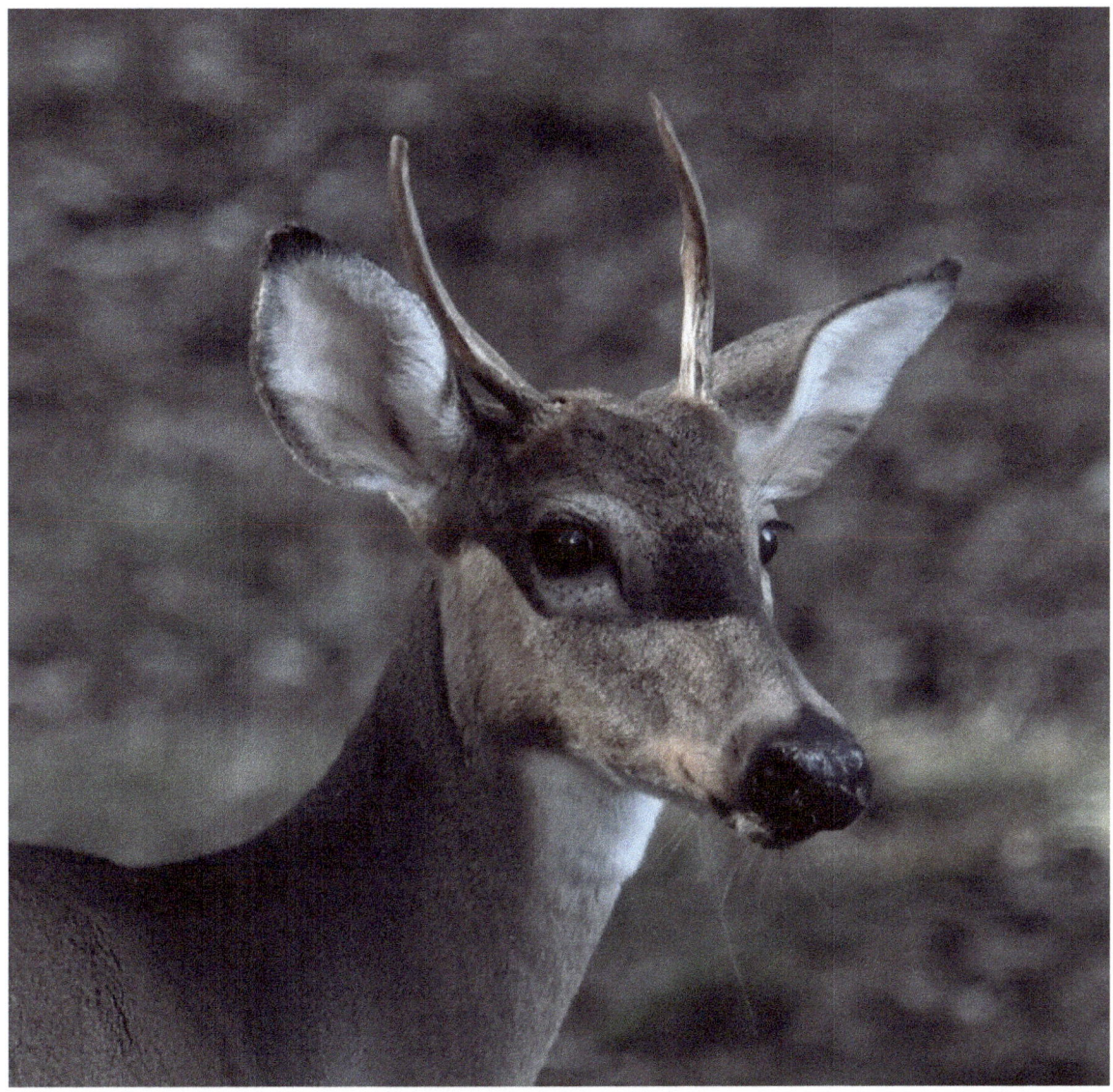

A spike can be as proud of himself as any ten-pointer. This one was not afraid to challenge bigger bucks in mock fights.

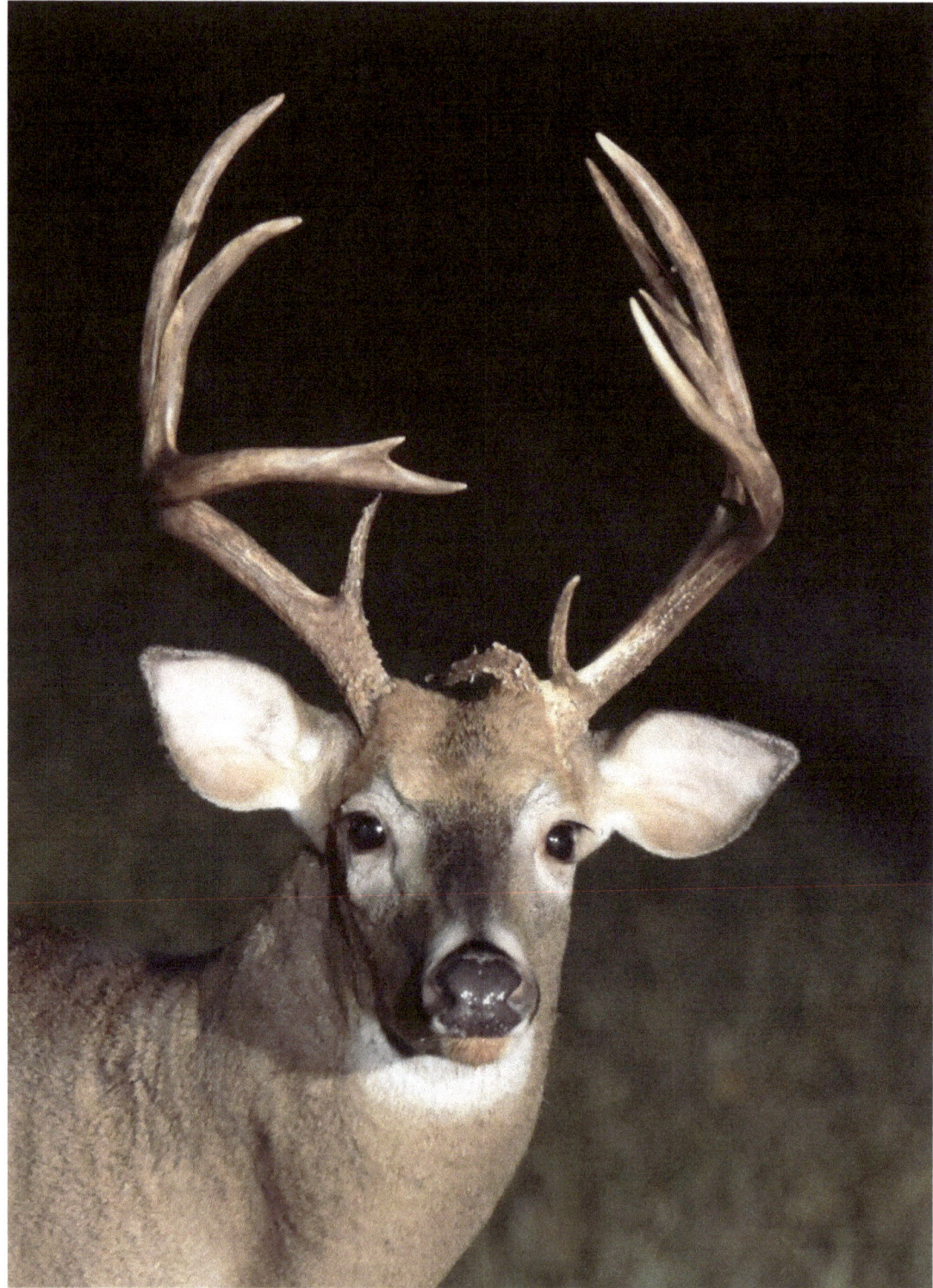

Note the atypical ear guard at the base of his left antler. He lost it in one of his pushing matches with a small three-pointer.

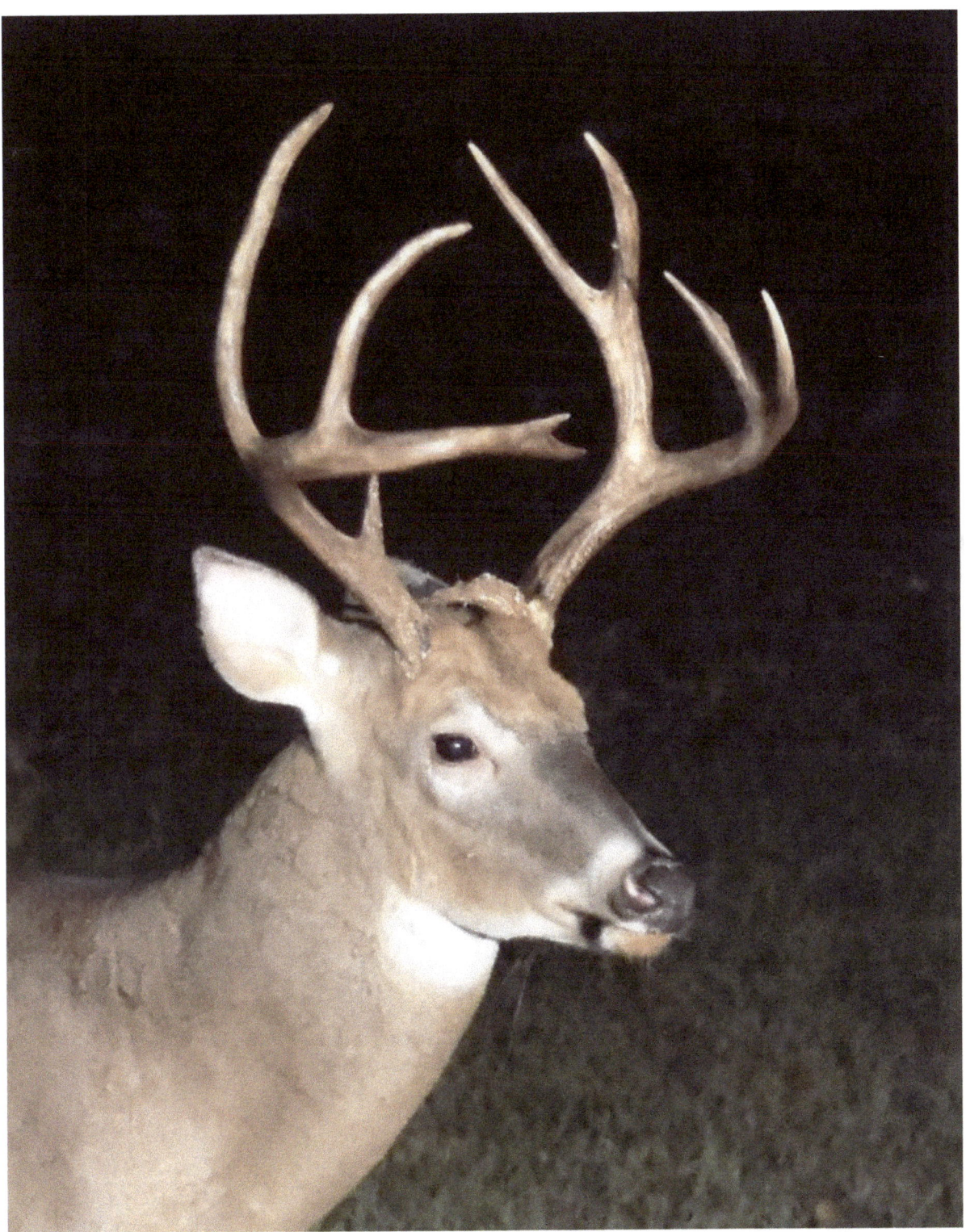

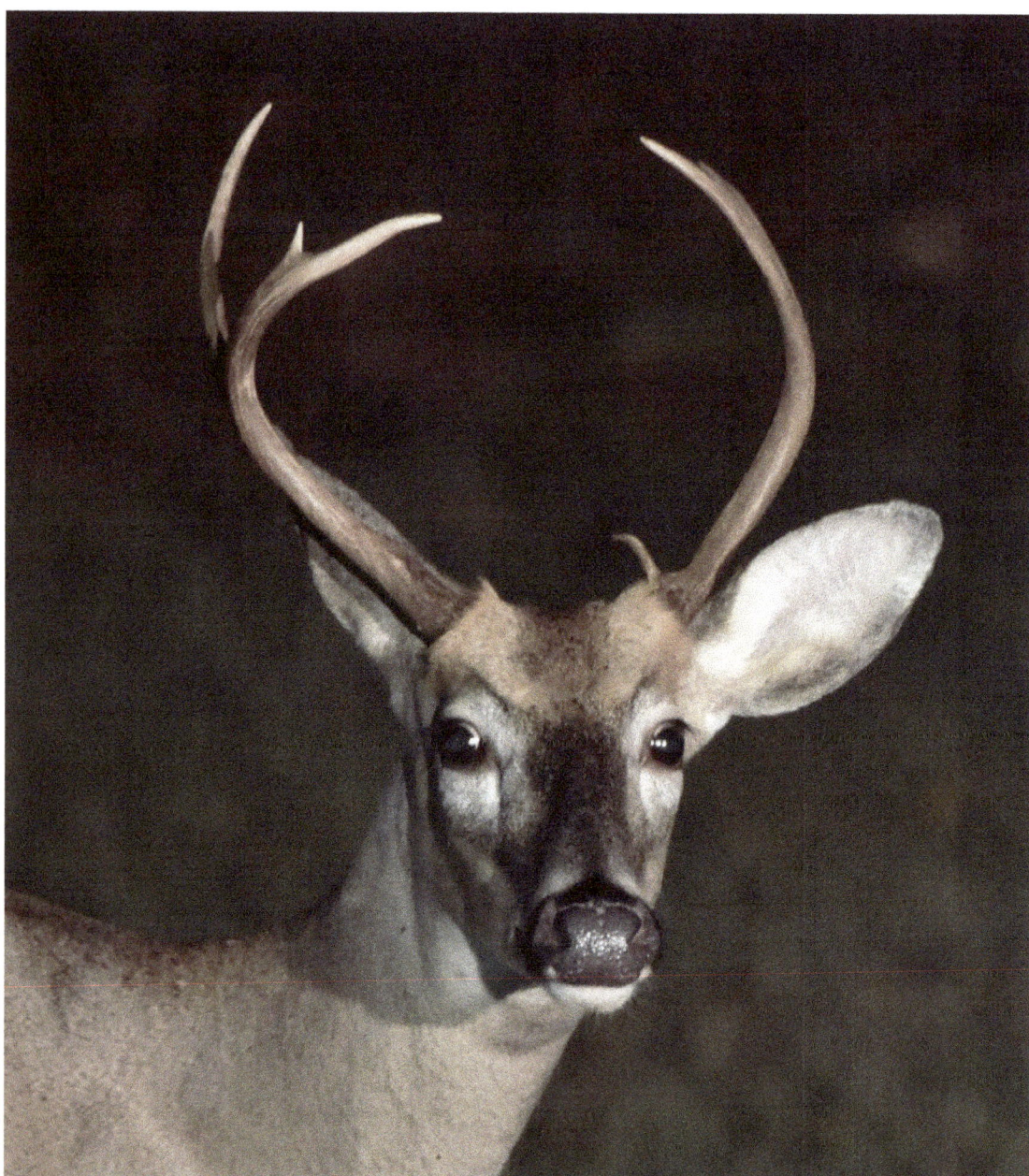

The tall rack and the crooked small tine at the base of his left antler makes me think this fella is perhaps son or brother to the one with the bent antler in the last two pictures.

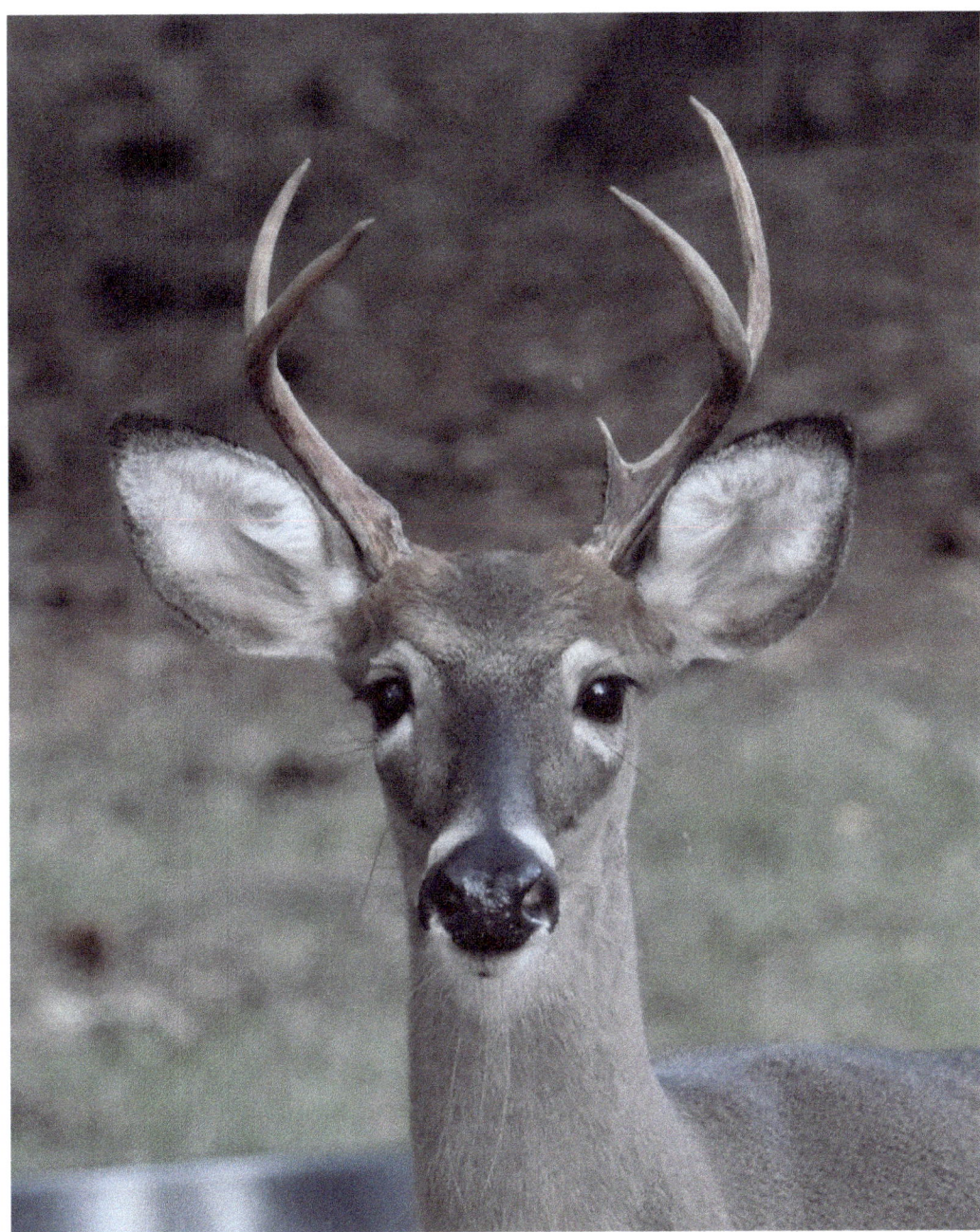

The five-point of several pushing matches I watched.

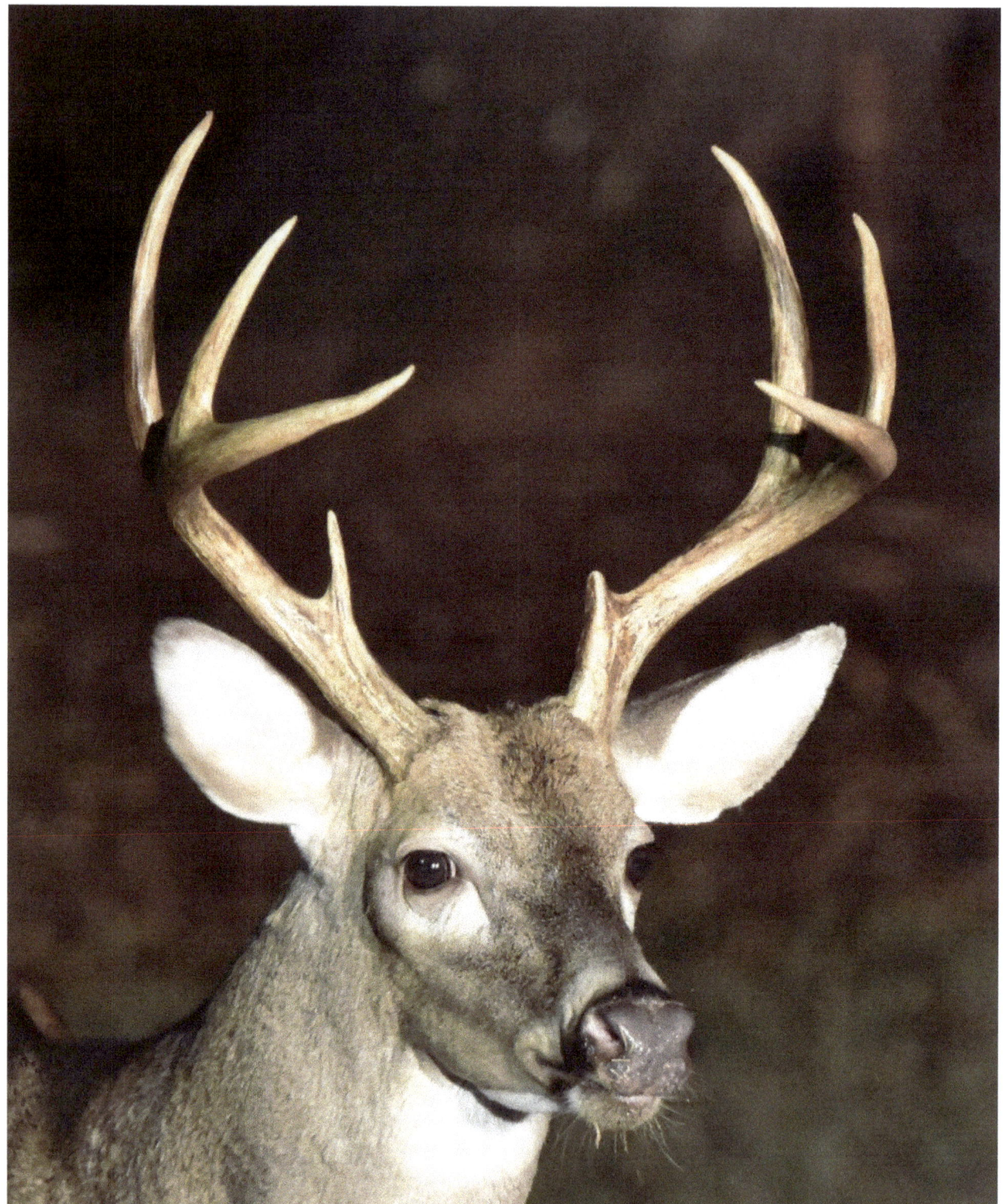

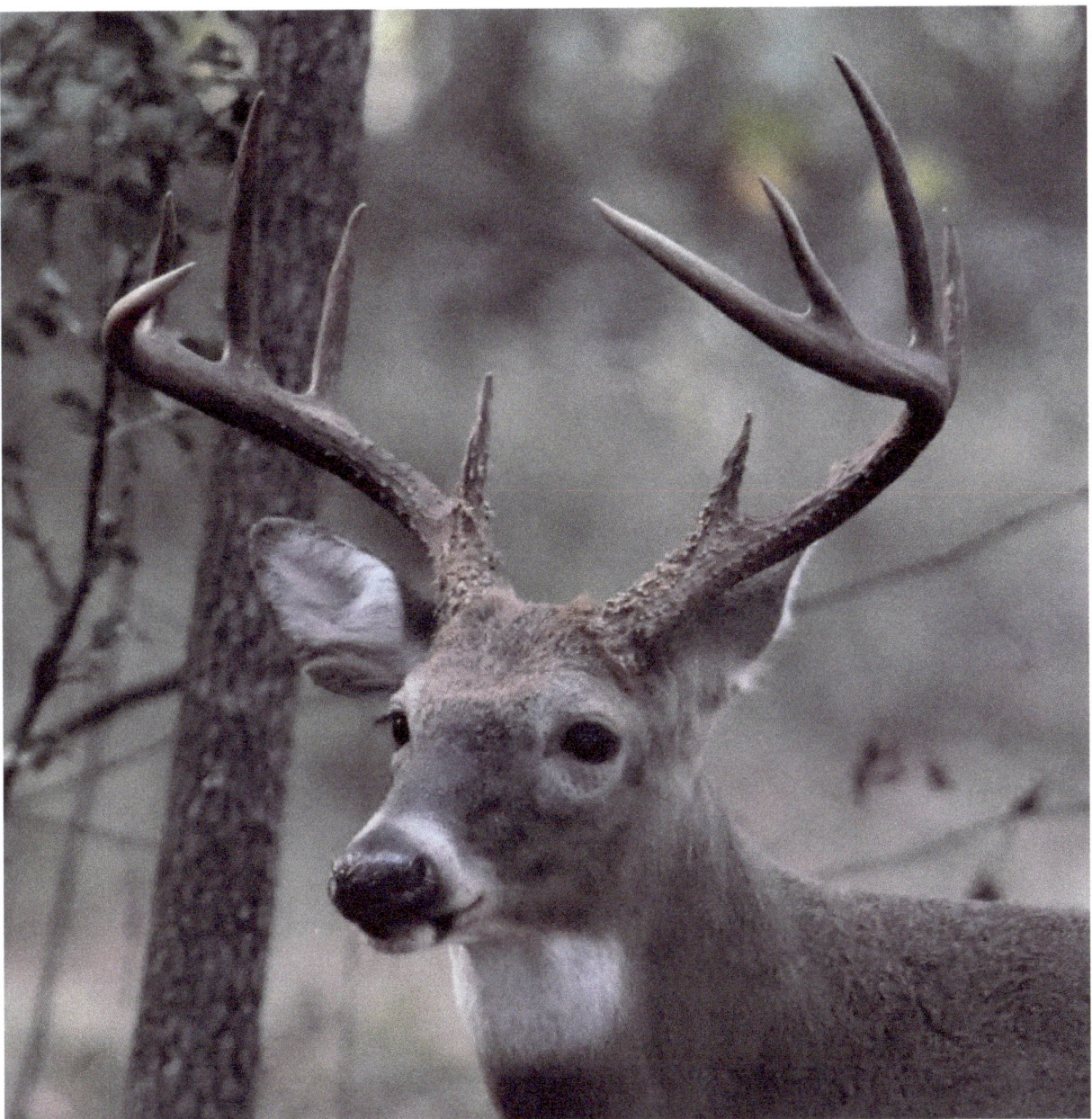

Big Ten showed up once after he'd had a pushing match with a tree. The light-colored matter at the base of his antlers and up onto the ear guards is tree residue.

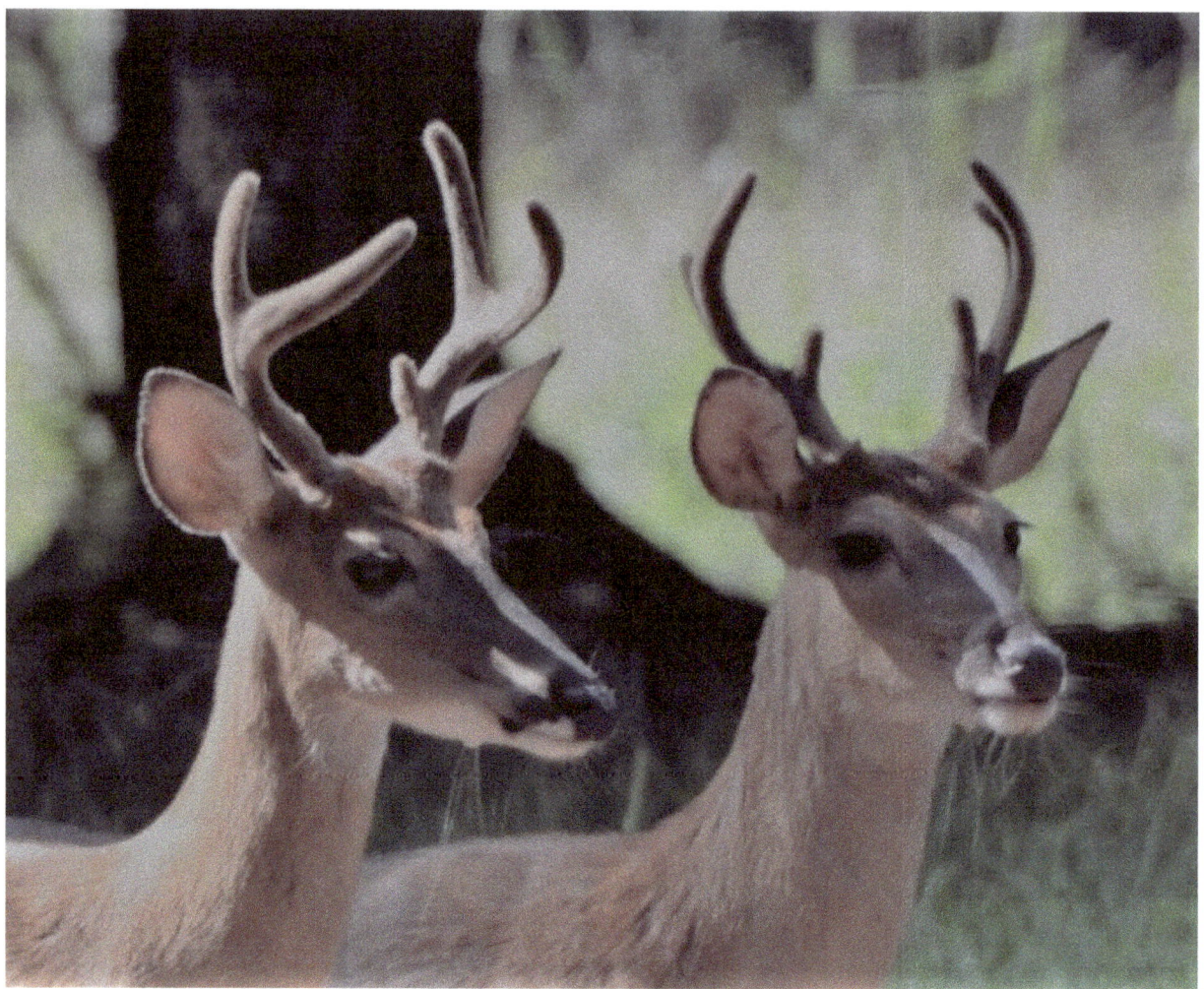

The Brothers, who will have a section of their own.

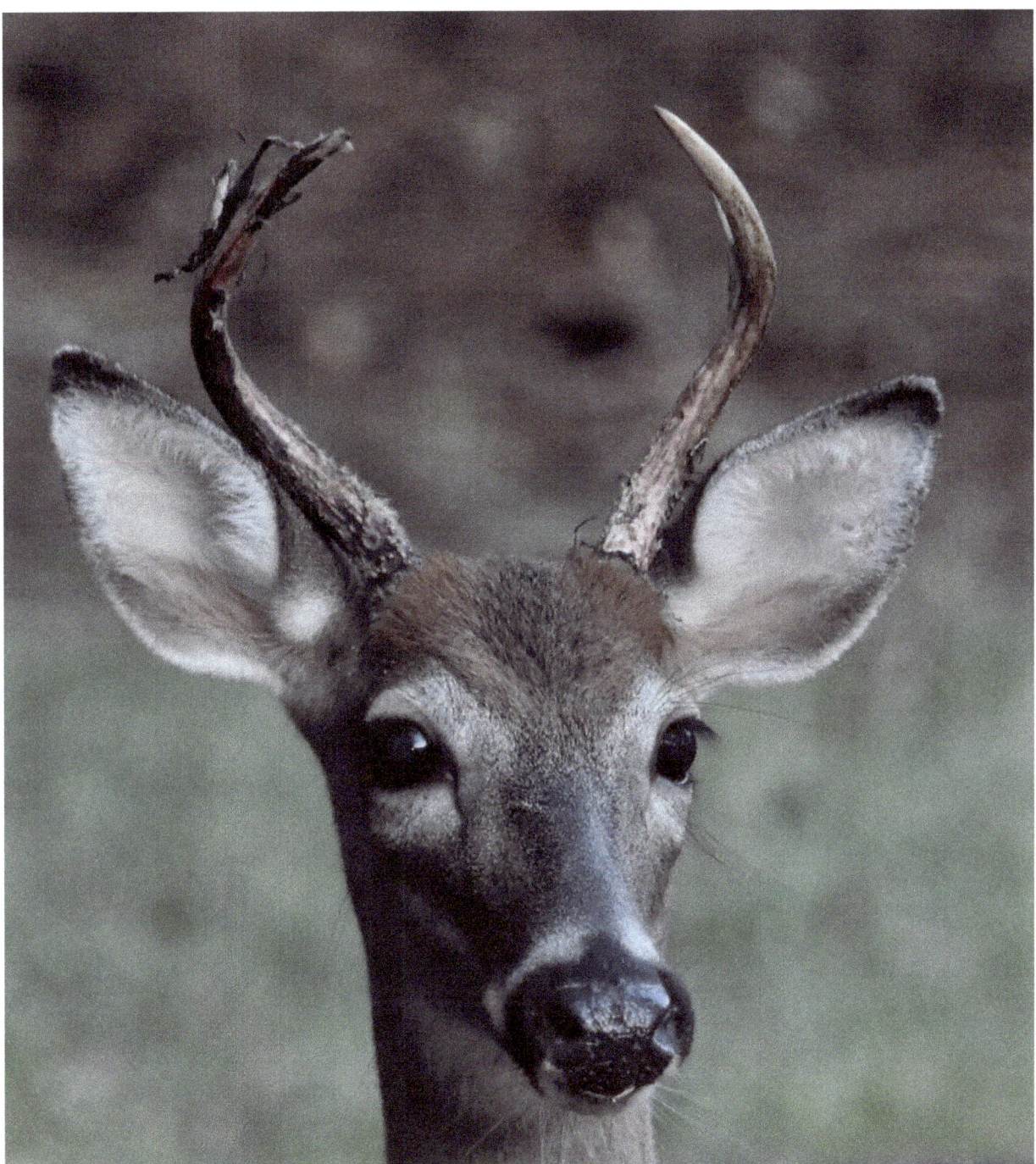

The crud on his antler is dried velvet. He eventually rubbed it off against a tree trunk.

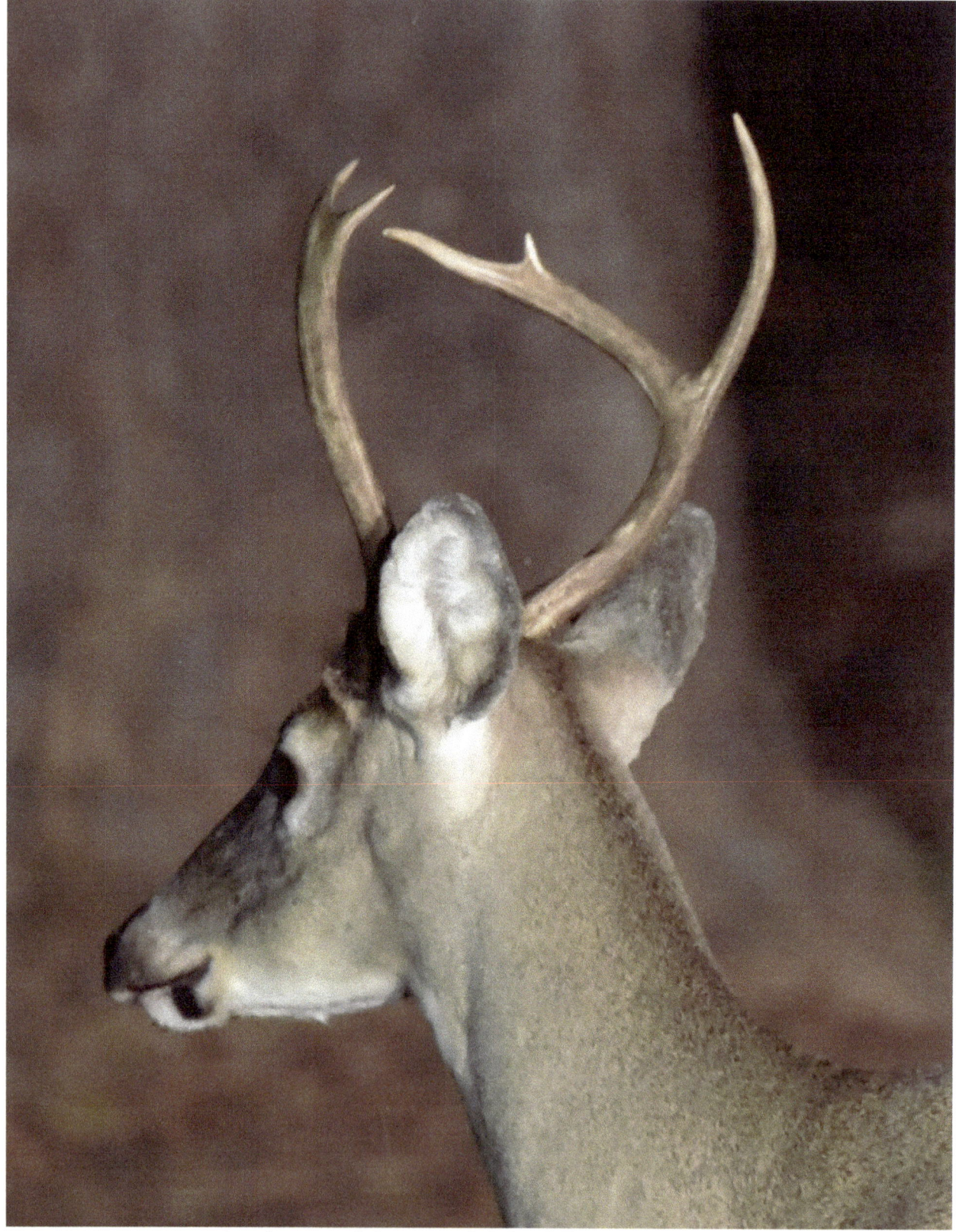

Another one of the young fighting fellas, the five-point.

THE BROTHERS
Totally Wild Teenagers

After hours of watching these two bucks, I decided they must be brothers. Where one went, the other followed. At the age of eighteen months, they would be considered teenagers in human terms. Their behavior showed a total lack of decorum as they sought their sexual maturity.

They ate side by side. One did shed his velvet a few days ahead of the other, but it's easy to see the similarity of their antlers and body sizes.

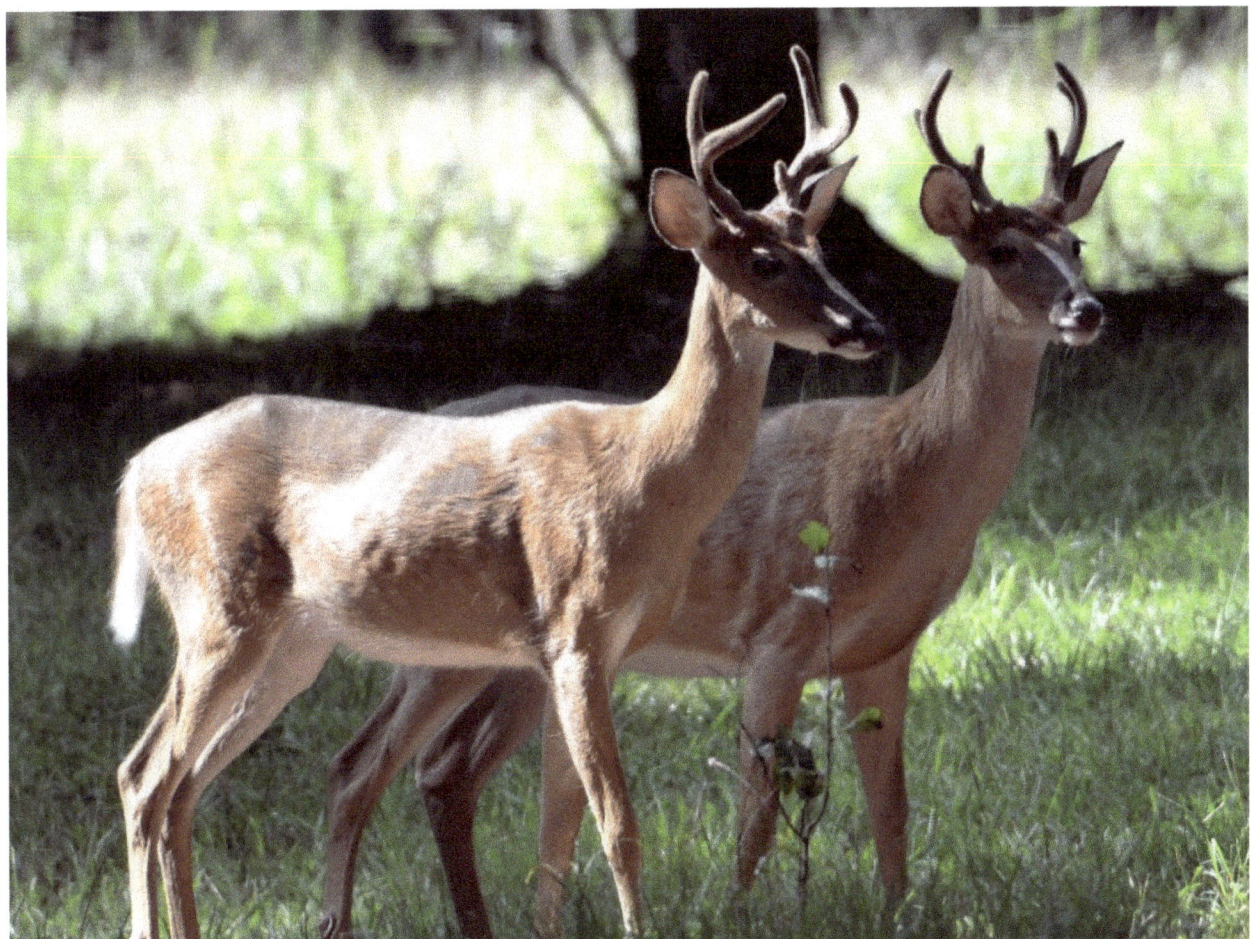

The boys are shedding their summer coats in August.

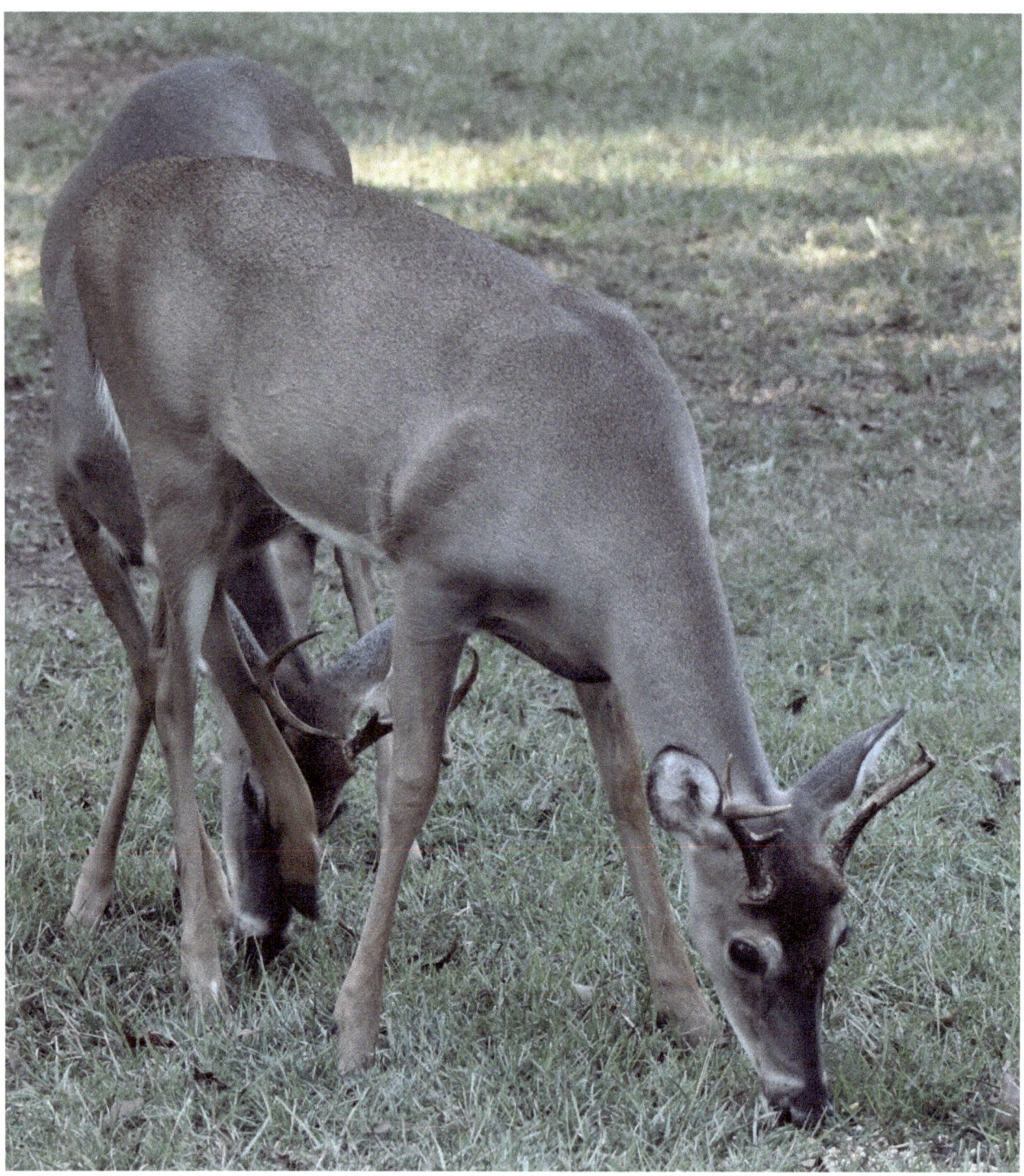

Not only did they eat side by side, but one never hesitated to feed beneath the other. The raised hoof did not slam the brother.

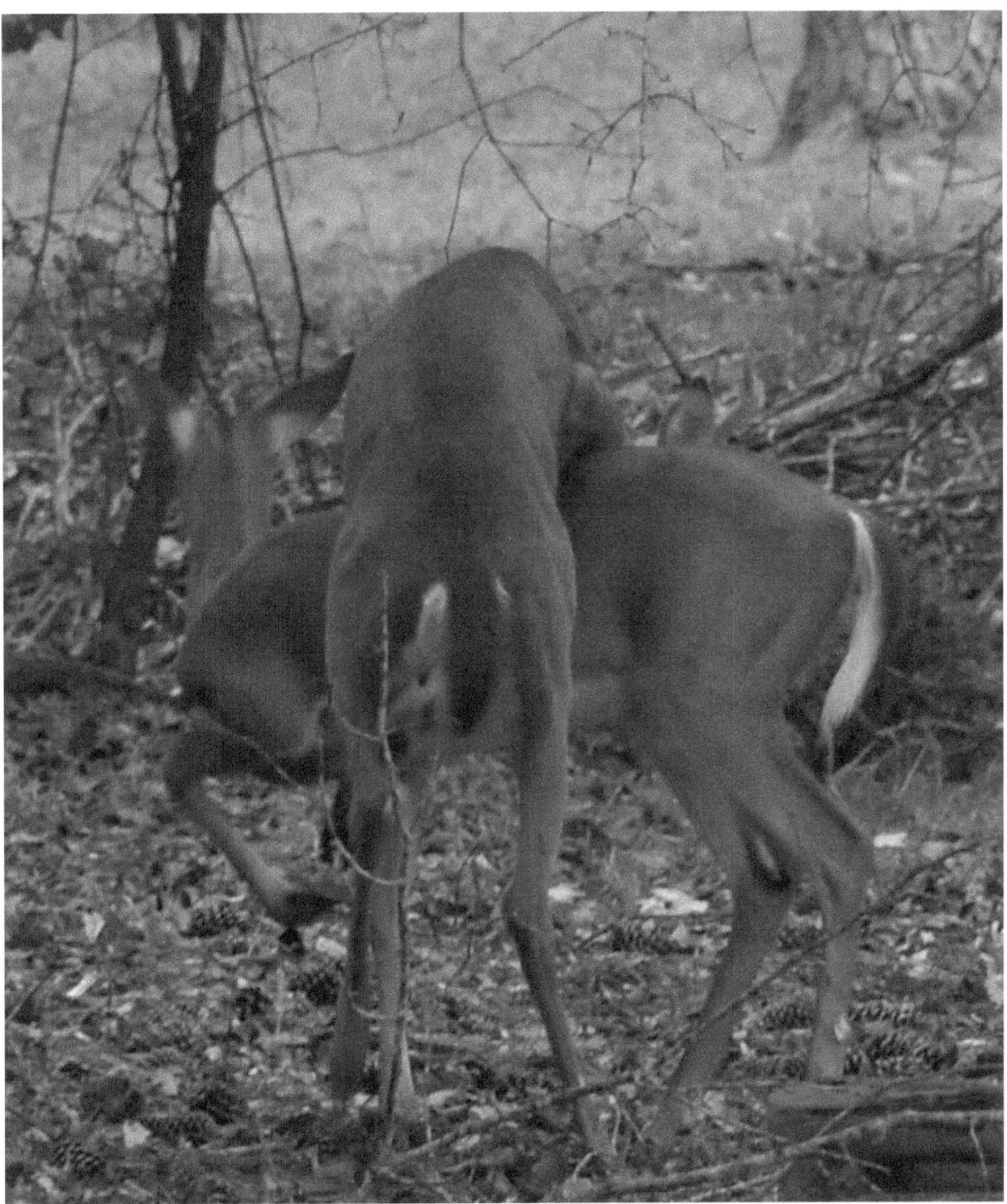

Inexperience in sexual matters showed in several other events. The next sequence of eight pictures was my first sighting of such an event. The black edge on the left side of some pictures is the trunk of an elm tree.

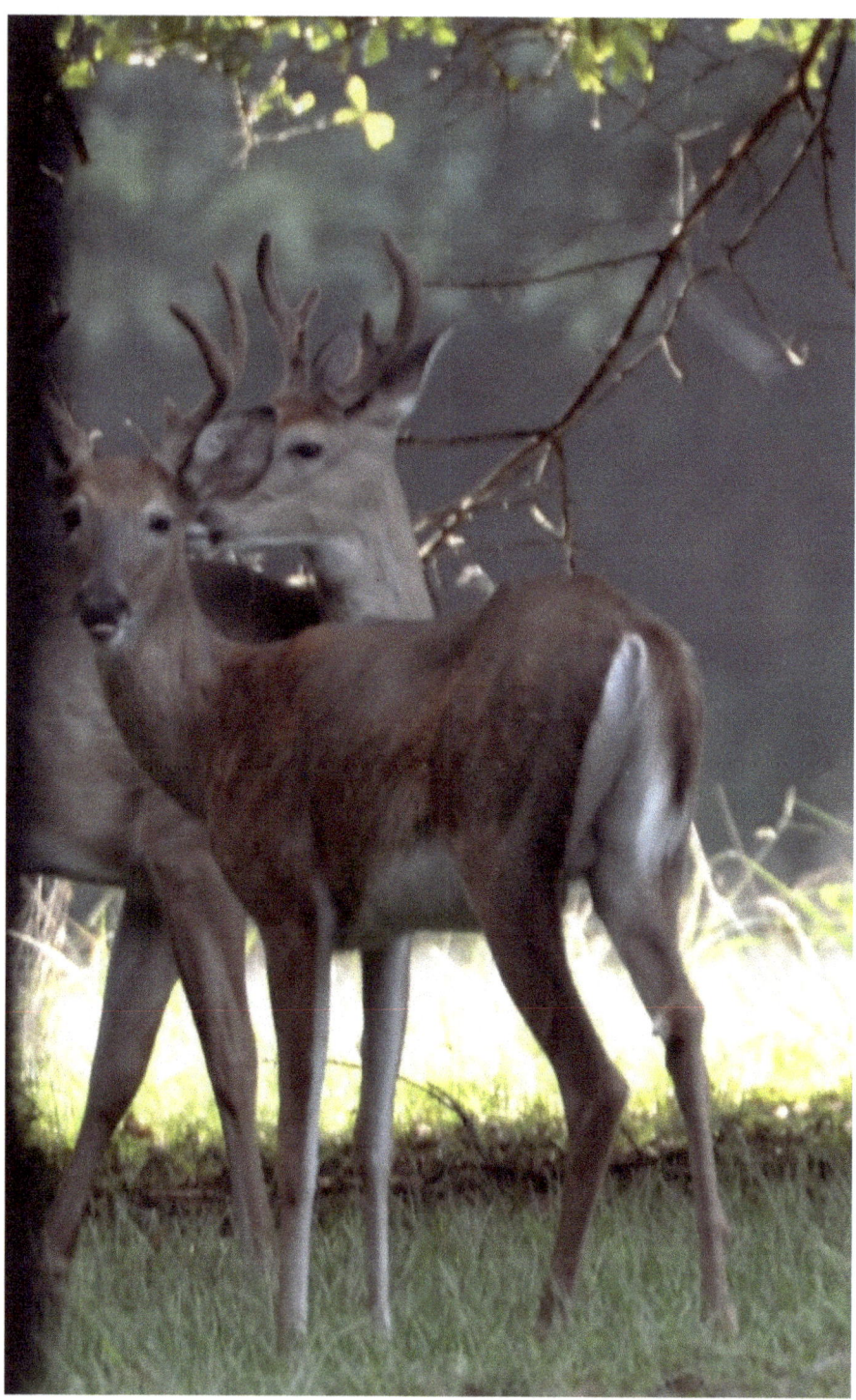

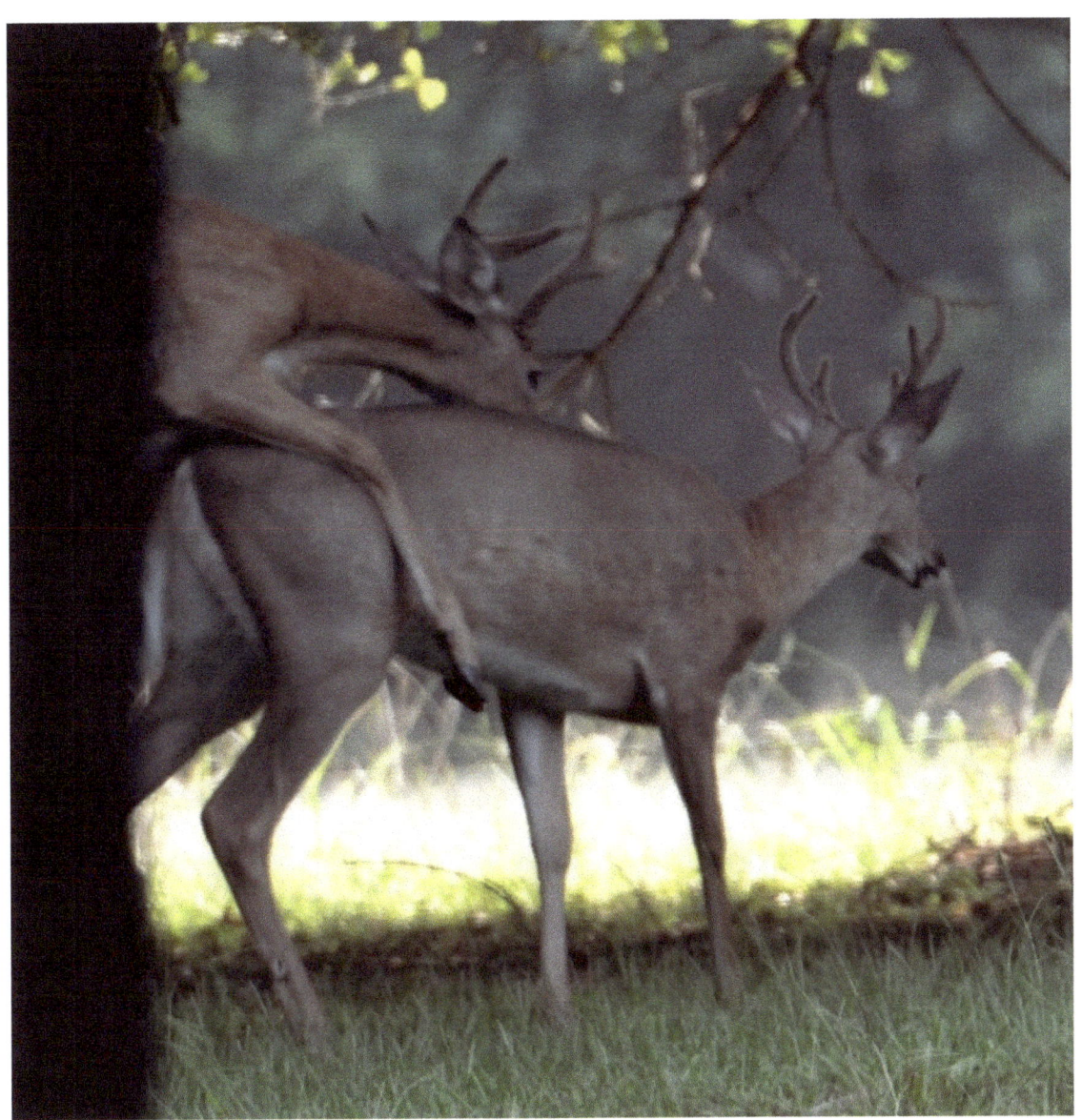

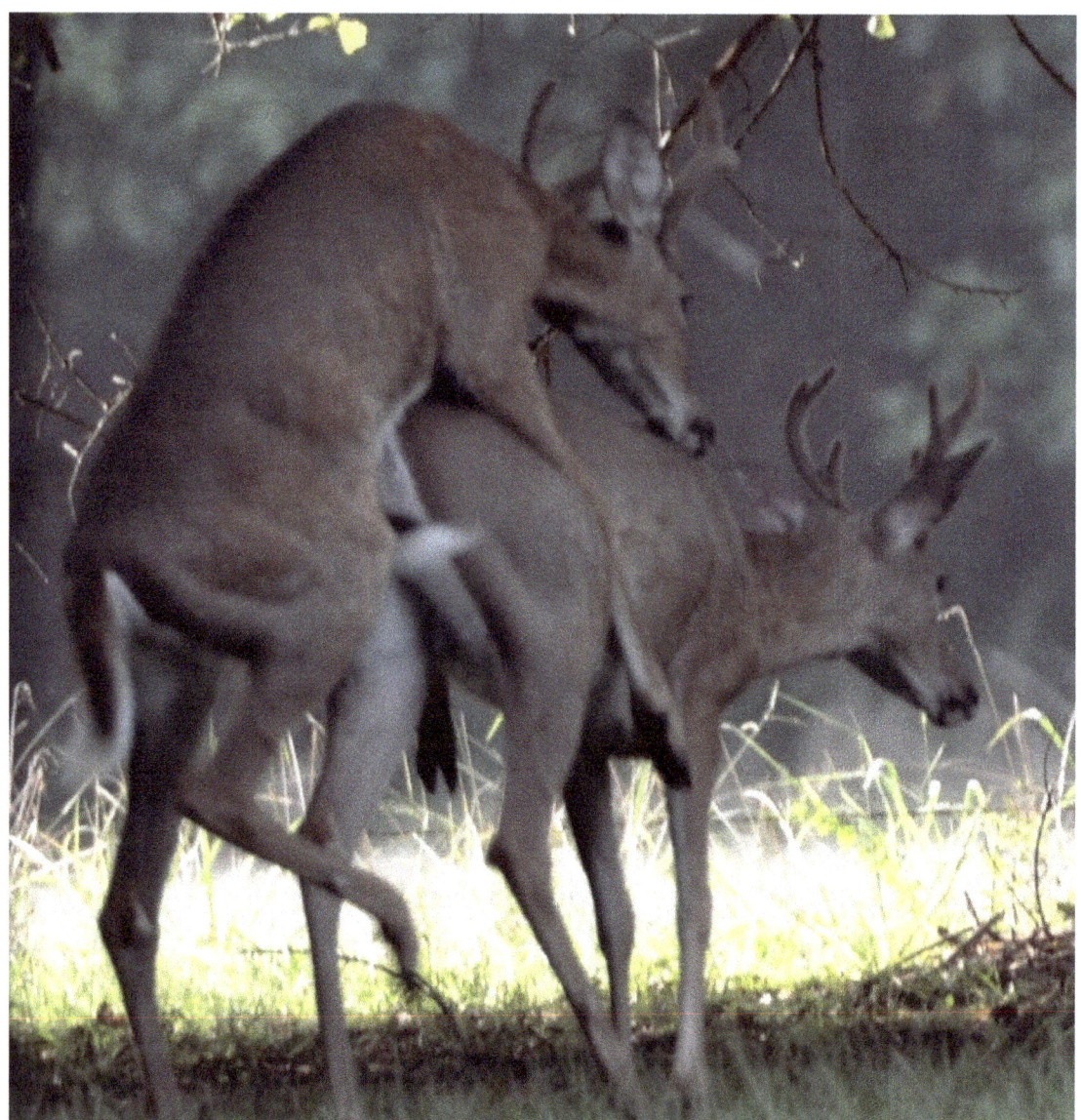

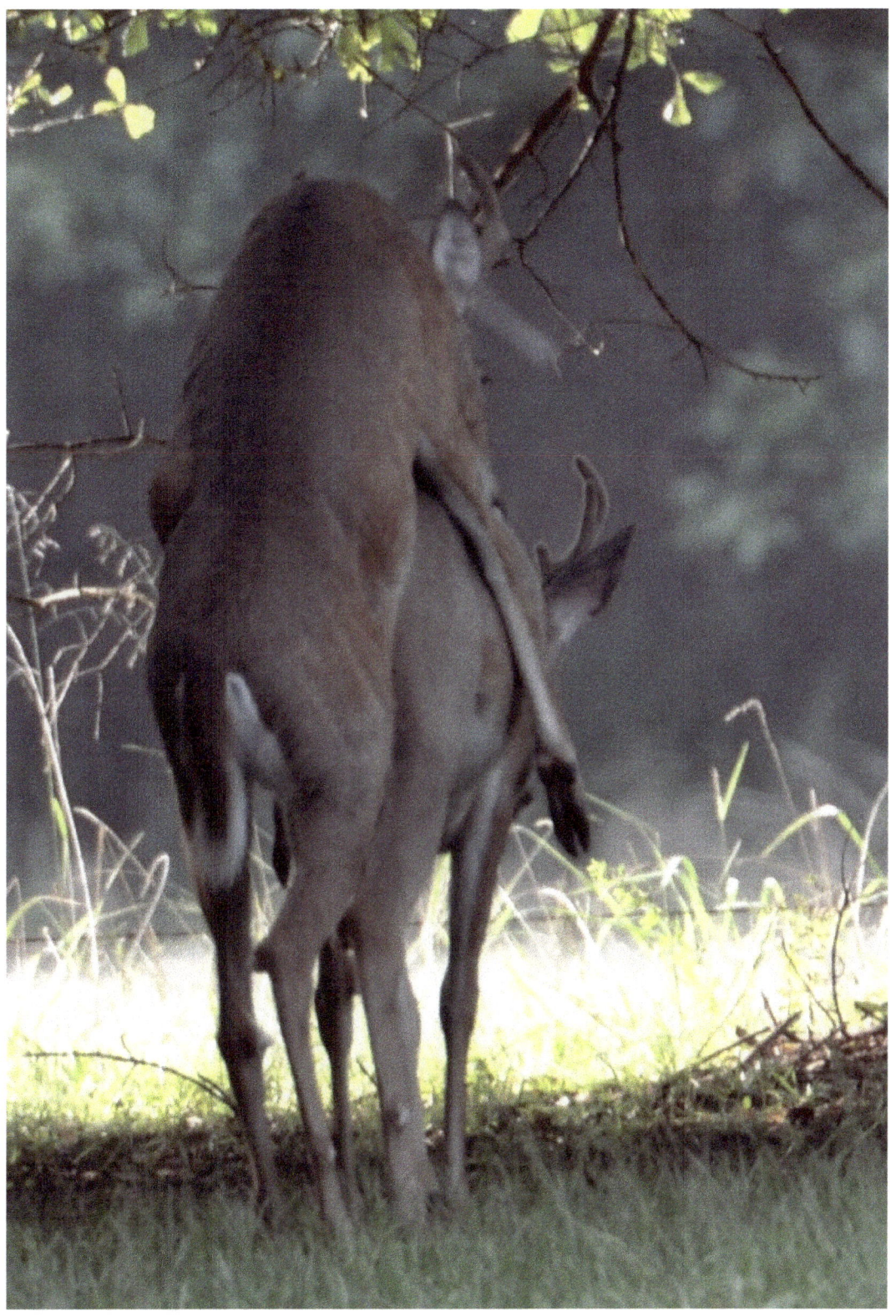

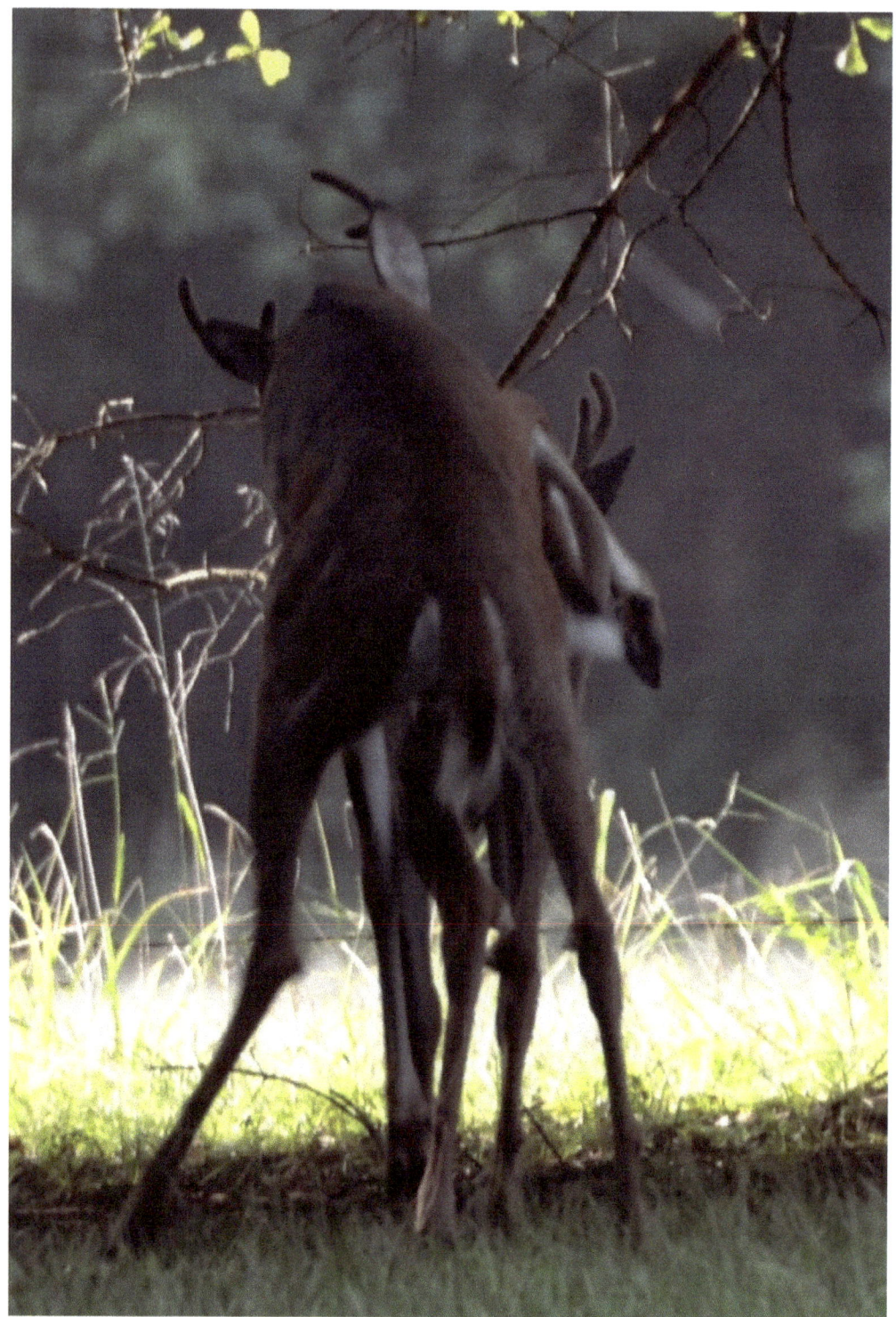

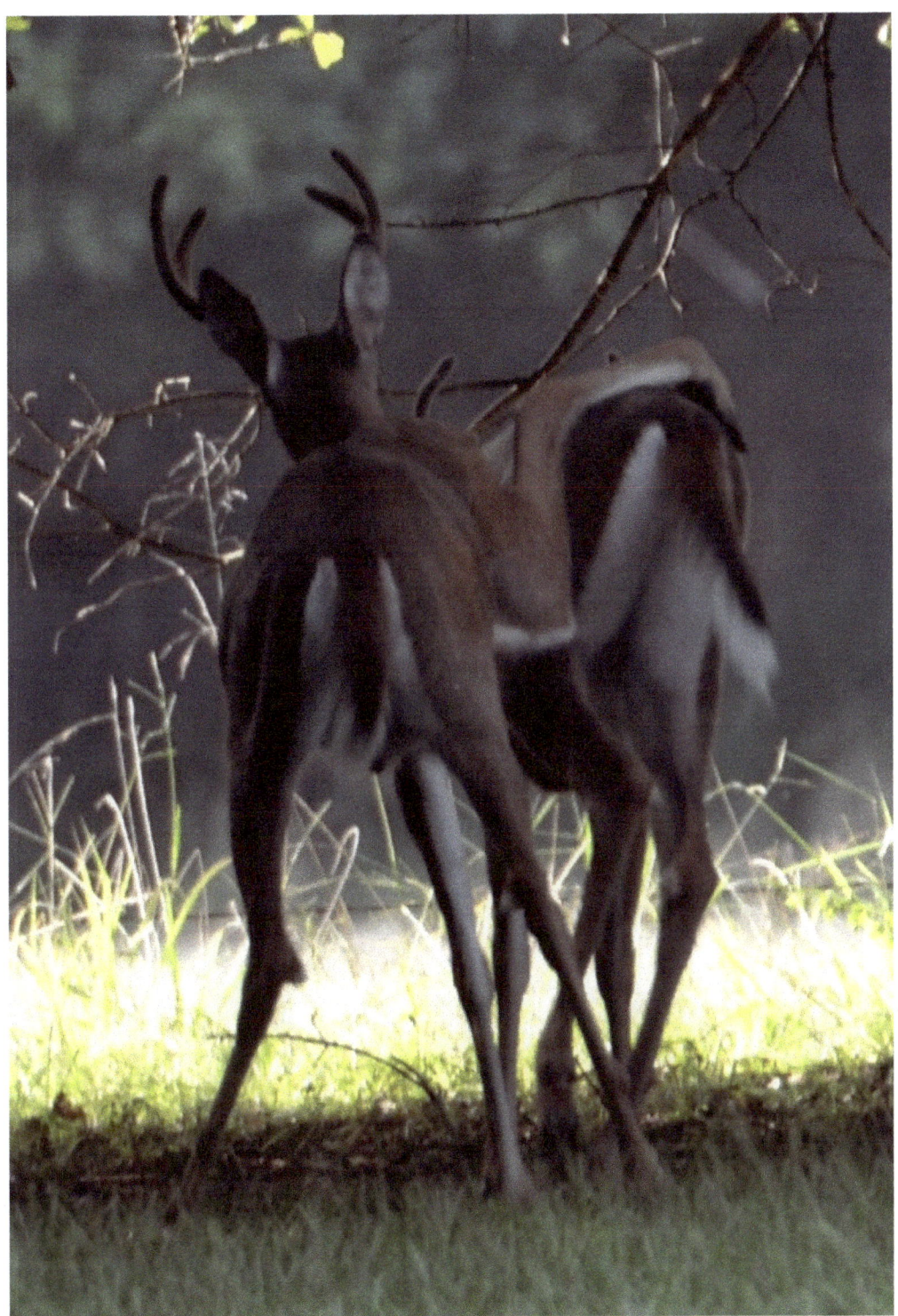

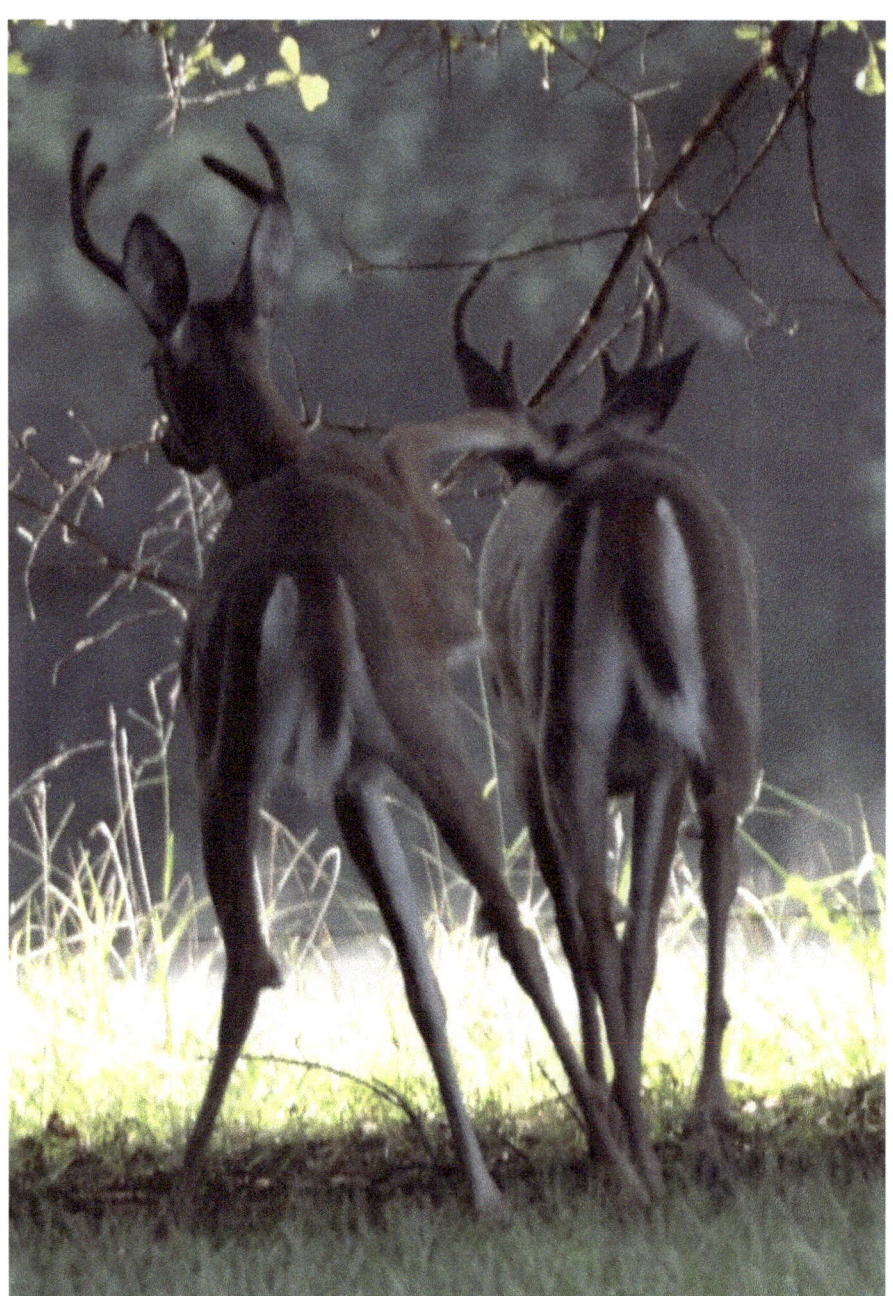

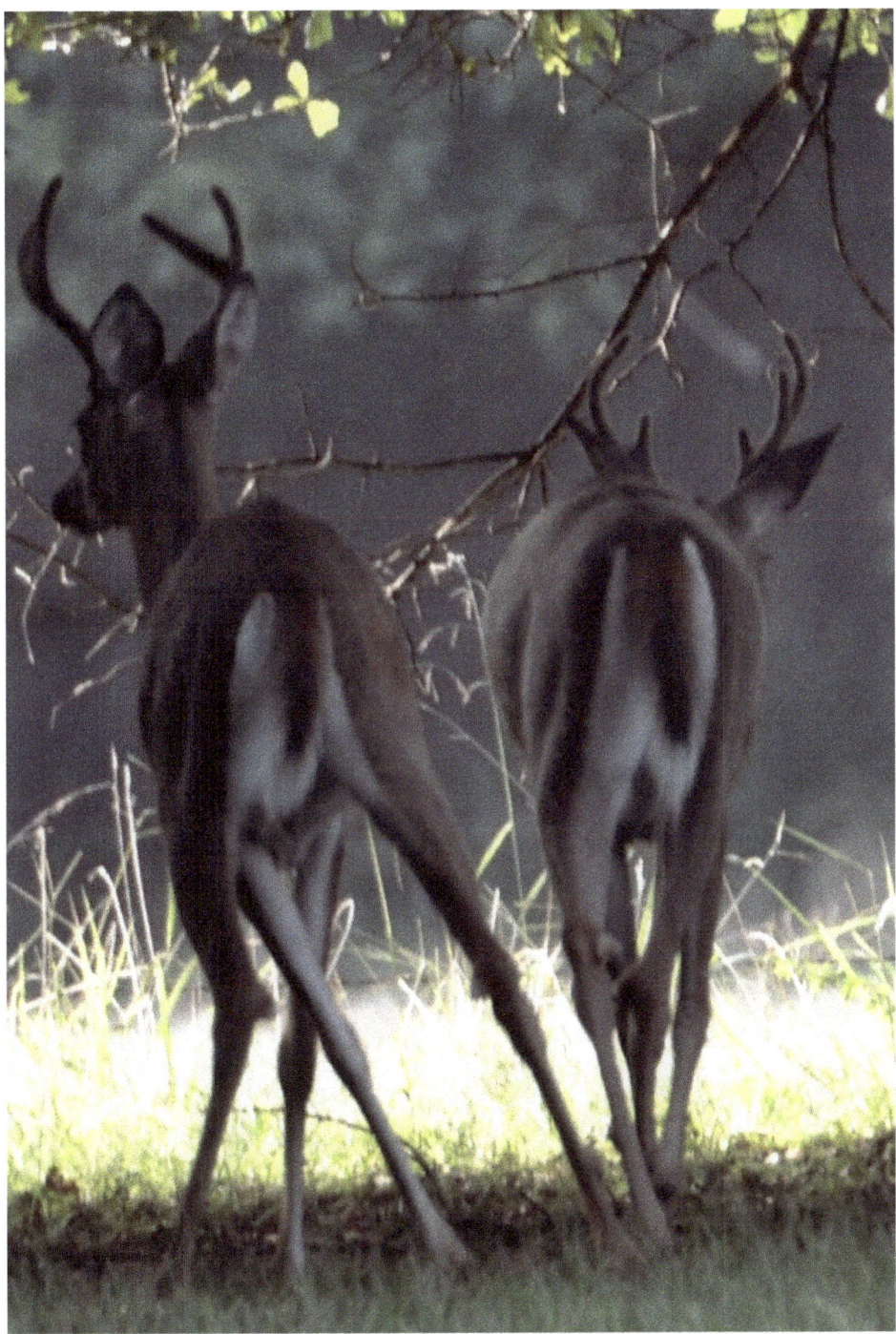

In my three weeks of observation, I saw this action repeated several times. The boys were practicing for the rut soon to come. Ironically, their behavior, from touching noses to mounting, was repeated by other frustrated bucks over the days I watched.

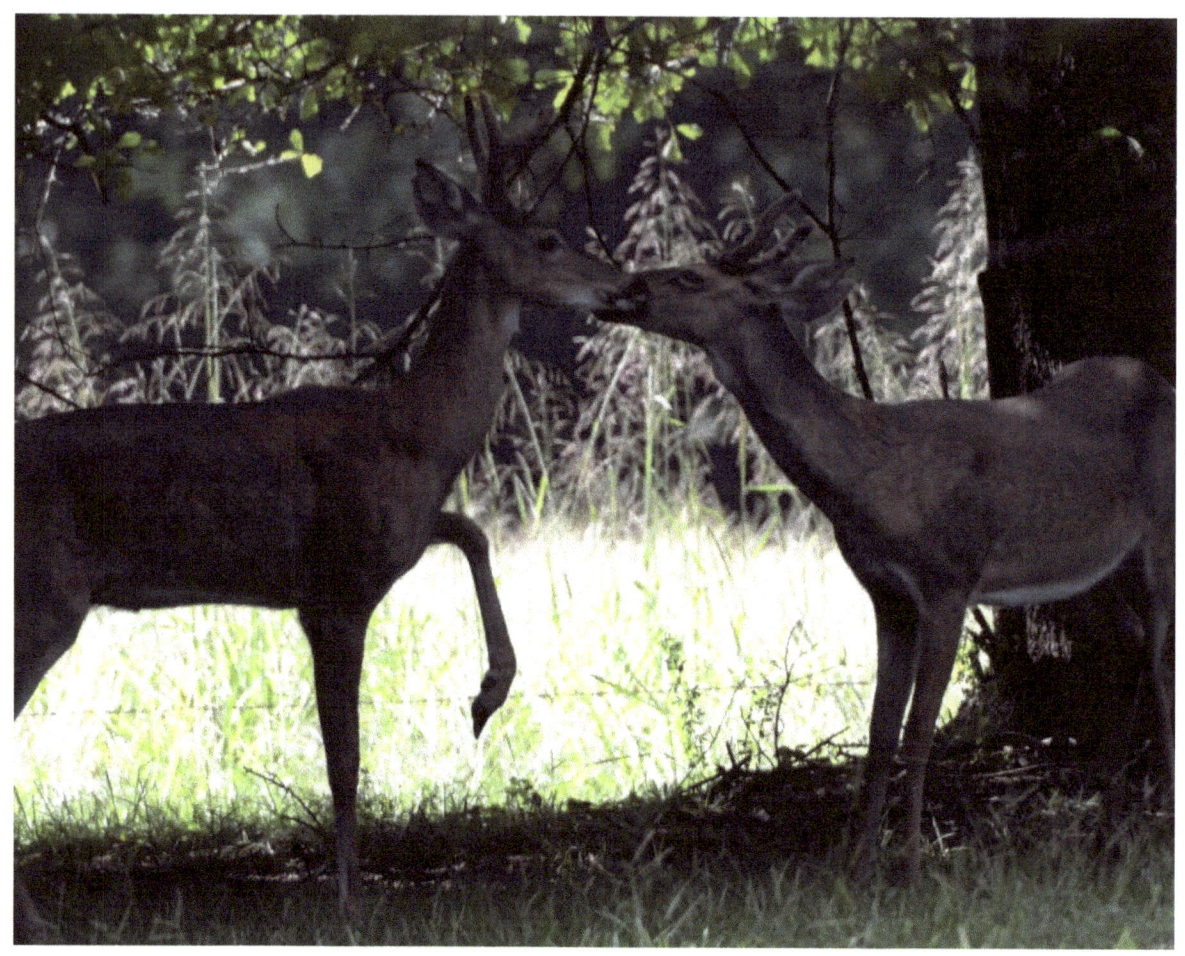

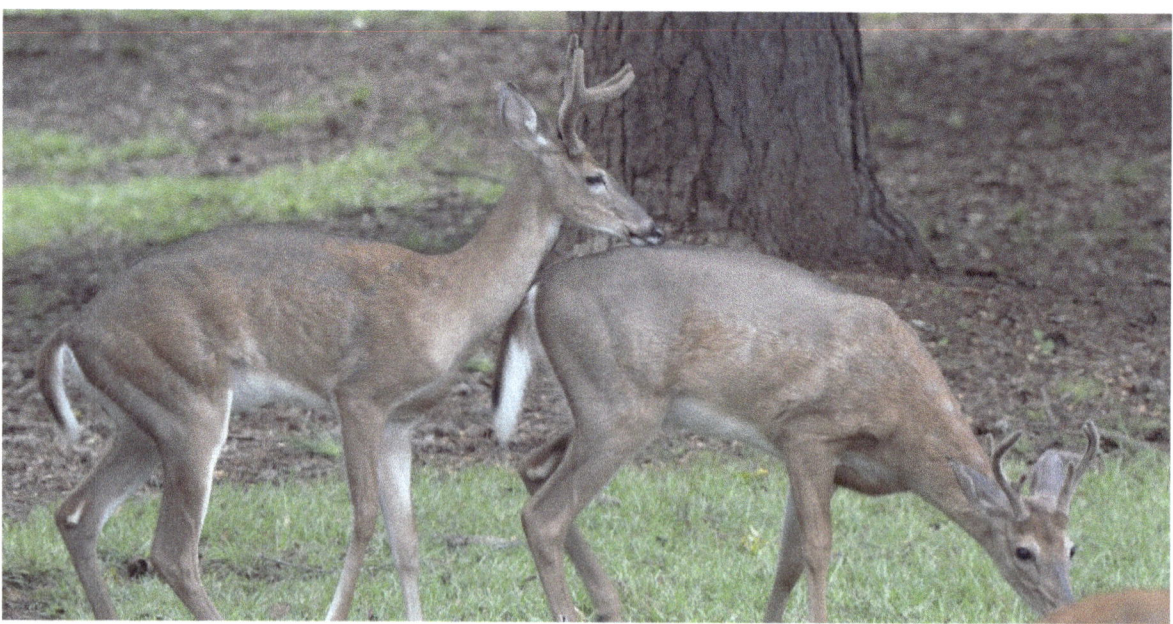

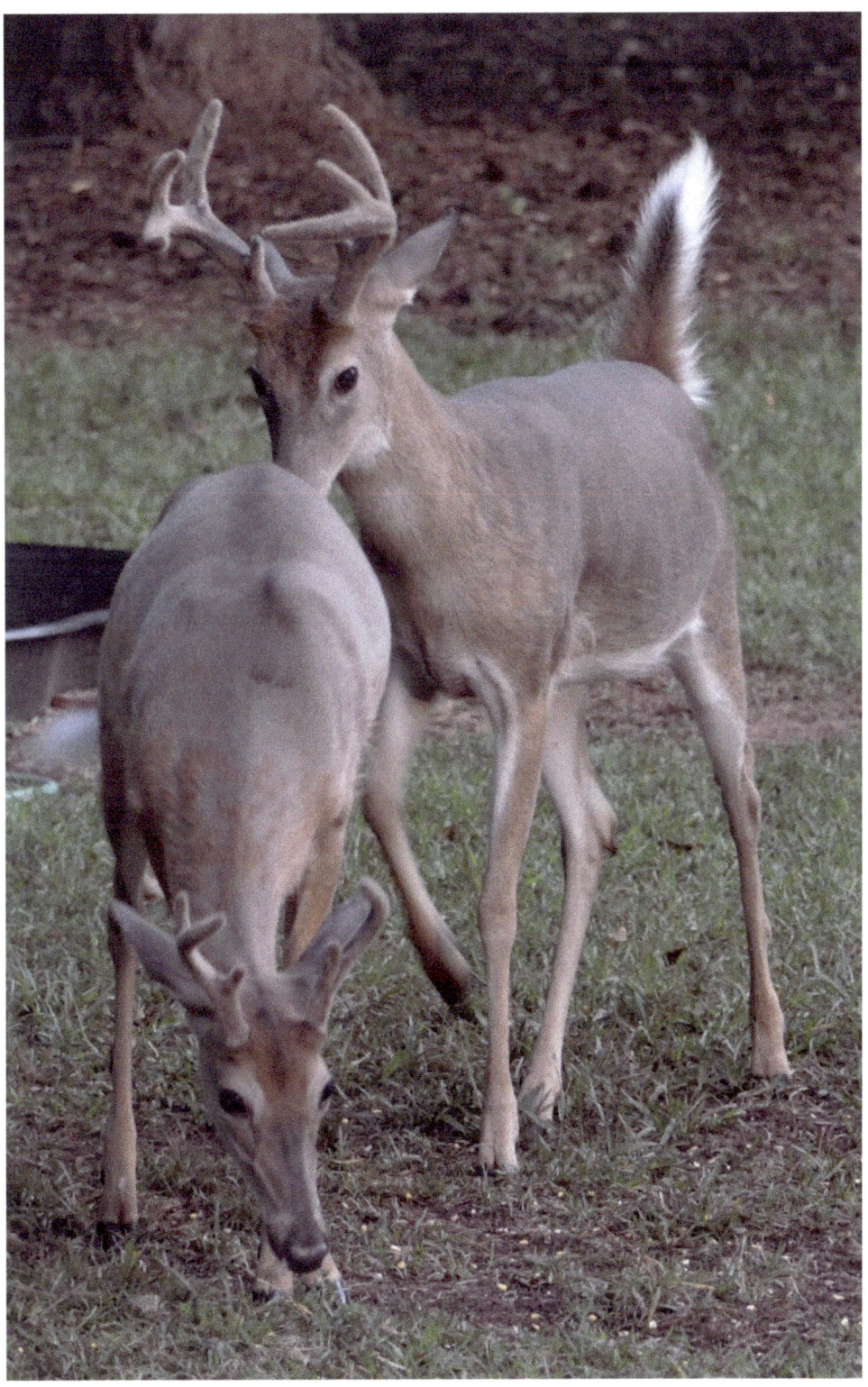

THE RUT

Bucks in all varieties of deer endure puberty every year. In late winter or early spring, bucks drop their antlers, their testosterone levels decrease and their testicles shrink. They return sexually to pre-teens, or prepubescent.

Soon after, they began to re-grow antlers. Around the first of September in my neighborhood, the bucks begin to transform into adults. Antlers change from growing flesh to bone and the velvet begins to dry and crack off.

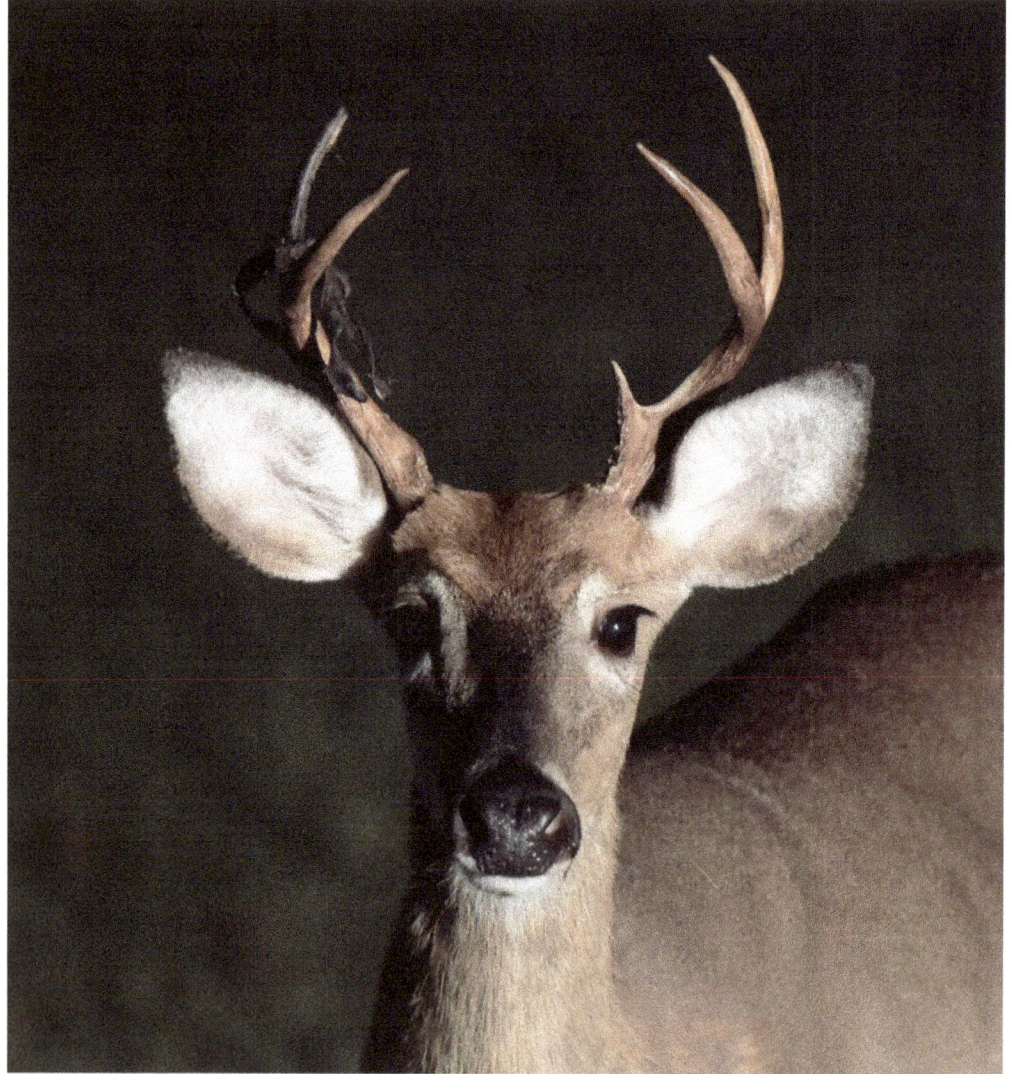

Their testicles drop and their testosterone levels rise. Their necks swell as the bucks begin to play-fight with each other. They are prepared to mate when the first local doe enters estrus. The half-play competition not only strengthens them for the coming battles for mating rights but also partly settles who will be the dominant buck.

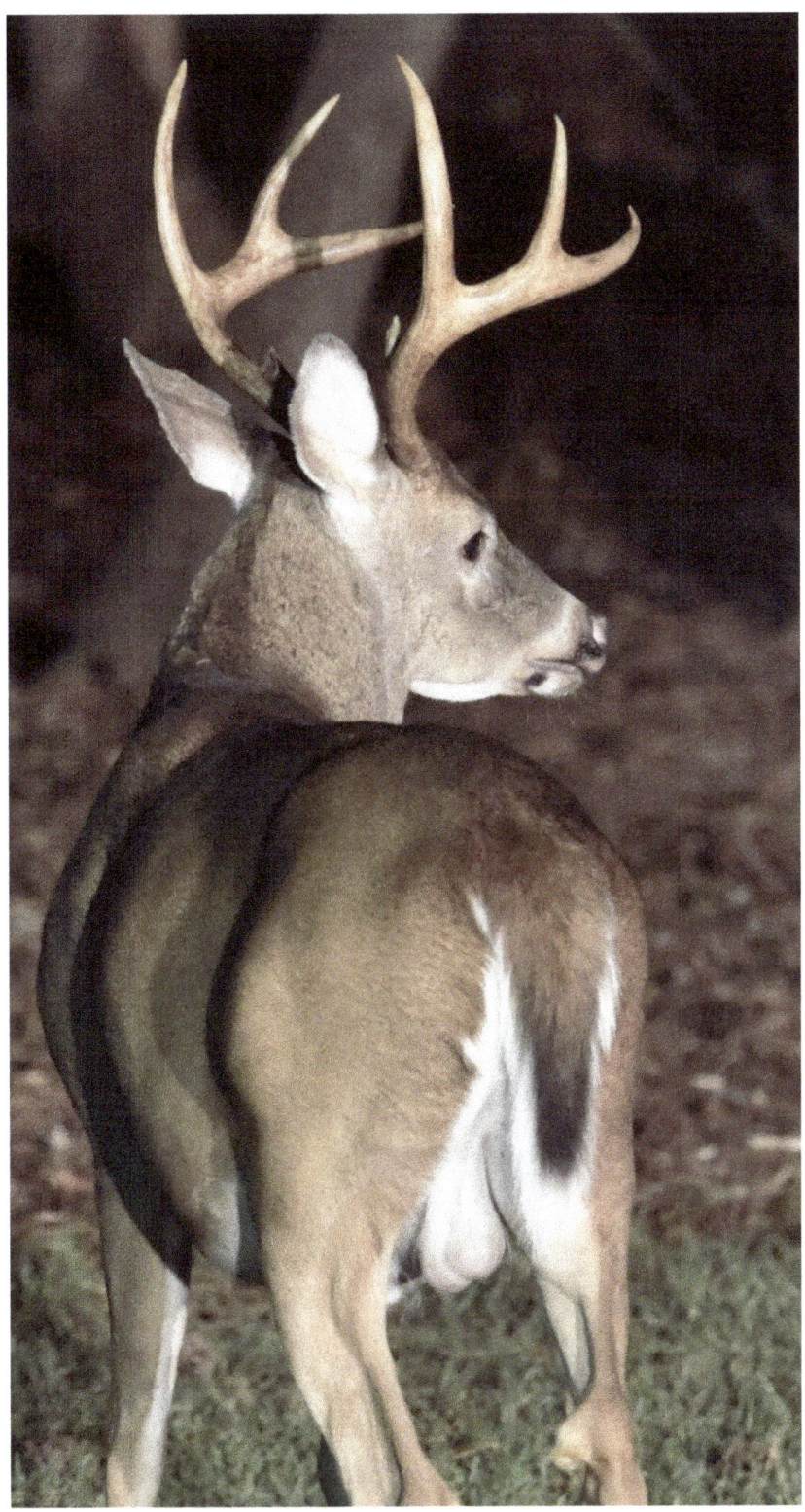

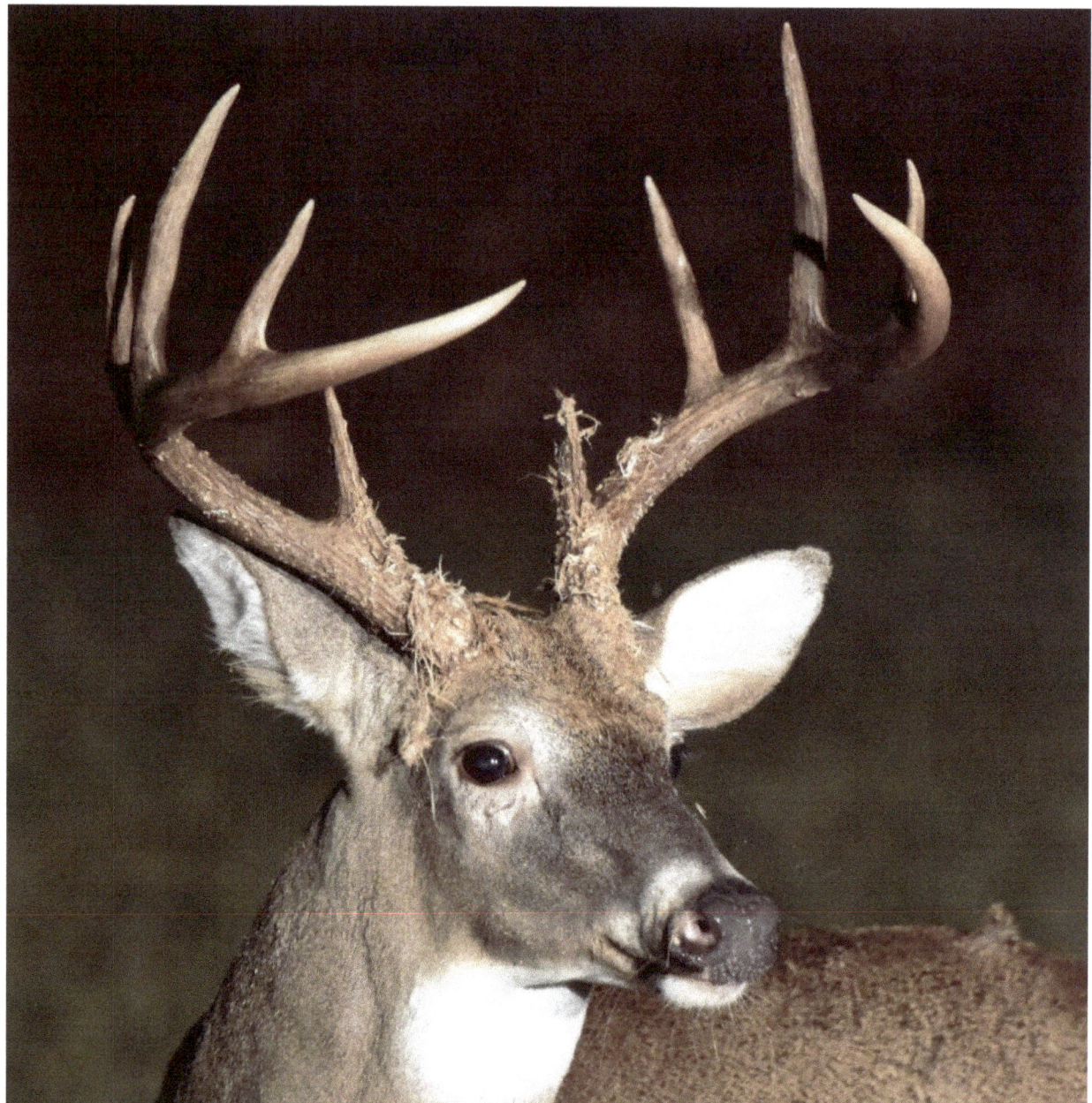

Big Ten showed up again after another battle with a tree and this time brought a lot more of the tree with him.

One of the bucks' courting behaviors is to paw the ground beneath a limb, usually of a hardwood tree, and urinate in the spot. They urinate down their back legs and thereby they run their scent onto their musk glands, which turn black and (for me at least) stink. When a doe in estrus comes upon a scrape, she will urinate in the same spot and wait around for the buck. If he doesn't show up before she becomes impatient, she will wander off, and when he returns, he will sniff the scrape and follow her urine-scent trail.

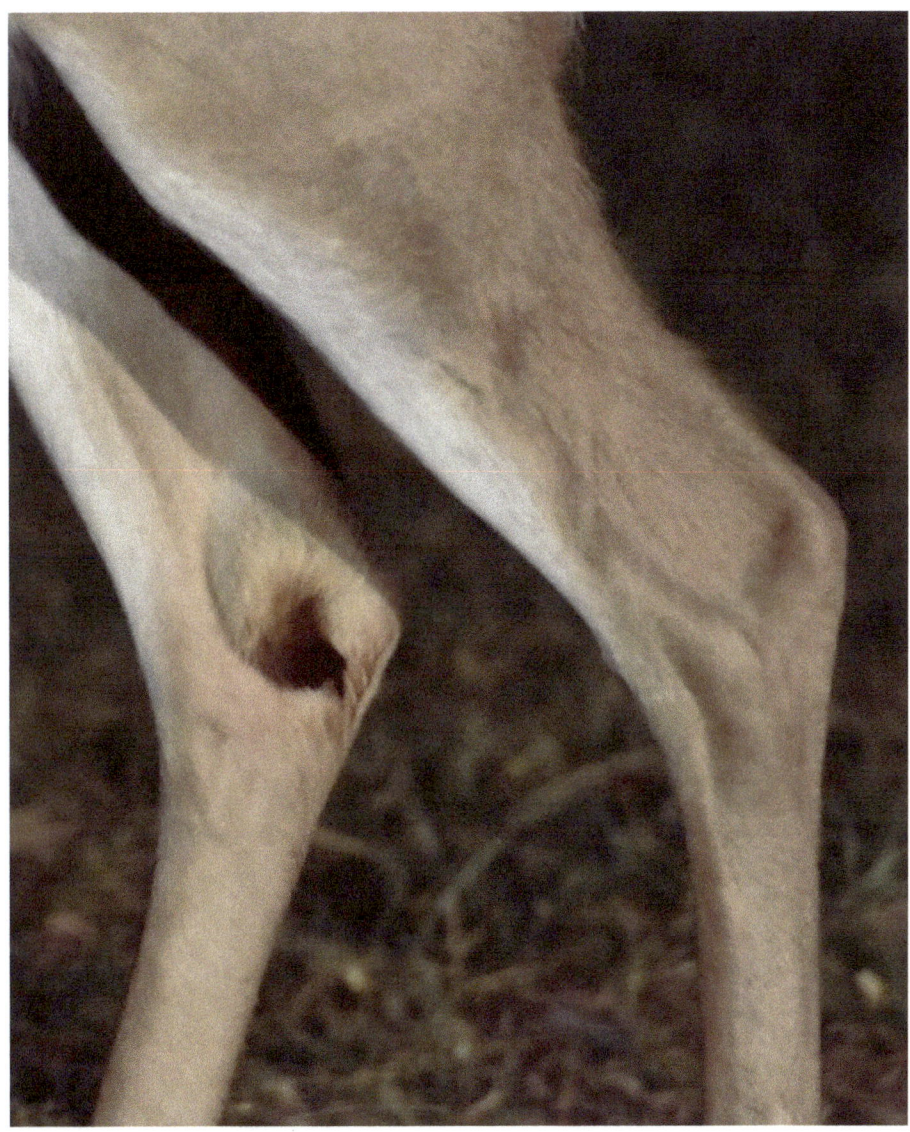

When I hunted, the first thing I did before dressing the deer was to remove the musk glands to ensure I did not get that scent onto the meat. I also washed my hands and tools before I continued to clean the deer.

BUCK v. BUCK

As the rut approaches, bucks begin to challenge each other in shoving matches, partially to begin to settle the pecking order for mating and partly to build up their muscles. Some spikes challenge older bucks with no fear, for the sparring is simply a game, until the does go into estrus and the competition begins in earnest.

All of these contests were ignored by the nearby deer.

I watched numerous contests, some half-hidden behind brush and some in darkness beyond the camera's ability to capture images. I am showing only a small portion of each contest. Each series will show a close-up of the combatants.

Spike v. fork-horn

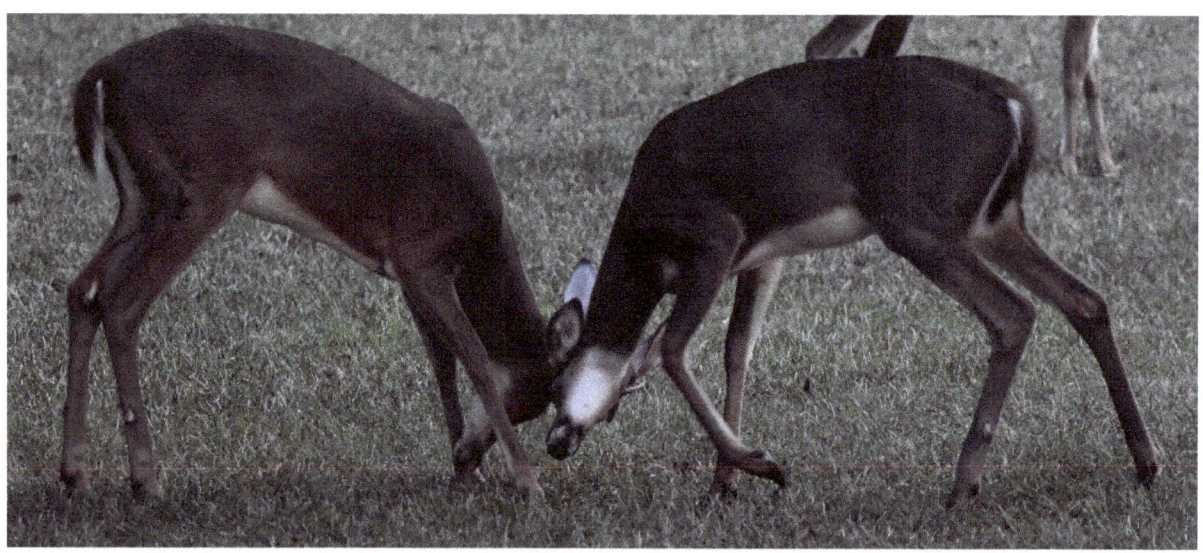

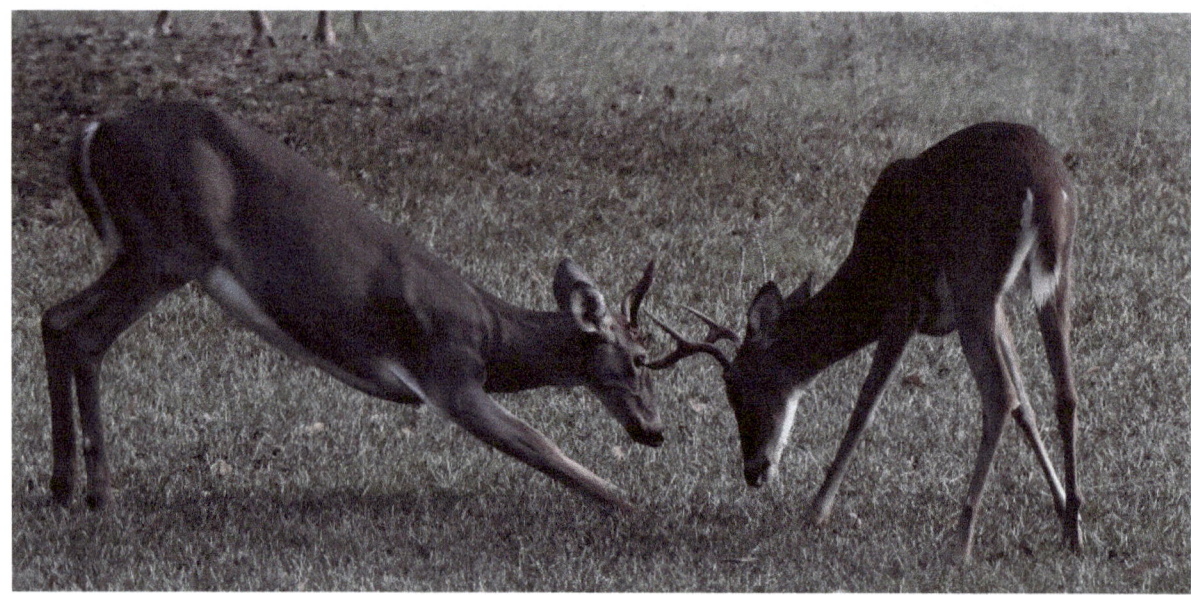

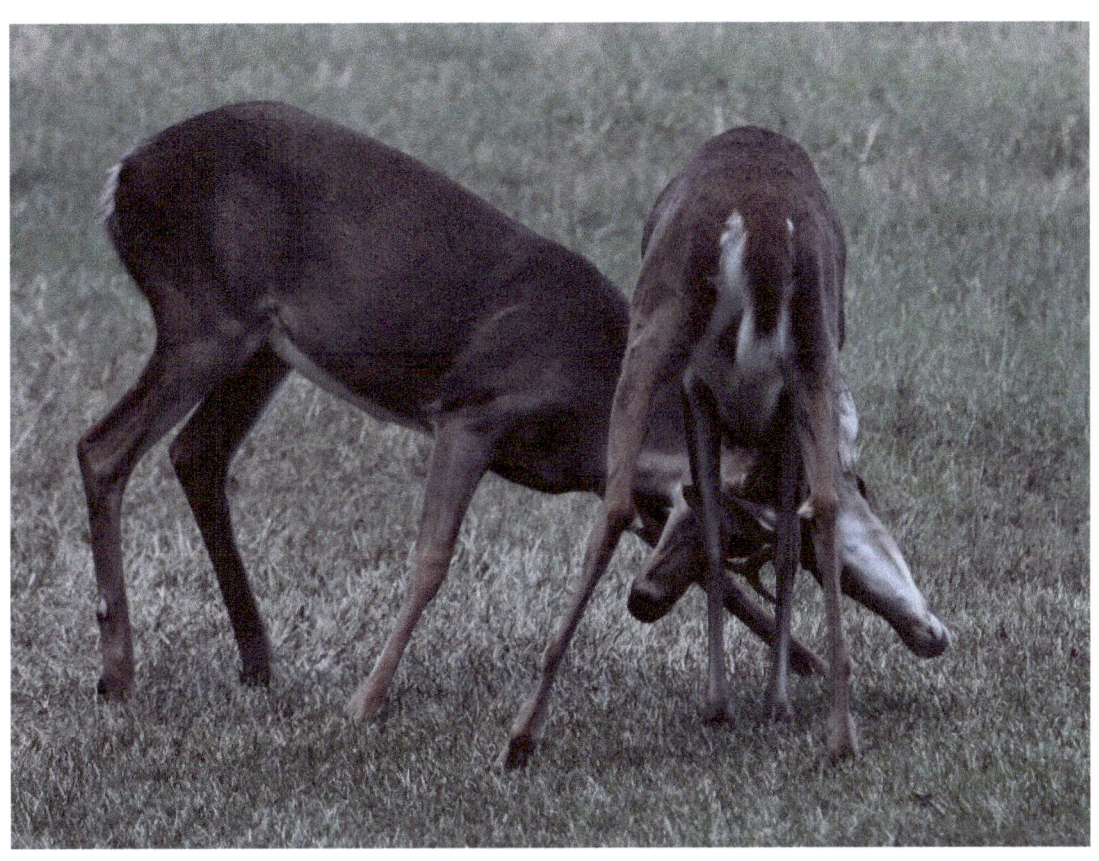

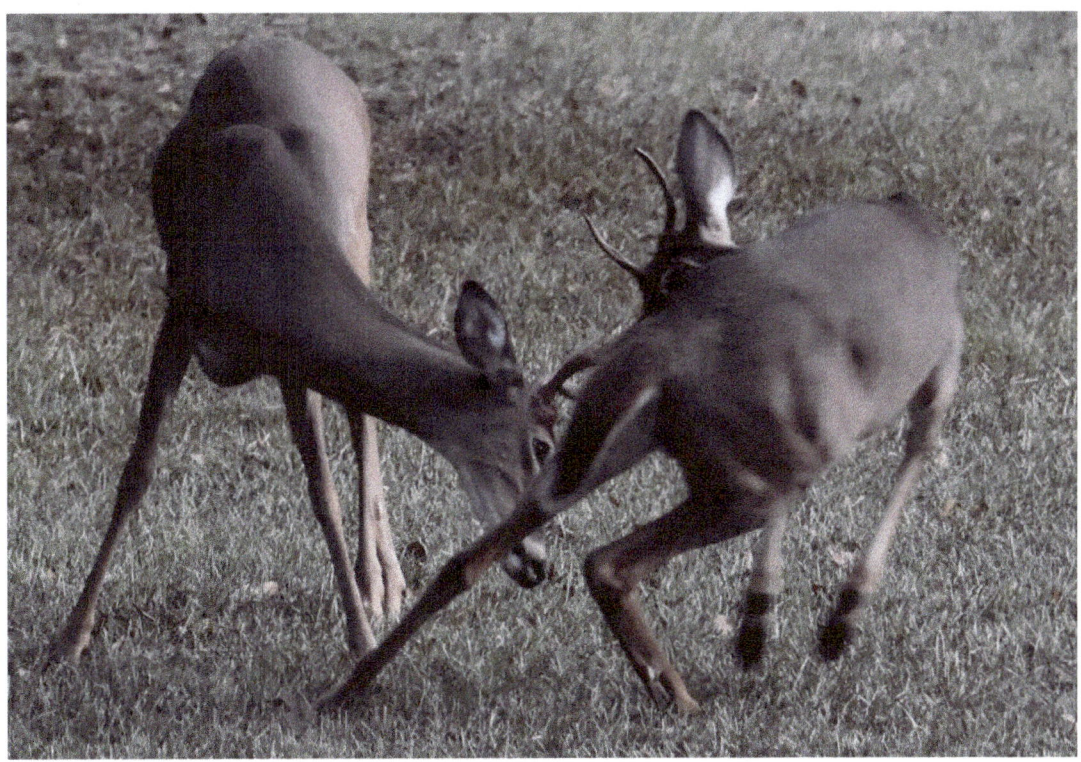

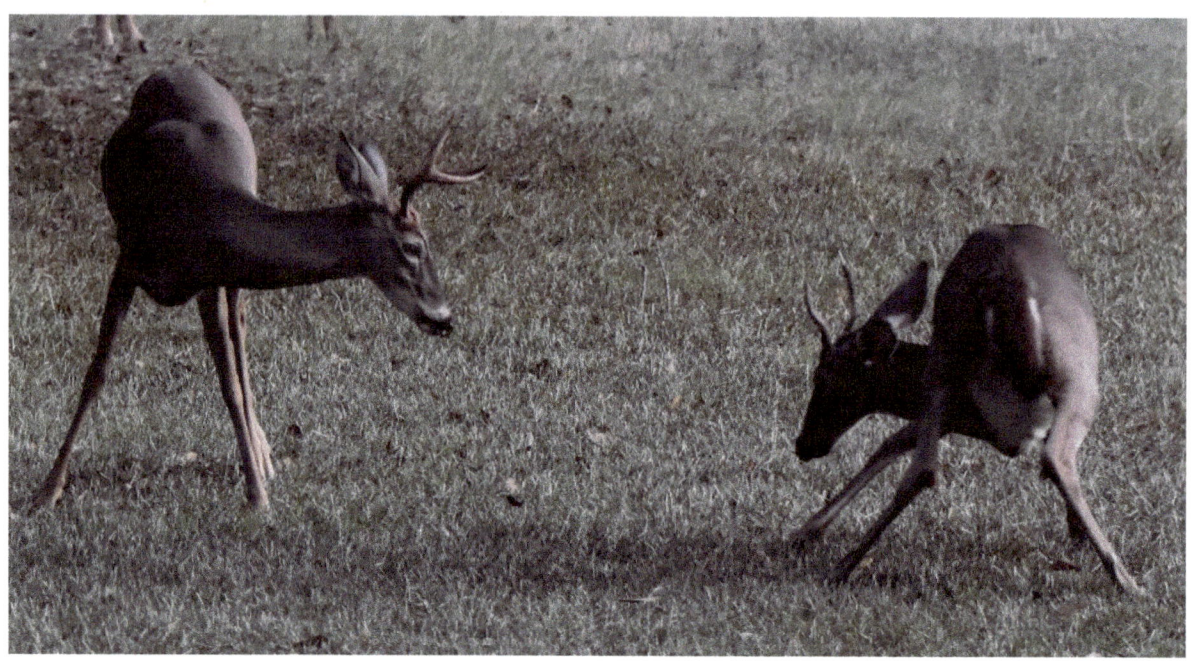

Spike v. five-pointer

The spike then challenged a five-pointer only moments after they shared the pool.

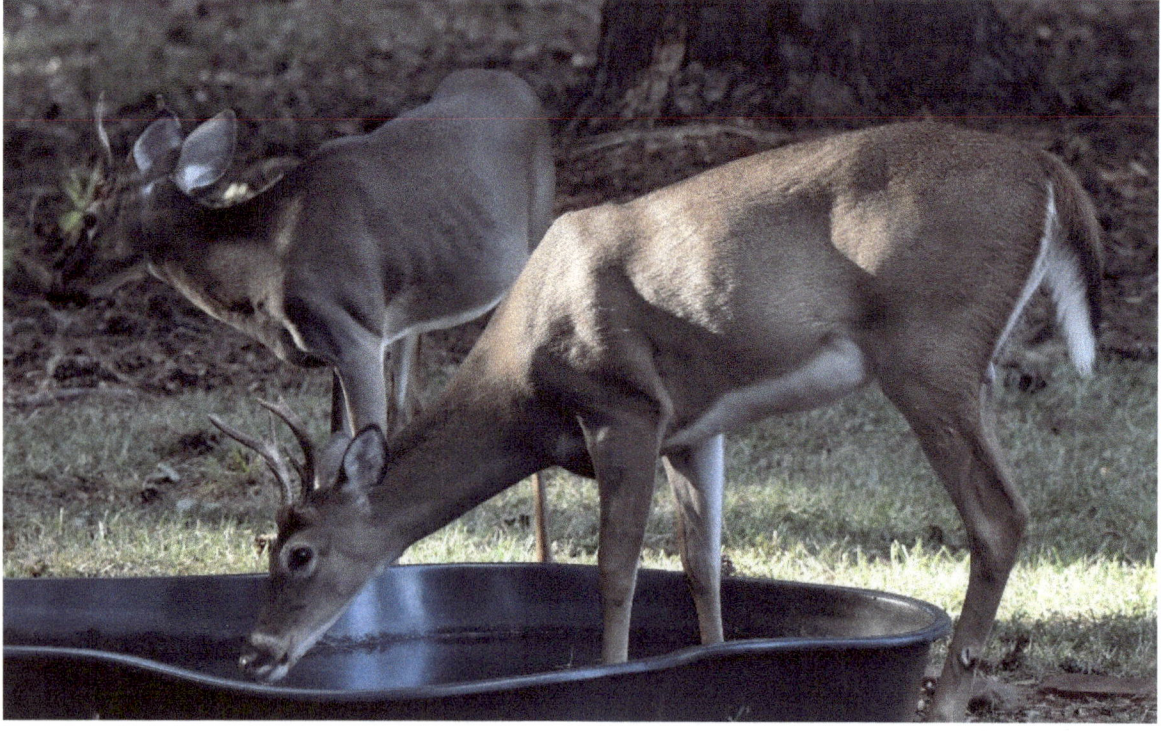

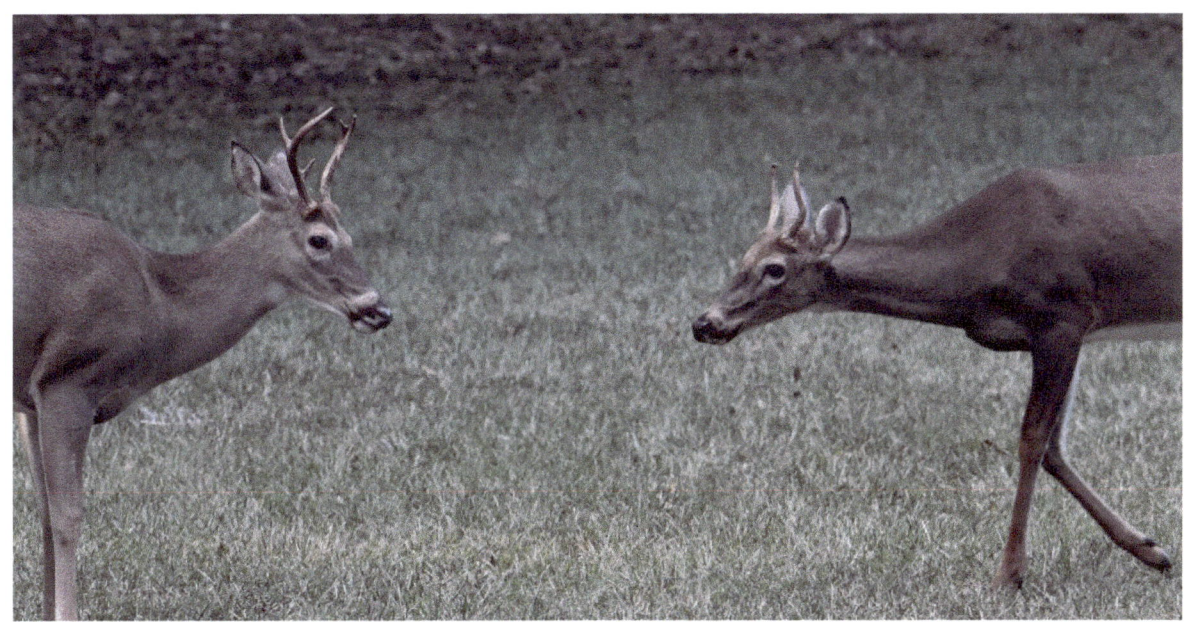

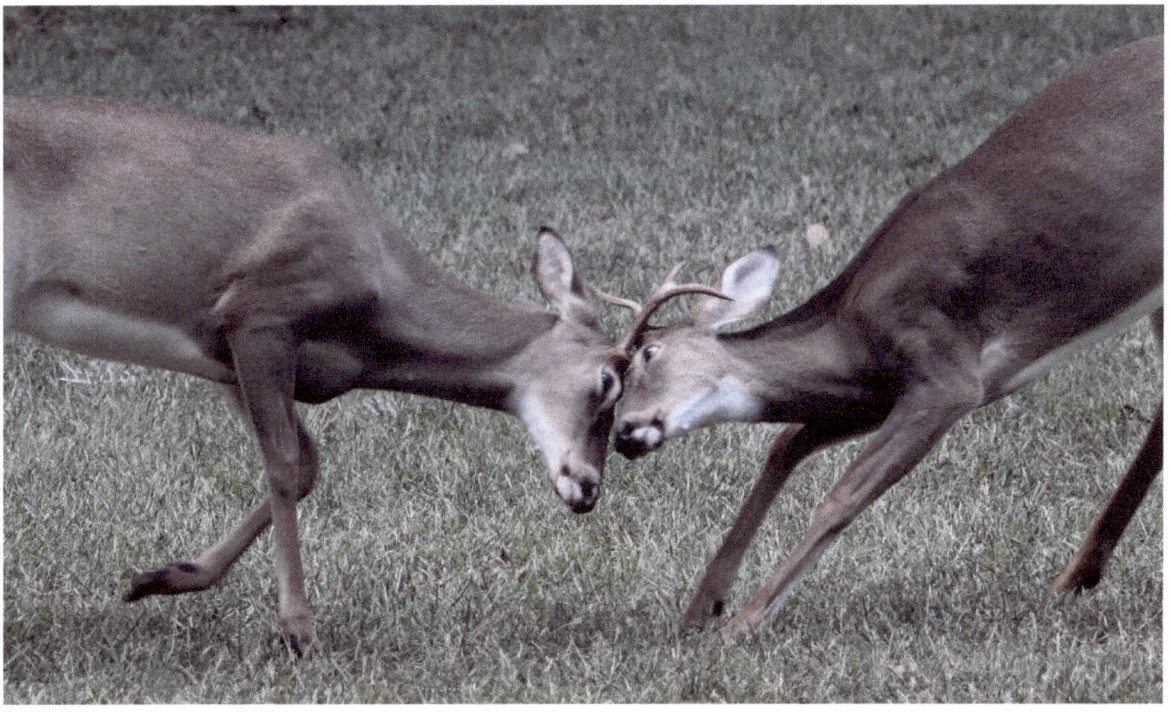

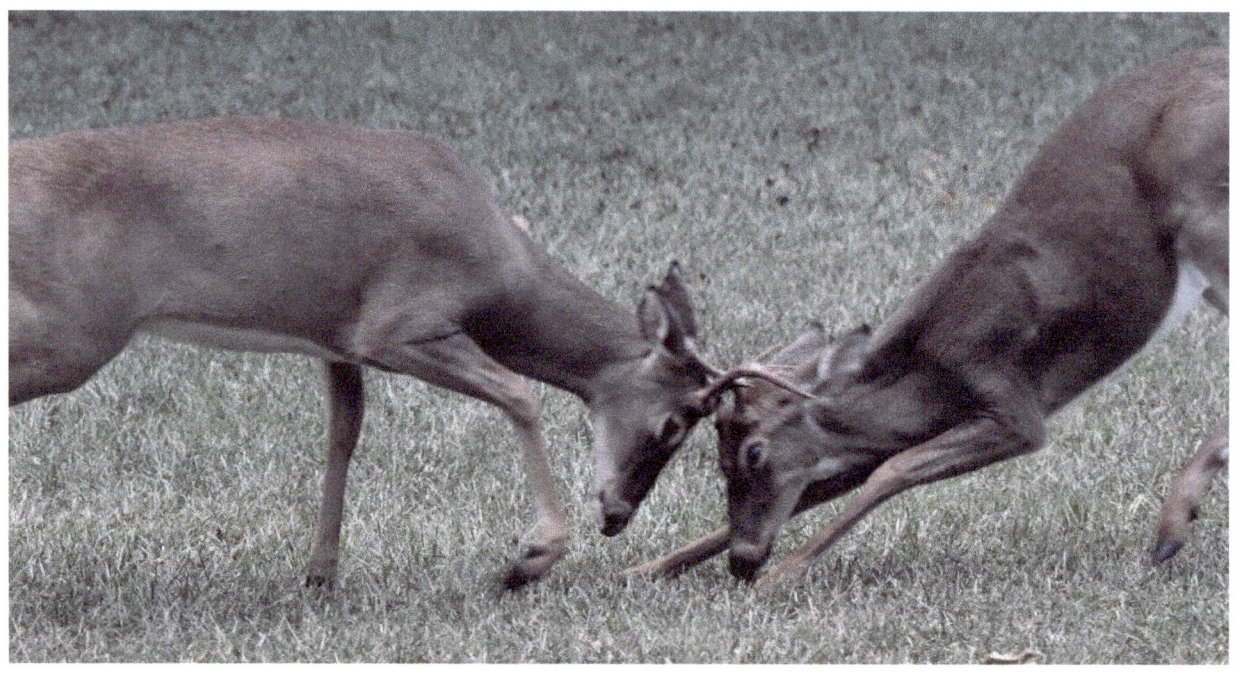

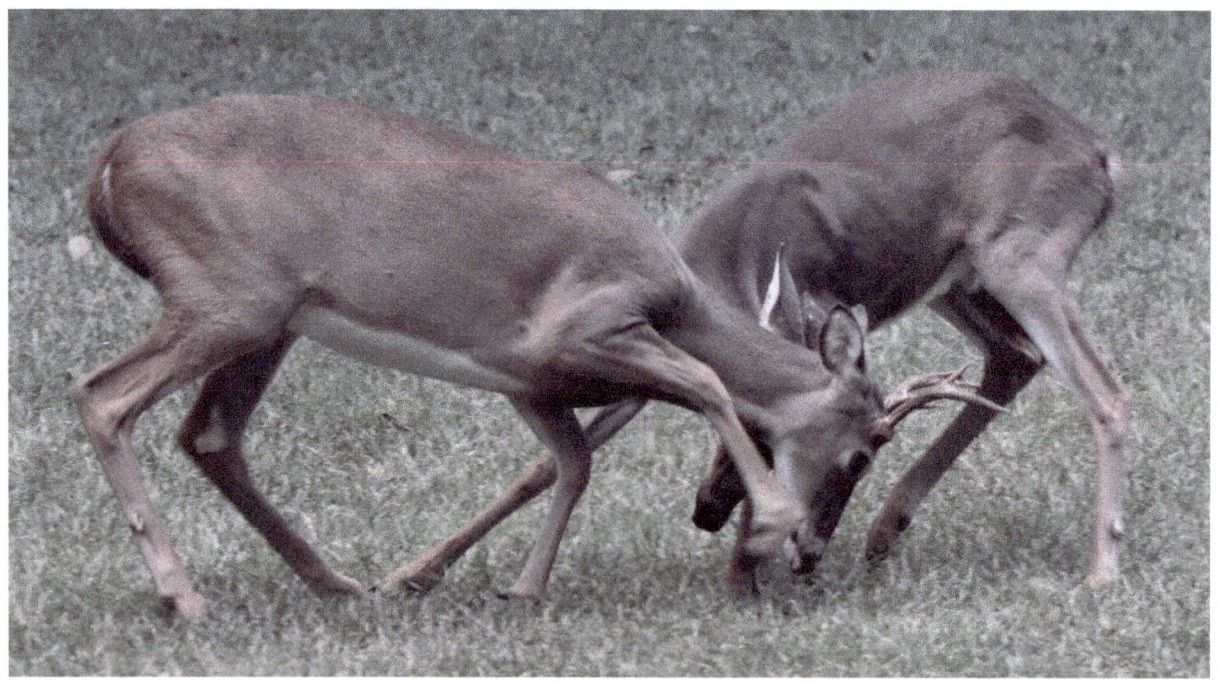

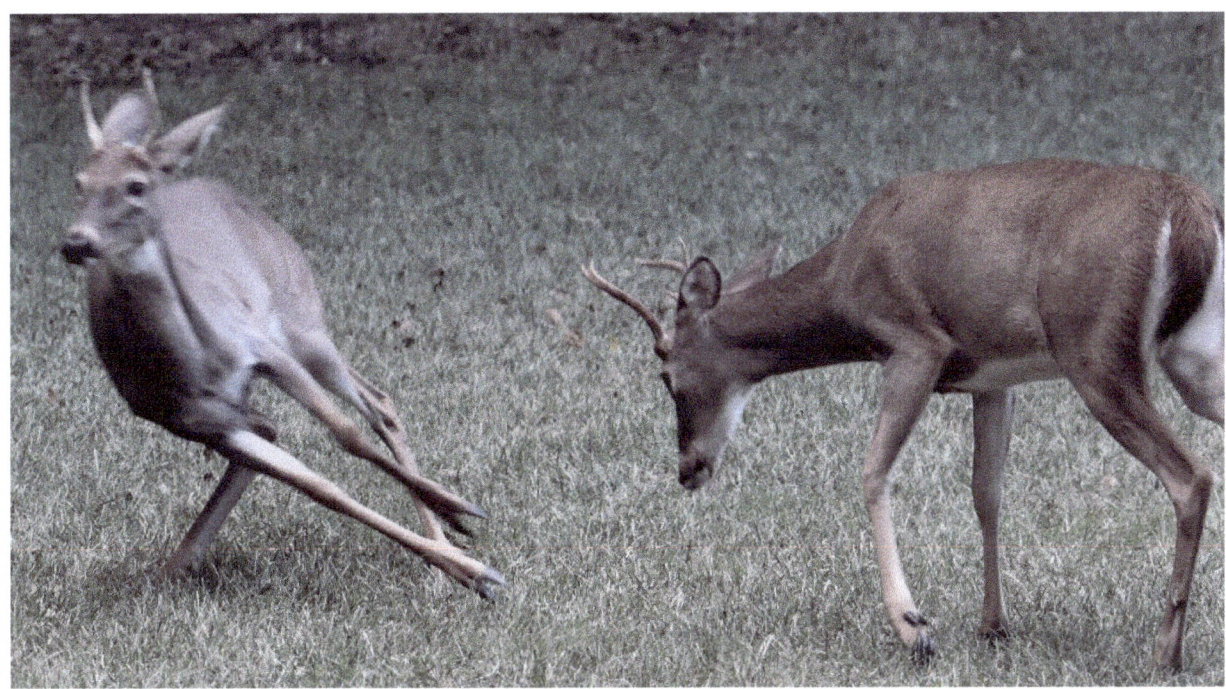

Five-pointer v. four-pointer

When this spike retreated, the five-pointer got into a match with the four-pointer that had defeated the spike earlier.

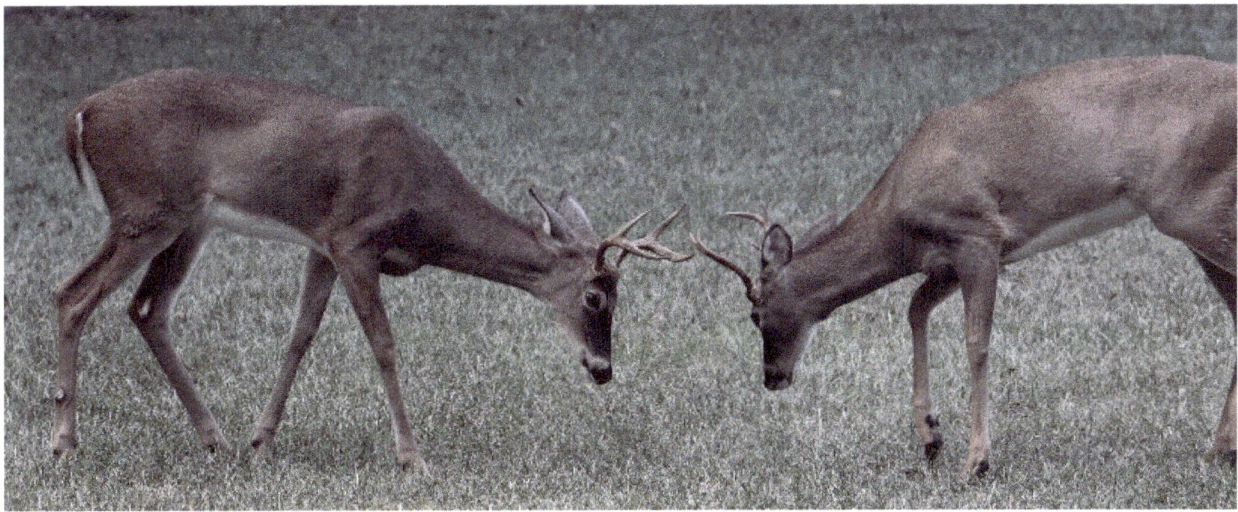

The spike retreats in the background. The new shoving match lasted only moments and then the two bucks strolled off.

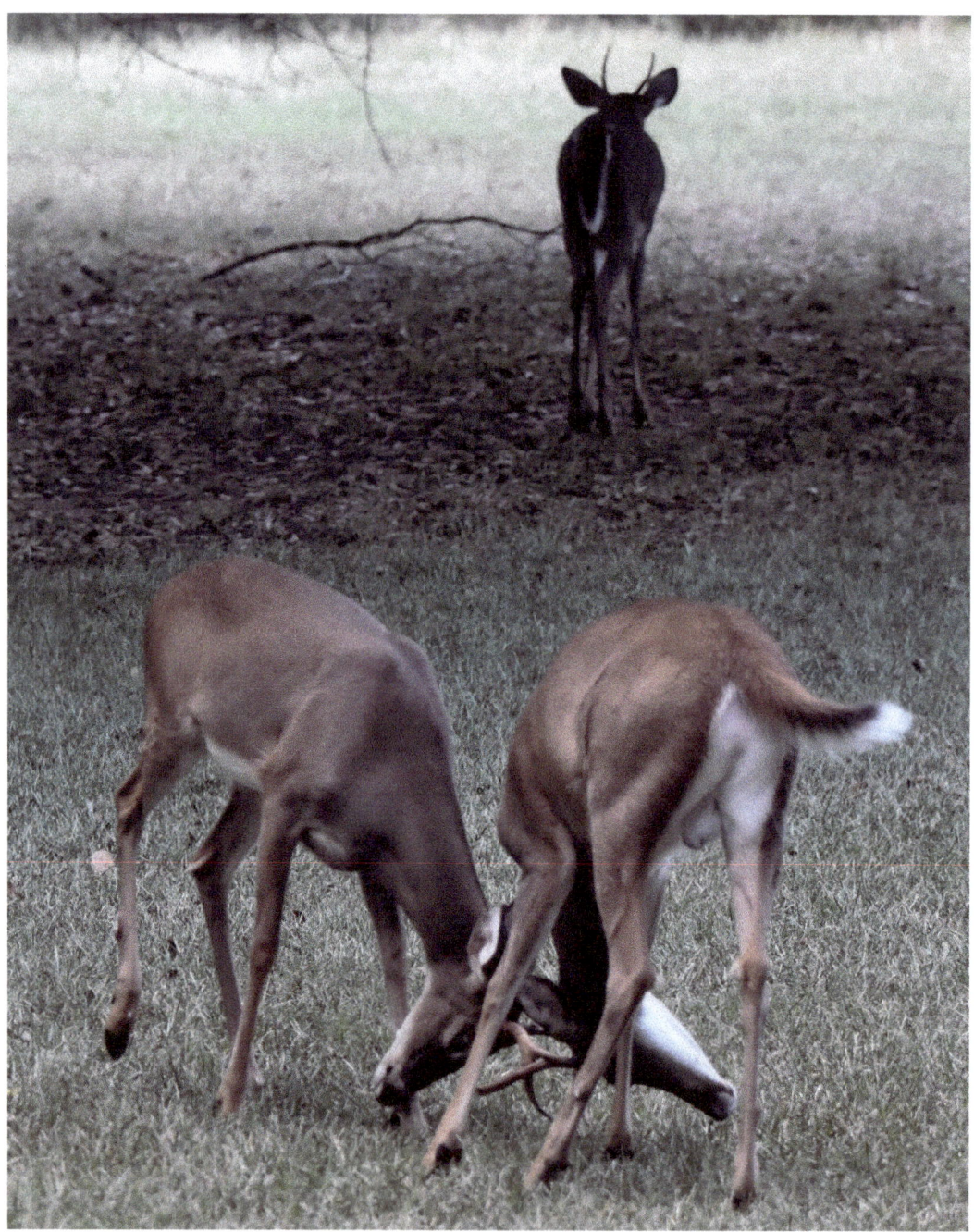

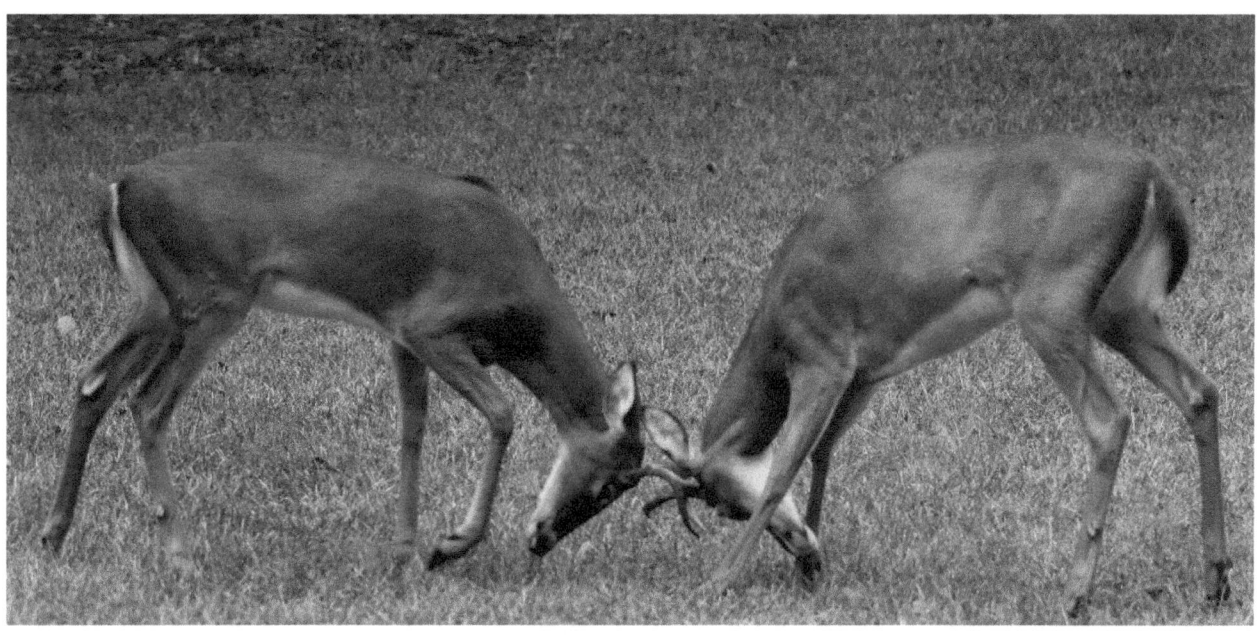

Eight-pointer v. Tall Rack

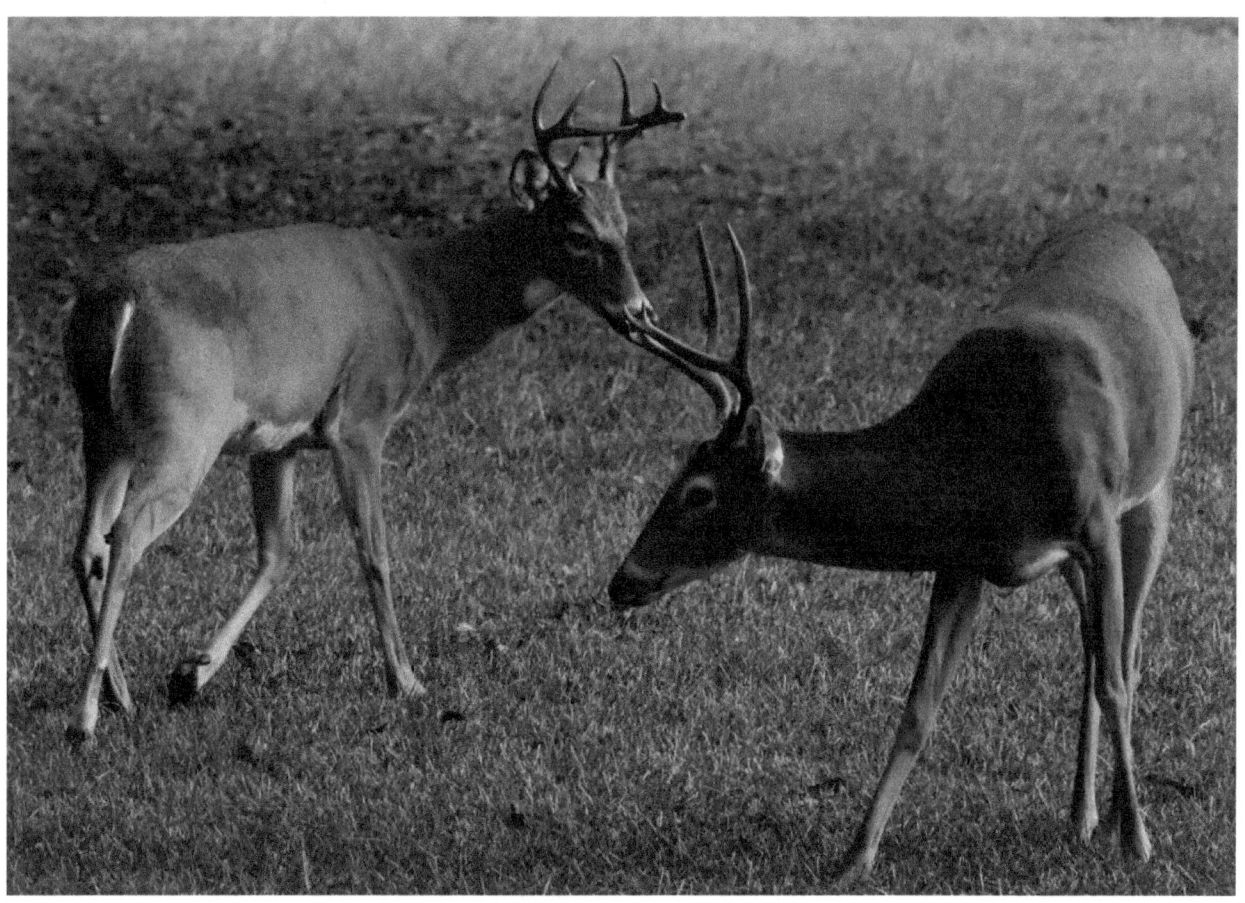

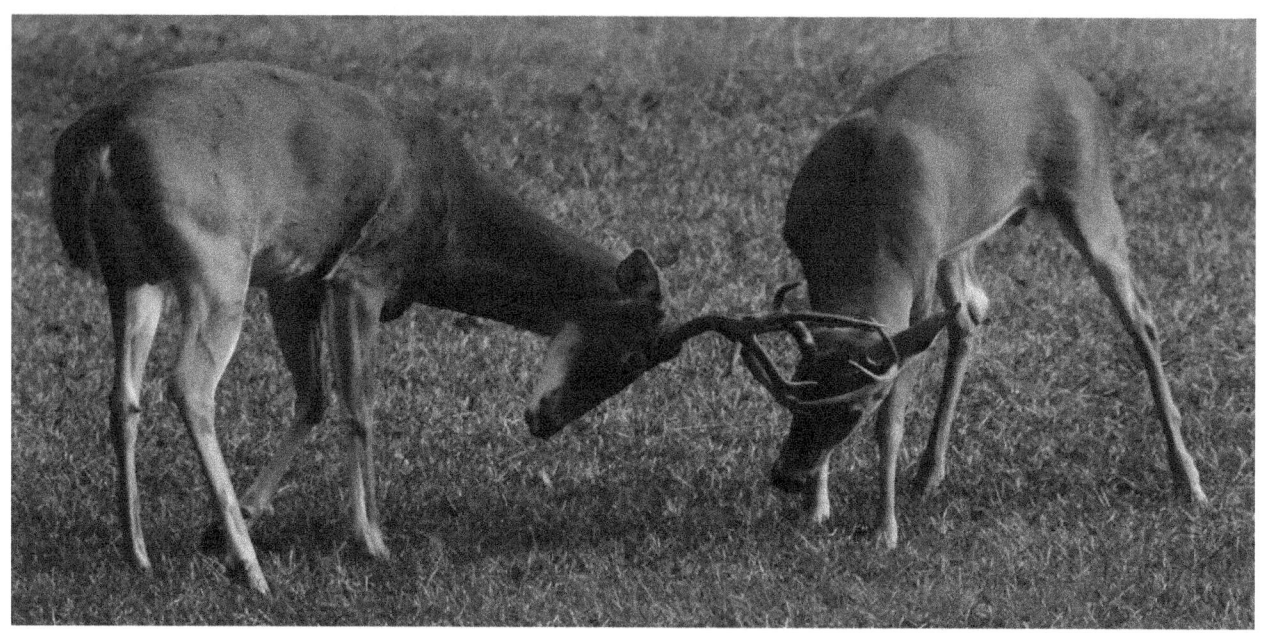

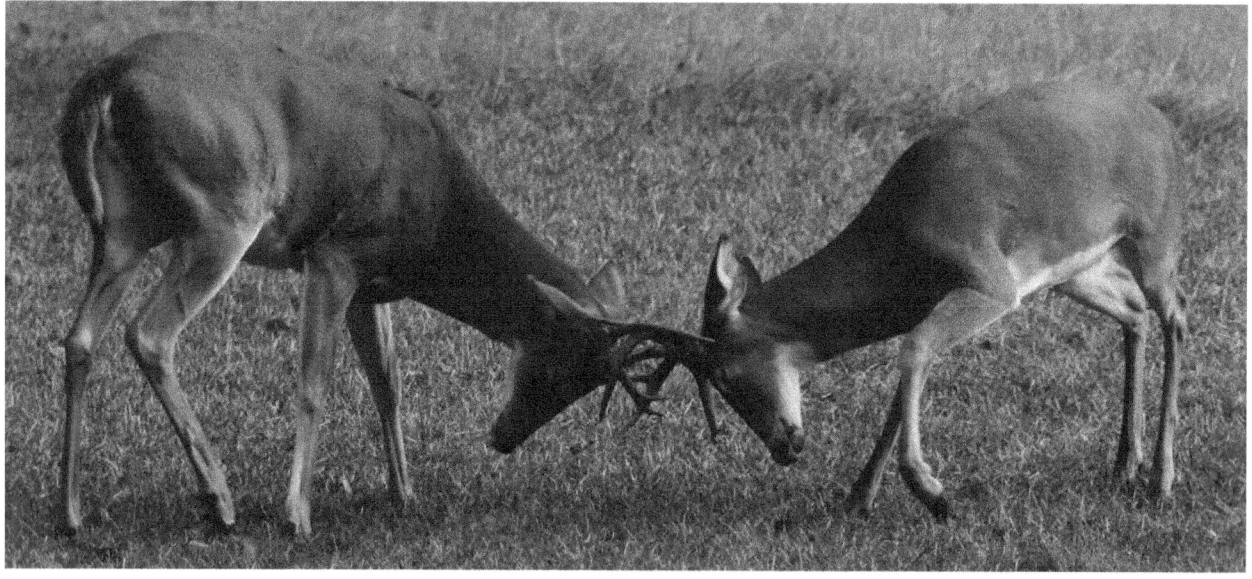

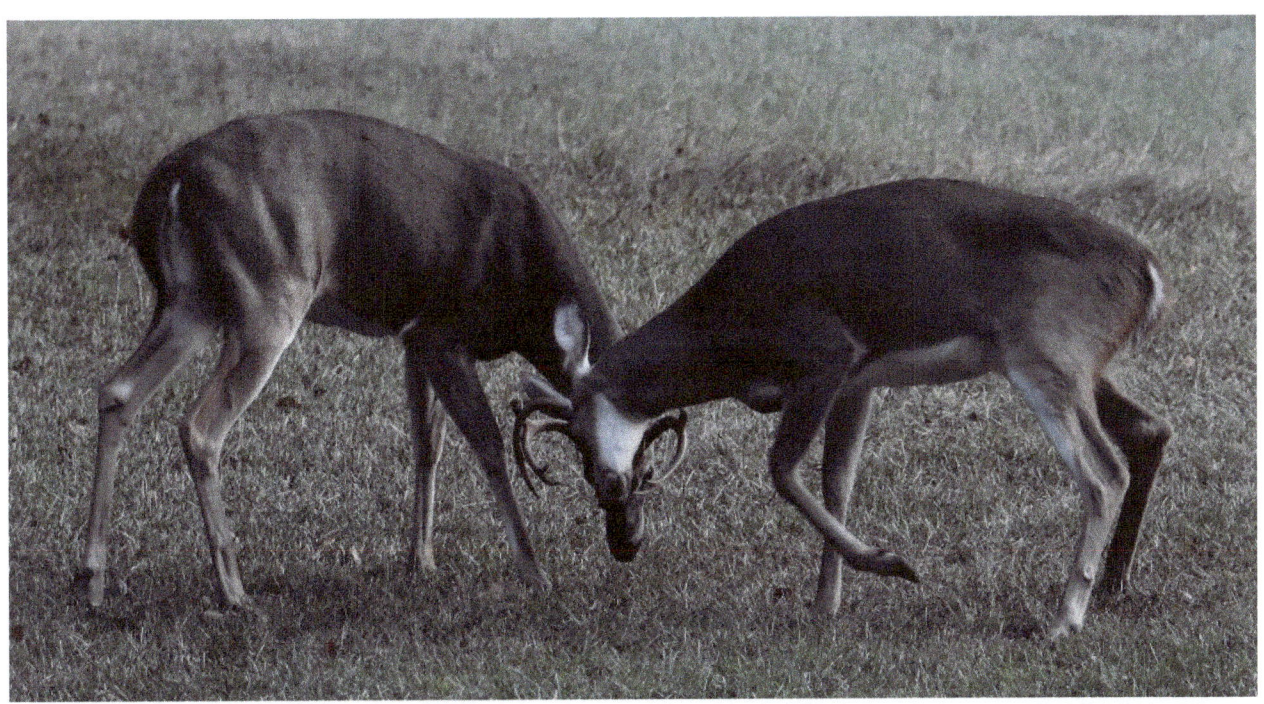

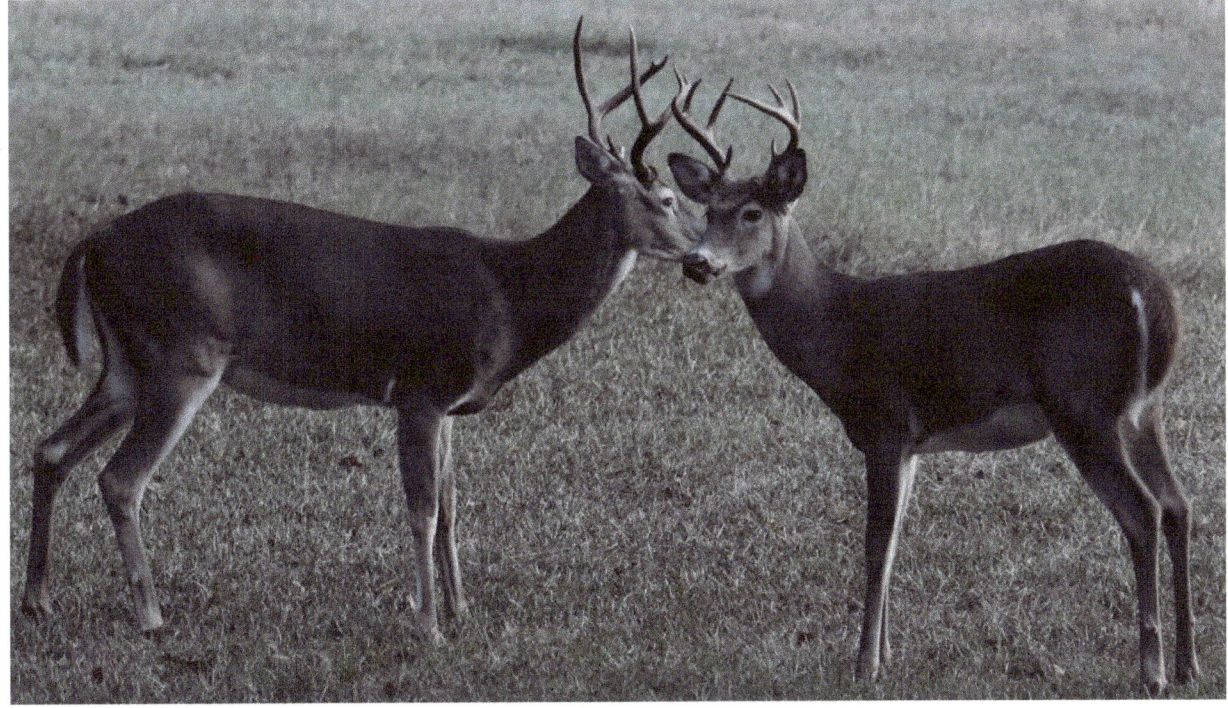

Tall Boy v. three-pointer

Clash of Tall Boy and a three-pointer turned into the highlight of the battles. They fought at night, and at times the camera could not keep up with the action. I have included a few blurred-action pictures because I was so surprised at the action.

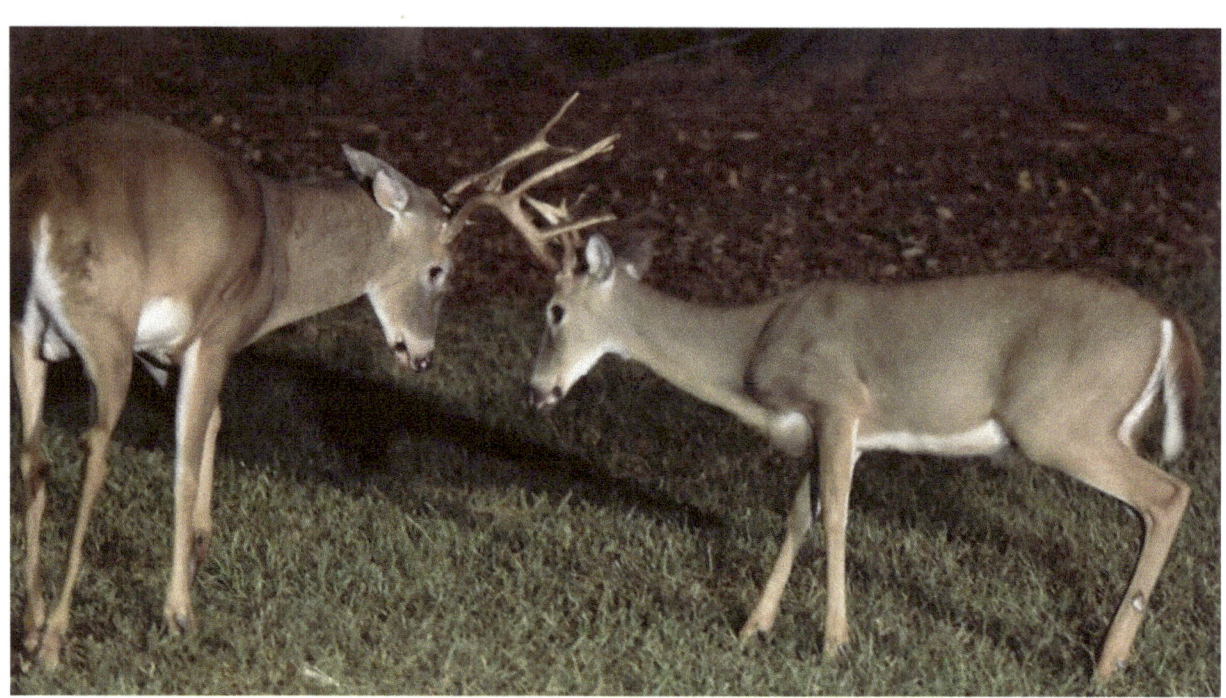

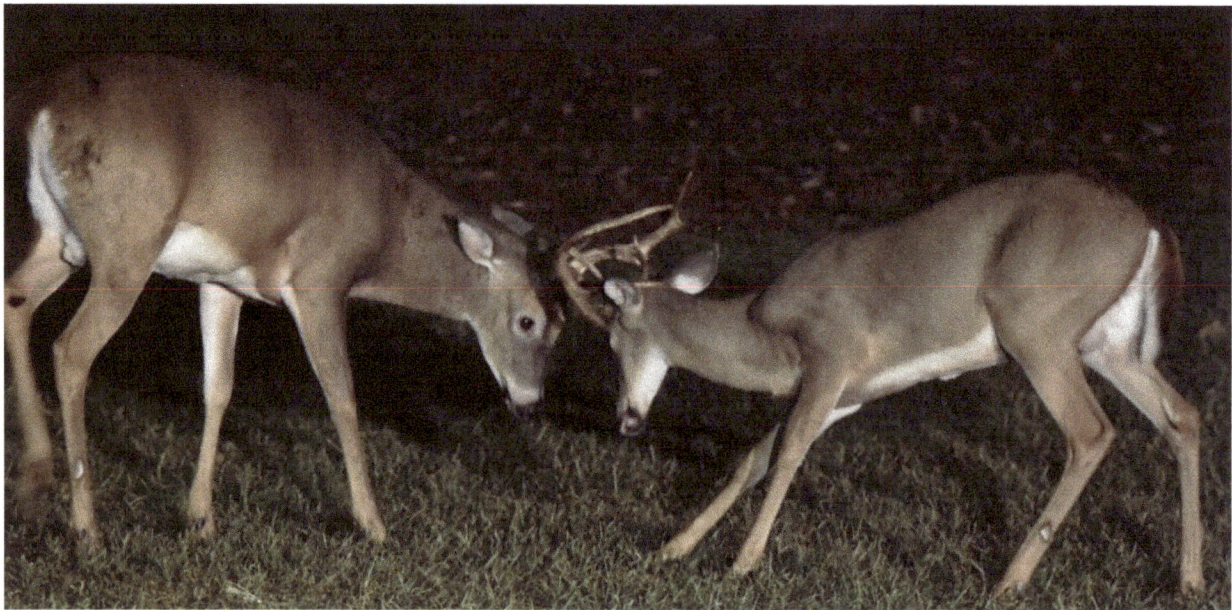

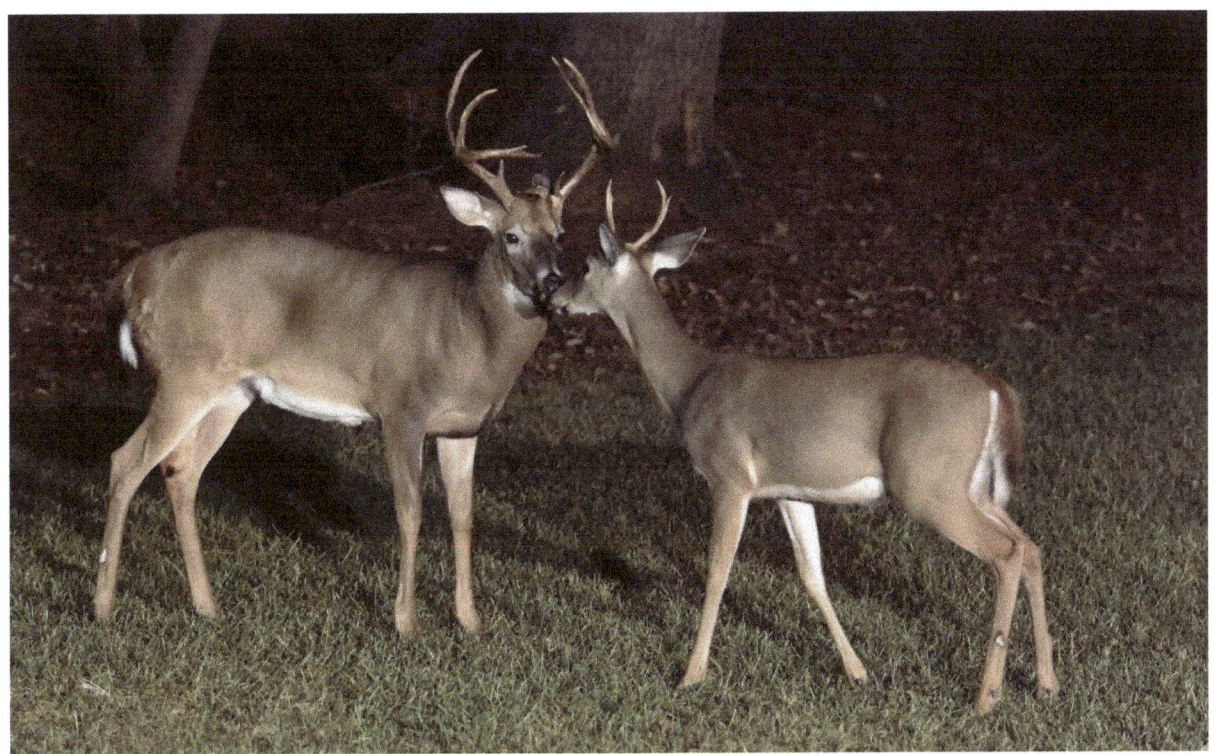

The boys often stopped shoving long enough to catch their breath and to say hello. Notice the dark musk glands on Tall Boy. And note the presence of the short tine beside the bent one.

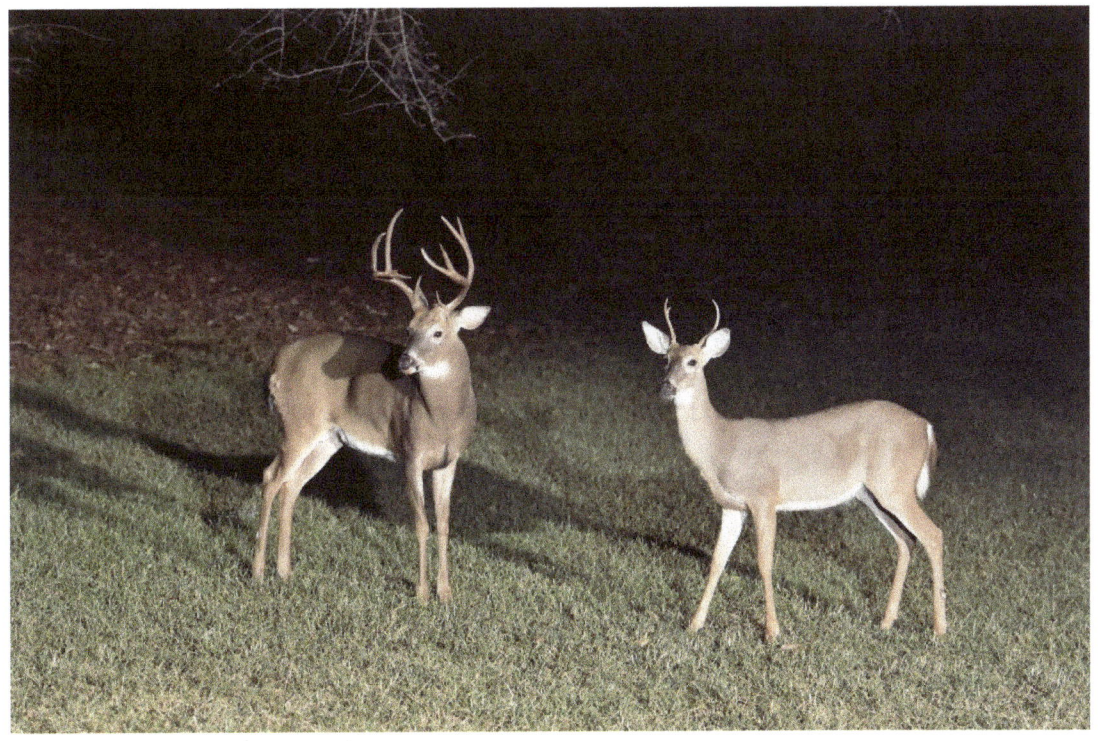

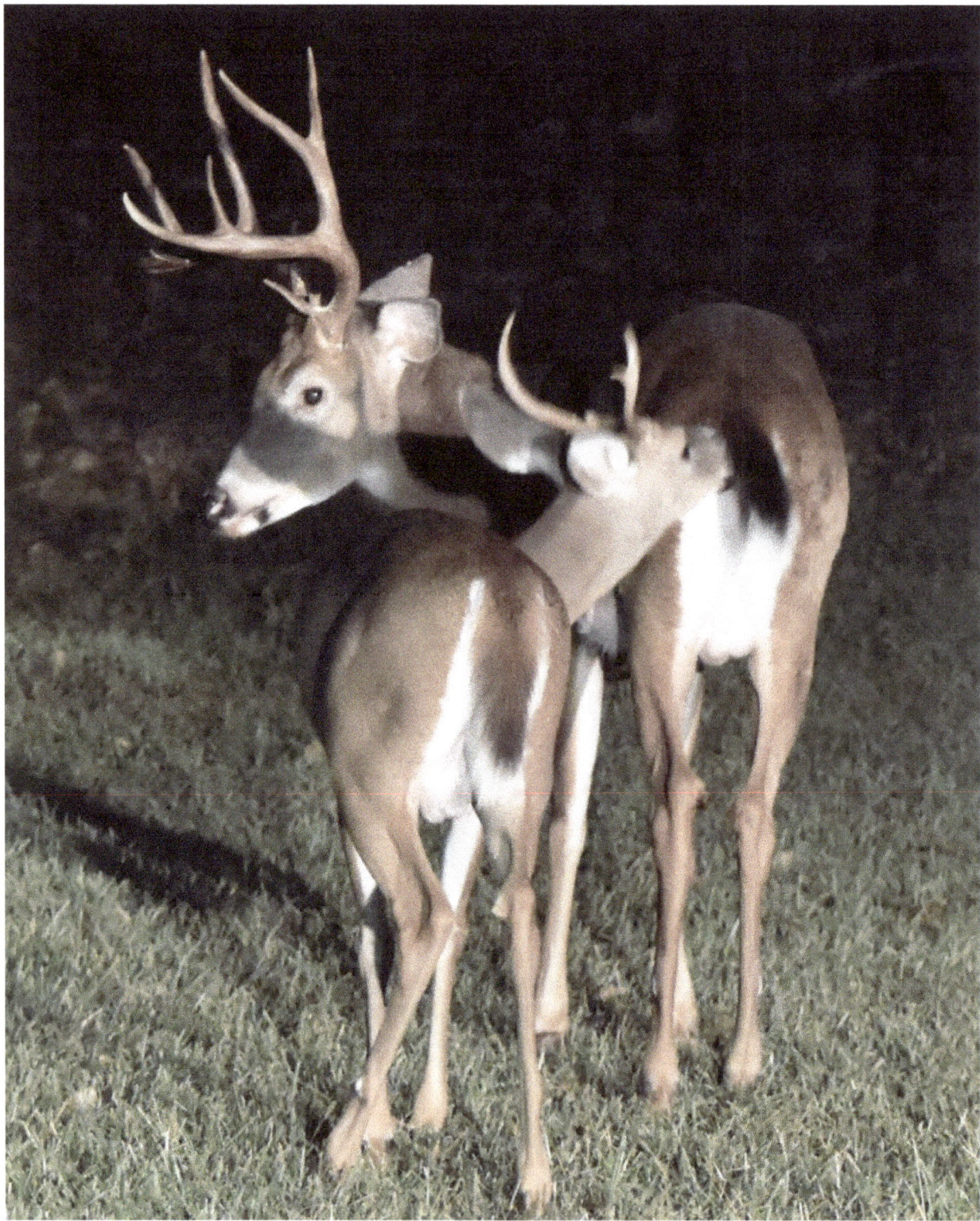

This greeting was enough for Tall Boy to move off into the shadows.

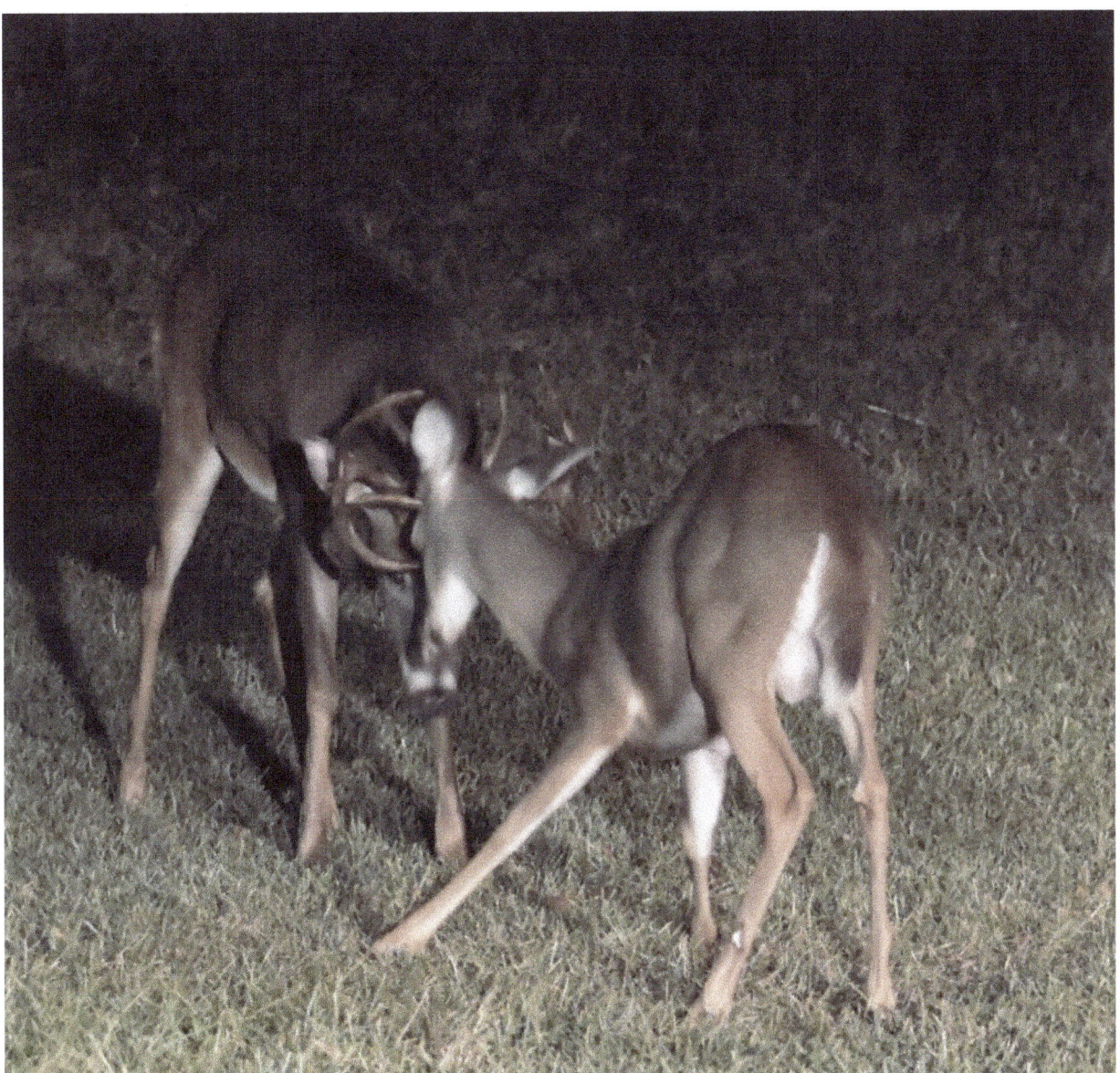

Unfortunately, they remained in the shadows as they resumed their battle.

In spite of the movements, I was able to capture the youngster's distain for Tall Boy. Forgive the blurring from the distance, the darkness and their movement, but I thought the pictures were worth sharing.

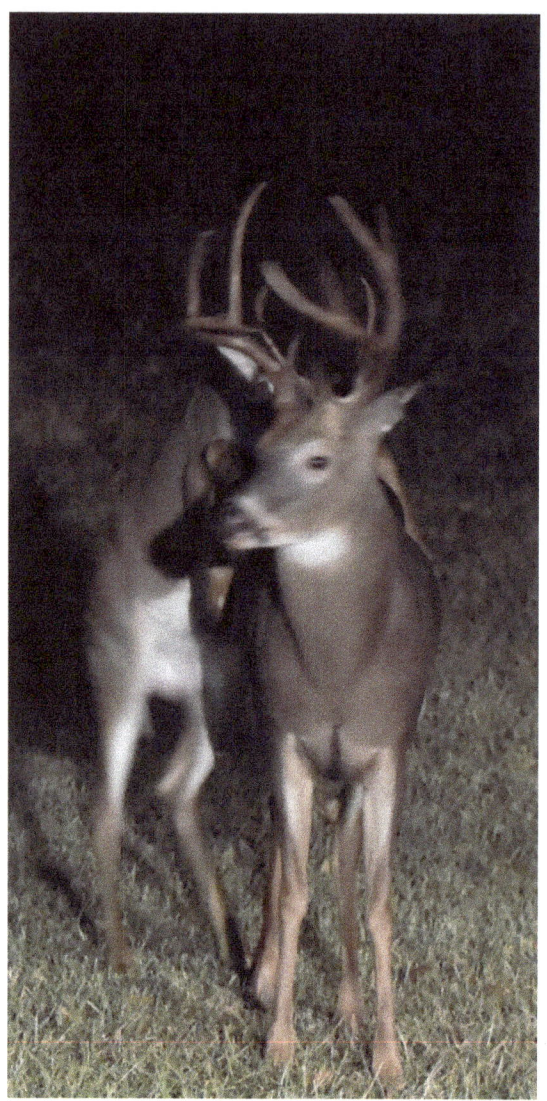

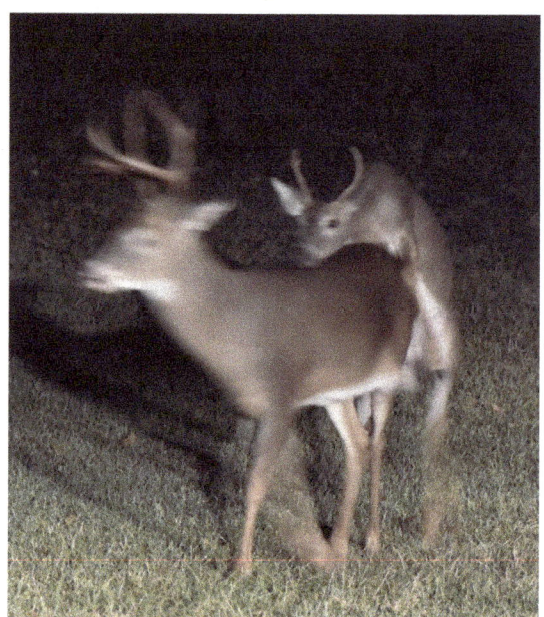

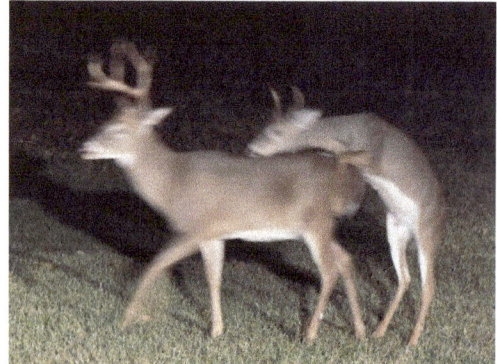

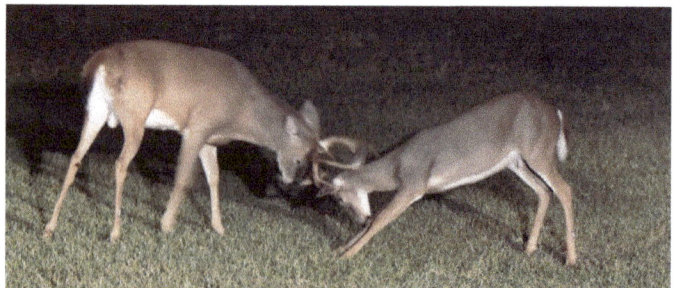

Tall Boy tried to put the youngster in his place.

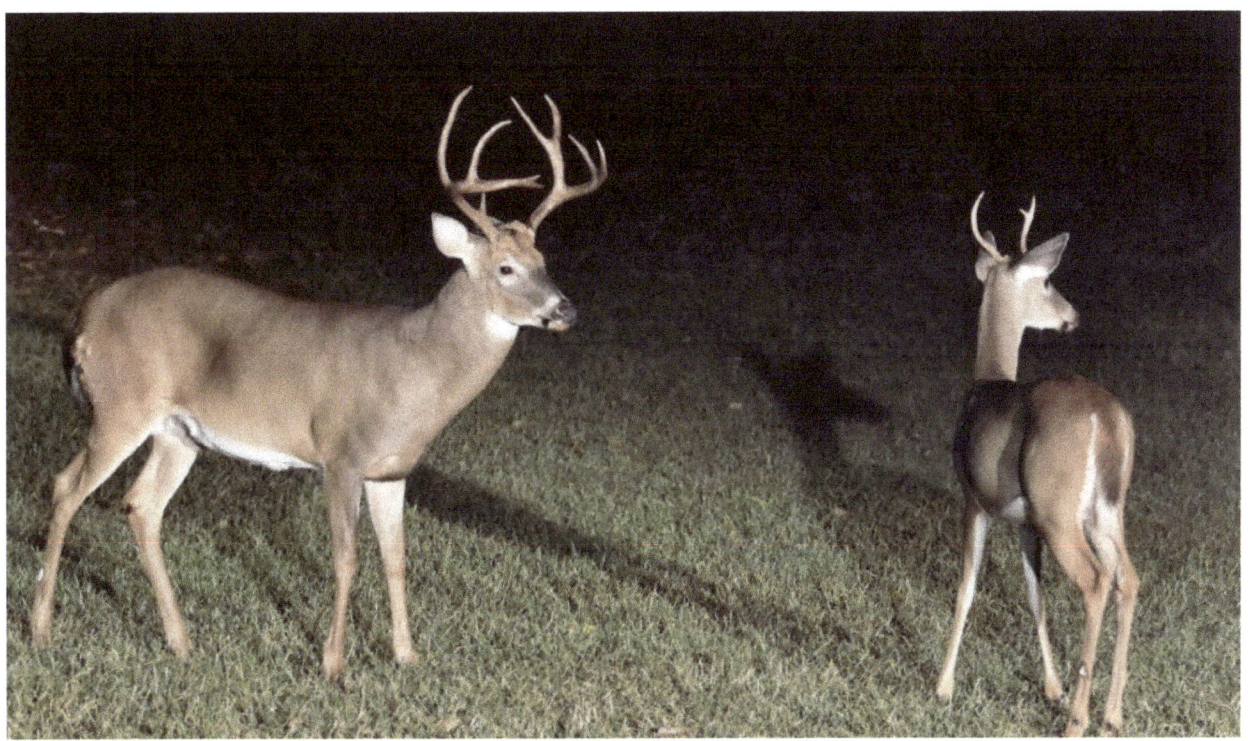

Tall Boy does not show any shame for having lost the small tine at the base of his left antler to the smaller buck.

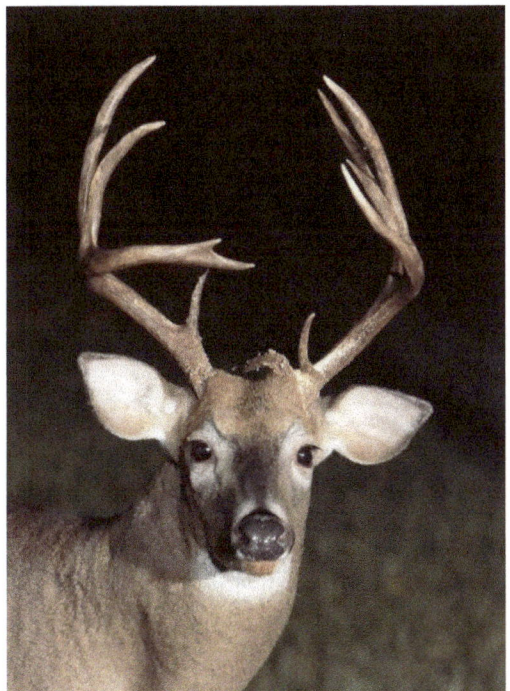 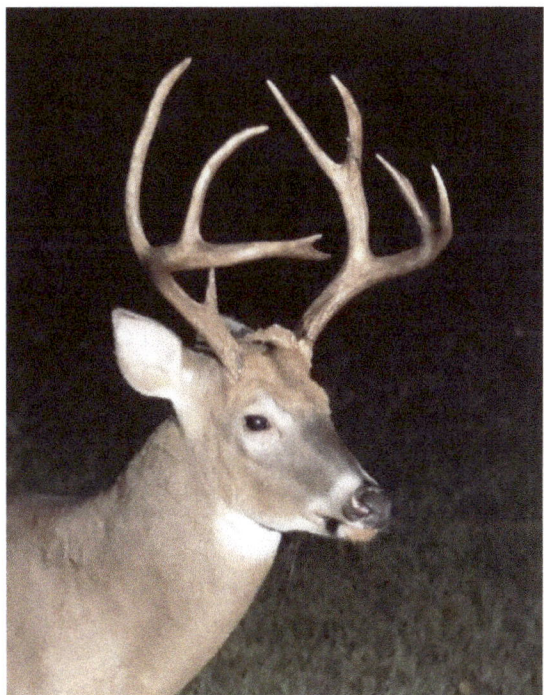

Before and after the encounter with the upstart three-pointer.

BROWSE LINES

Most of the deer who walked beneath the hanging oak limb as they left the yard would stop for a snack of salad to go with their vegetable. Fawns fed on the lower limbs, while bucks and does reached higher. Over time, however, the limbs become bare. From a distance, these oaks show a *browse line*, which often indicates a too-high population.

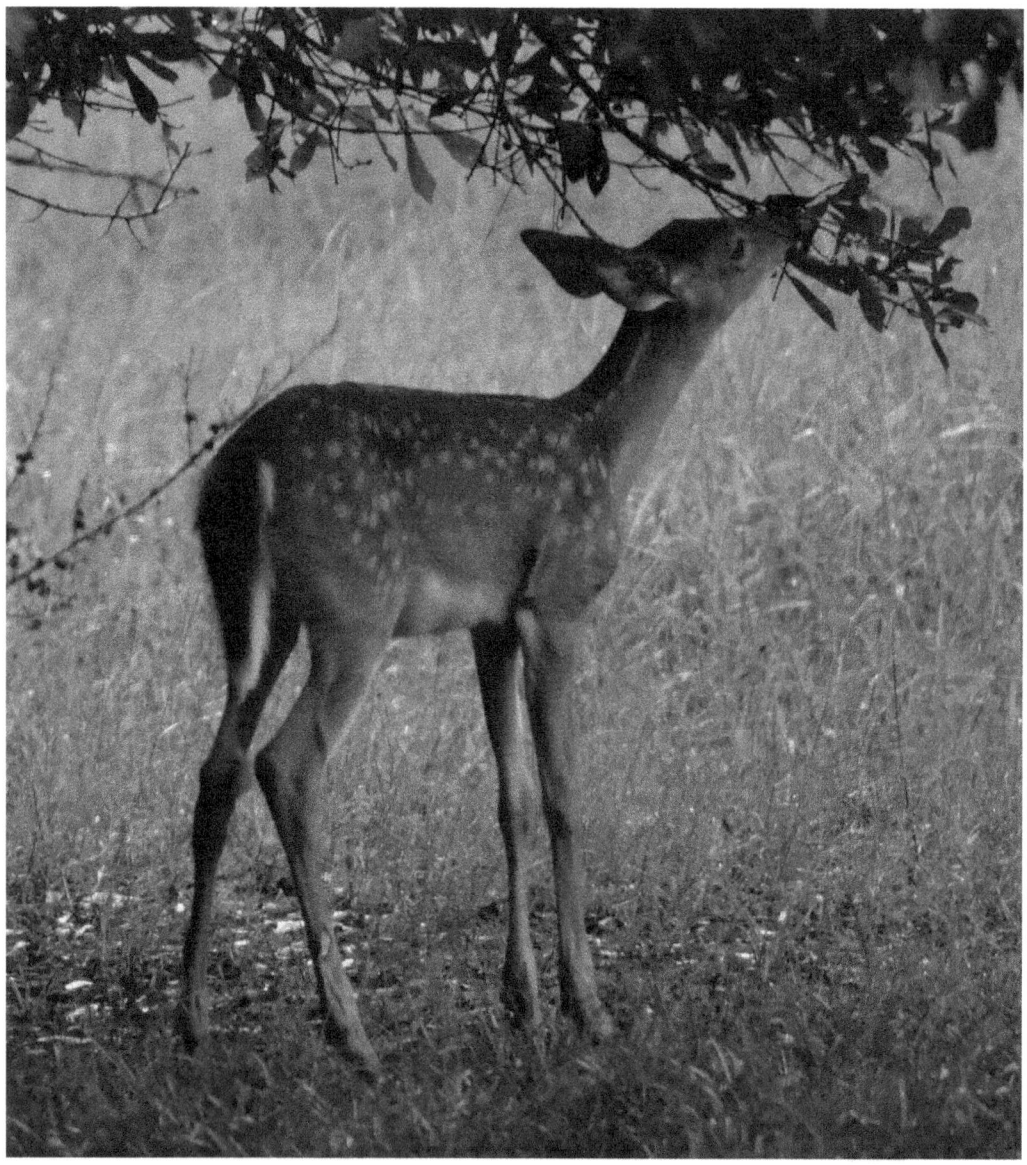

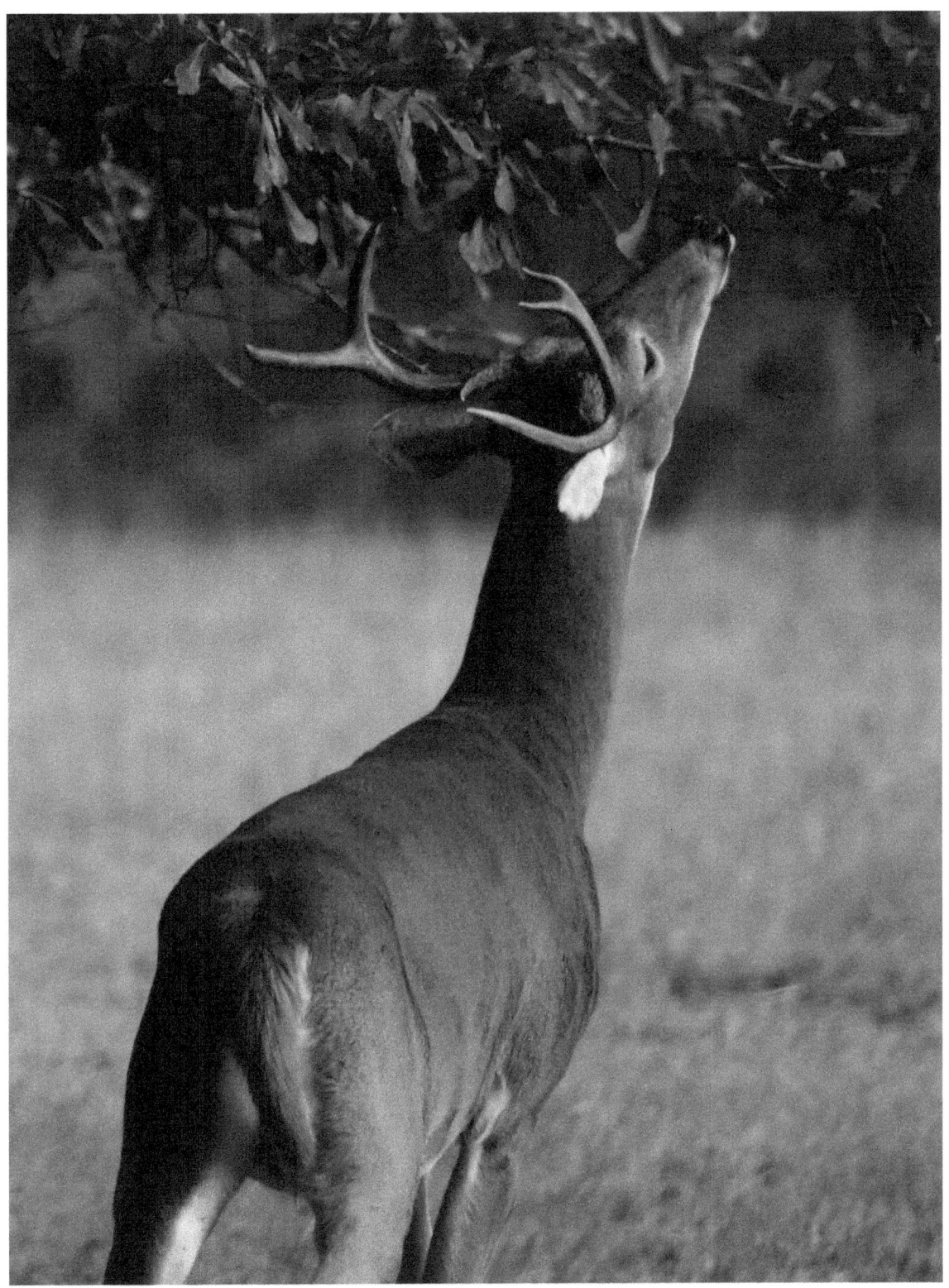

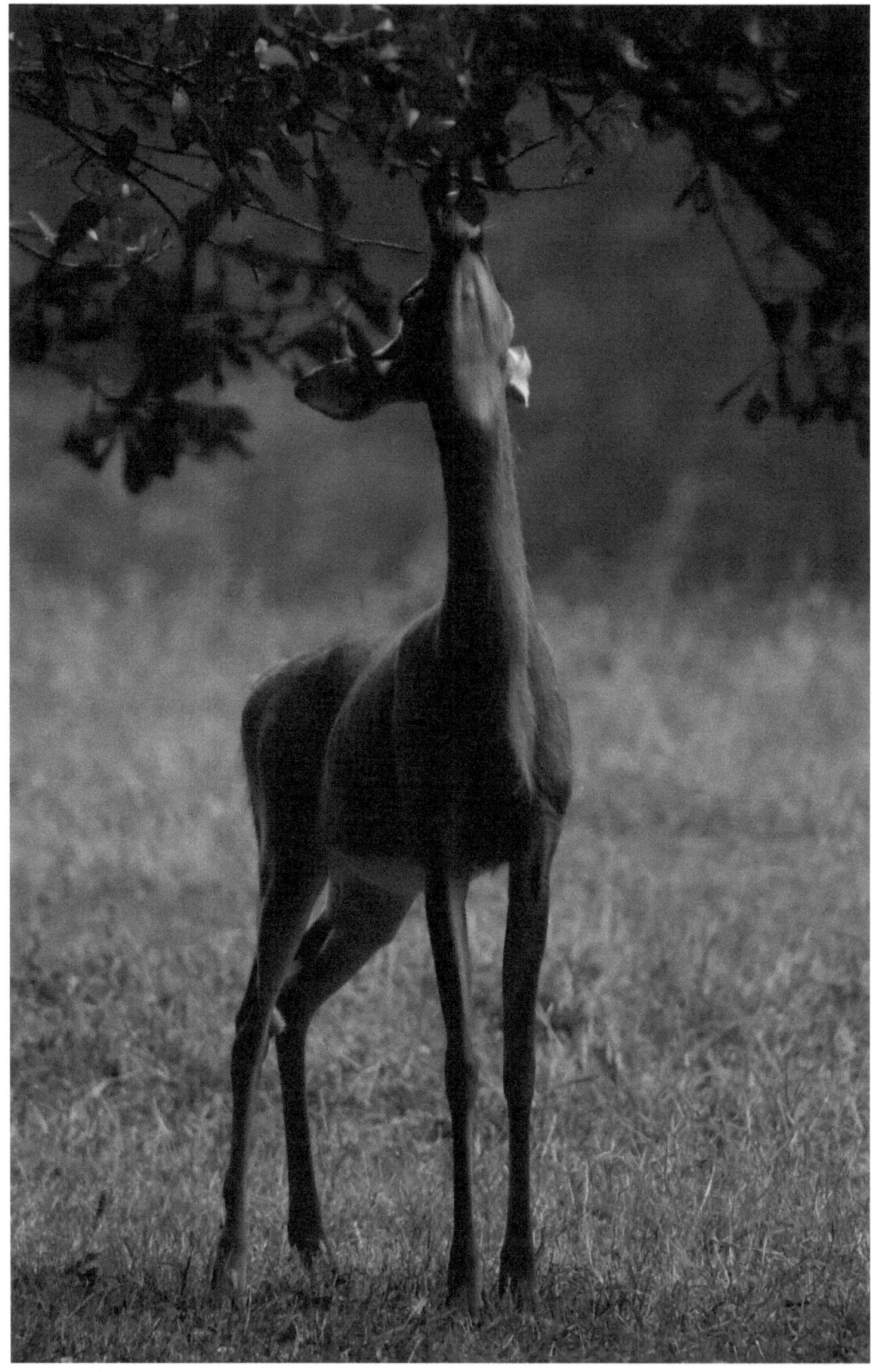

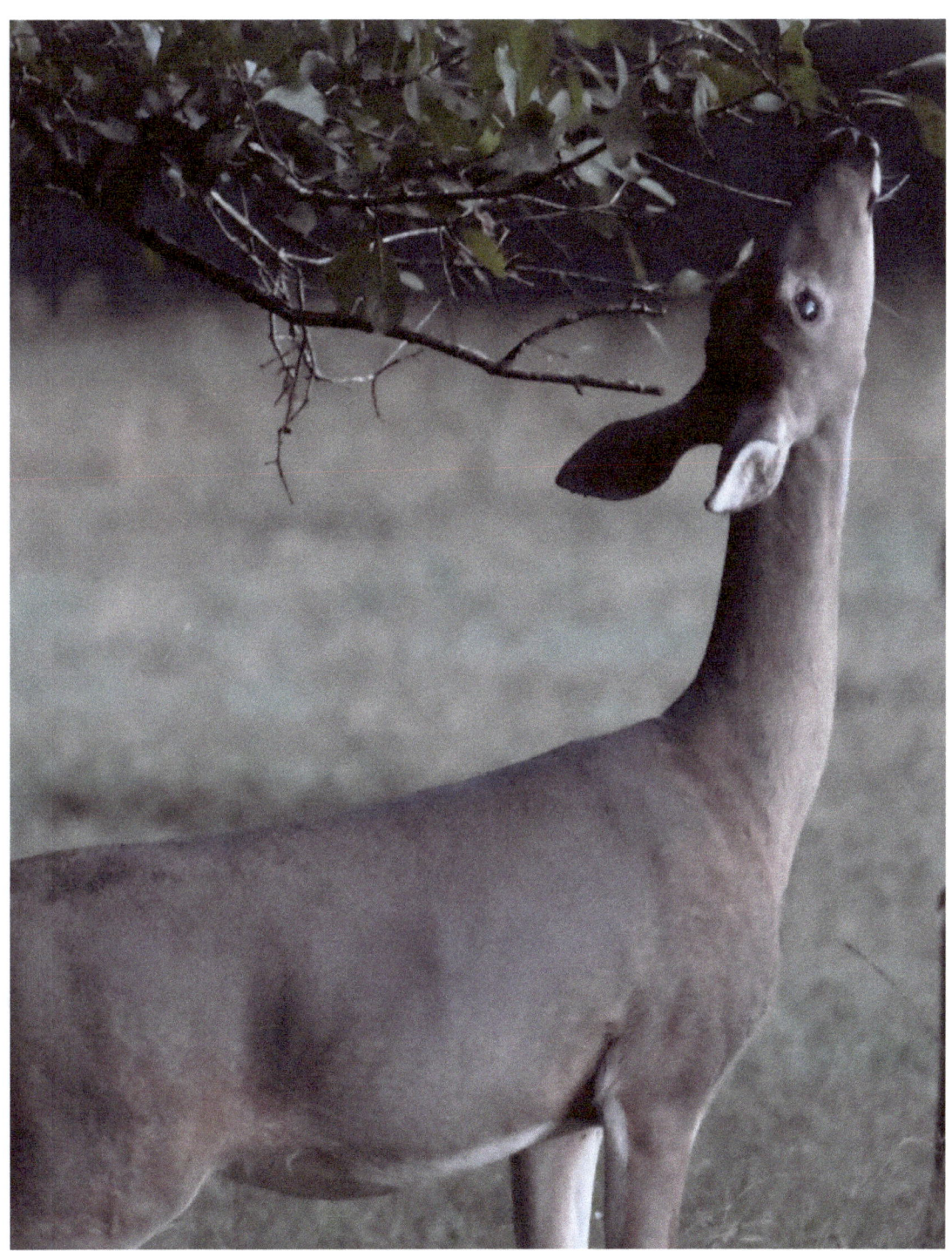

MOTHERHOOD

Does give birth about mid-May to mid-June, and must wean the fawns in late September to mid-November when the rut is underway in Middle Georgia. But for those months the doe tends to her young and shows affection in many ways.

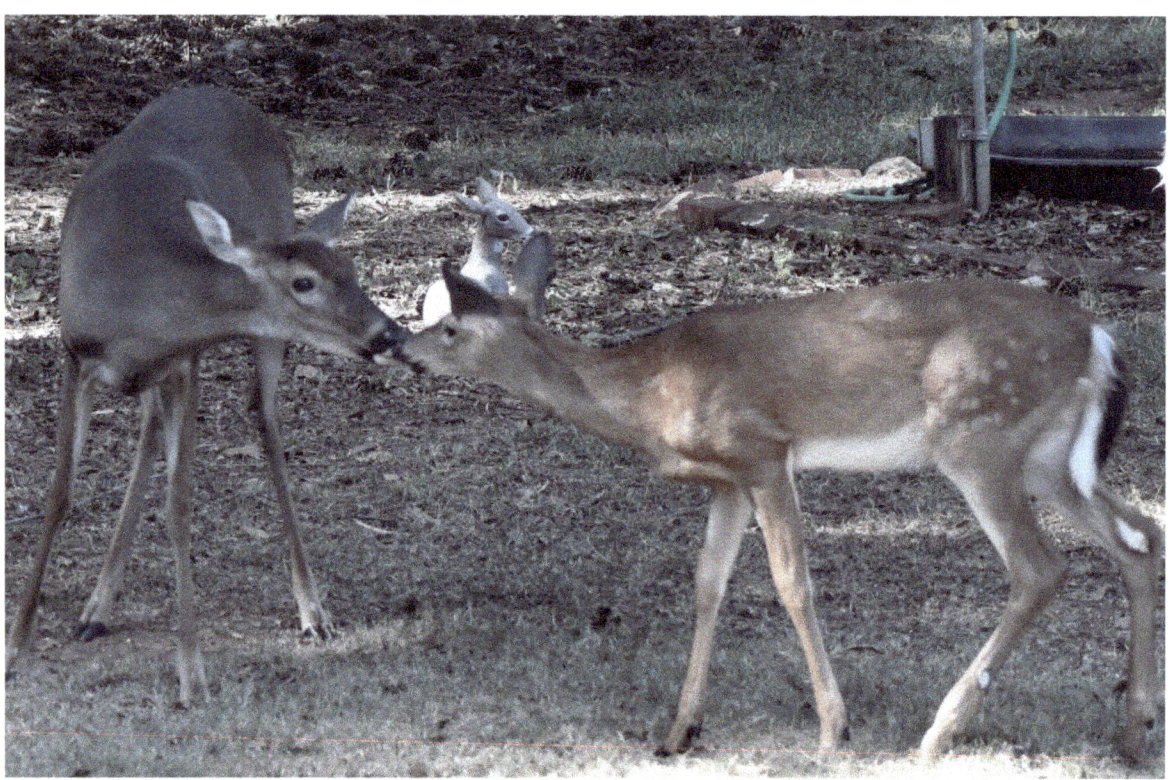

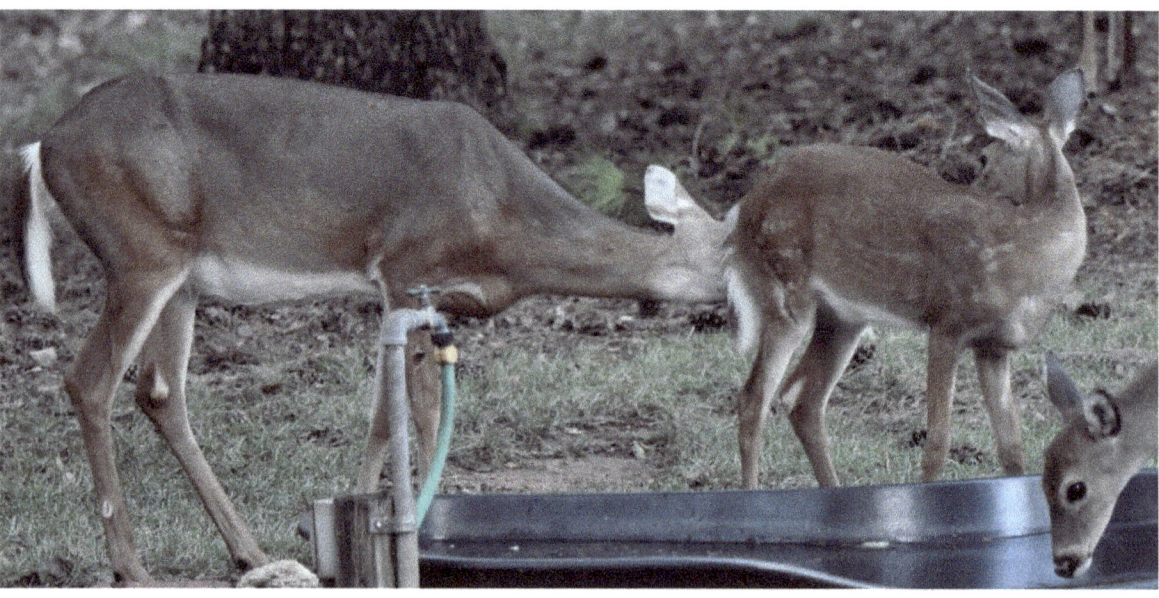

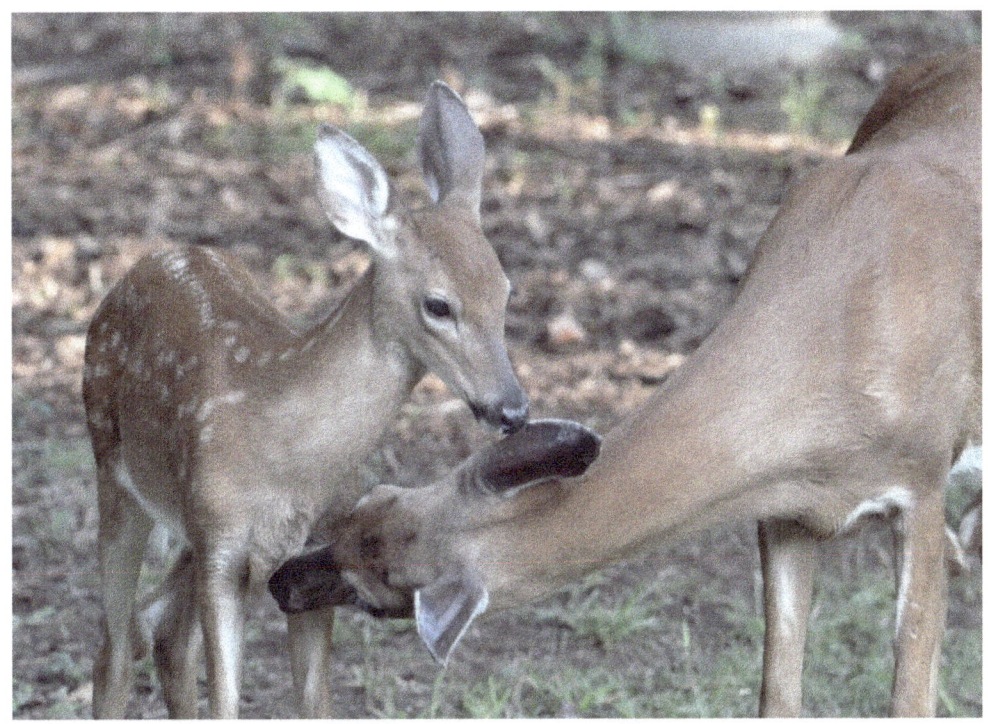

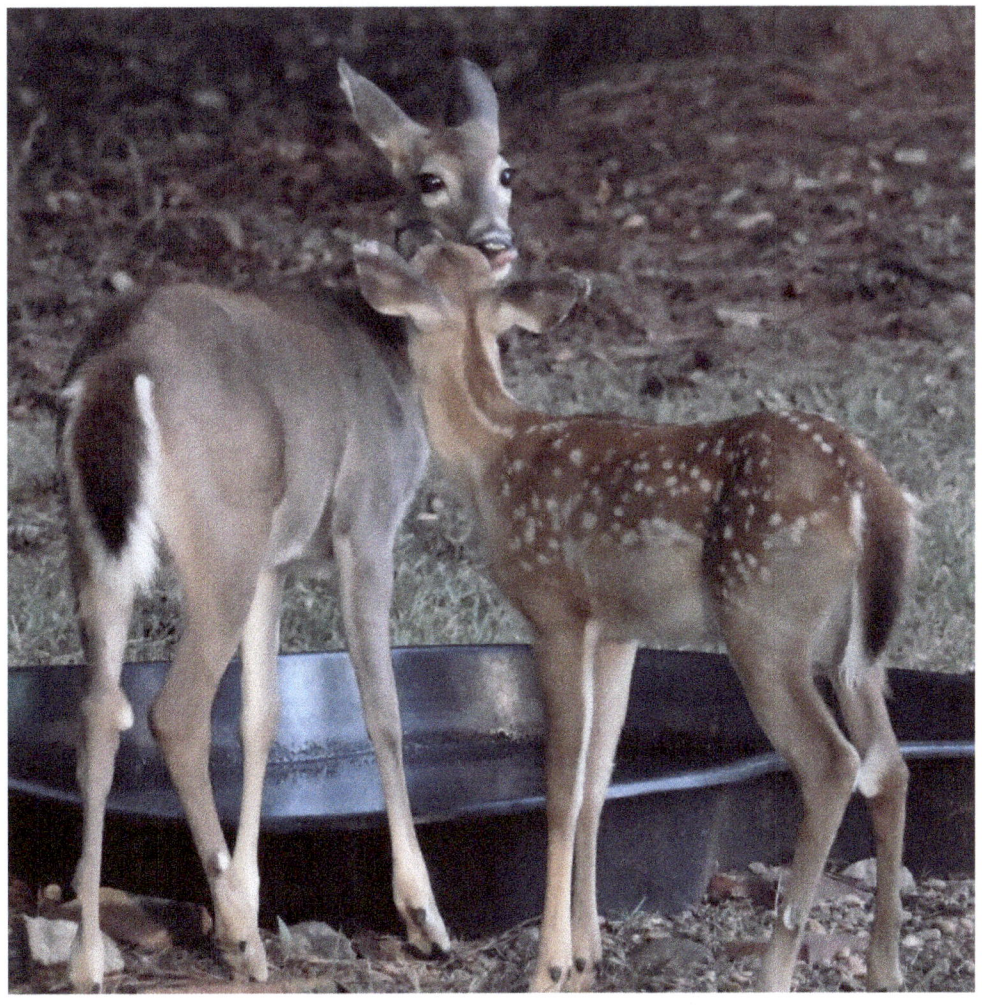

Mama is not always available for a milk snack, but when she is, she bleats for her baby. The fawn is one happy critter—the youngster gallops to mama, butts her to remind her to let down the milk, and wags its tails with delight. She will step over the youngster as she walks away.

I saw fawns nursing every day, and once they reached the spout, the babies wagged tails like a puppy getting fresh steak. They approached the mamas from any direction.

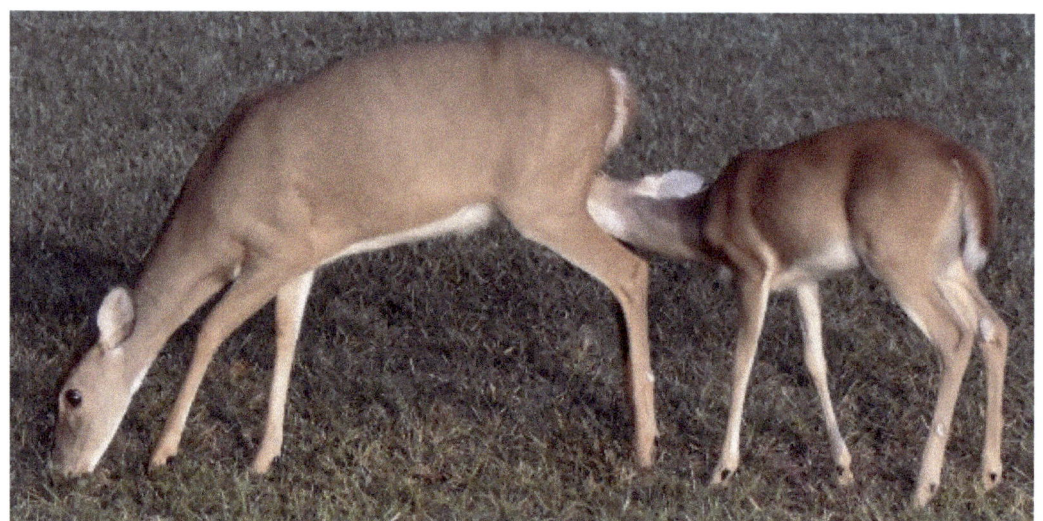

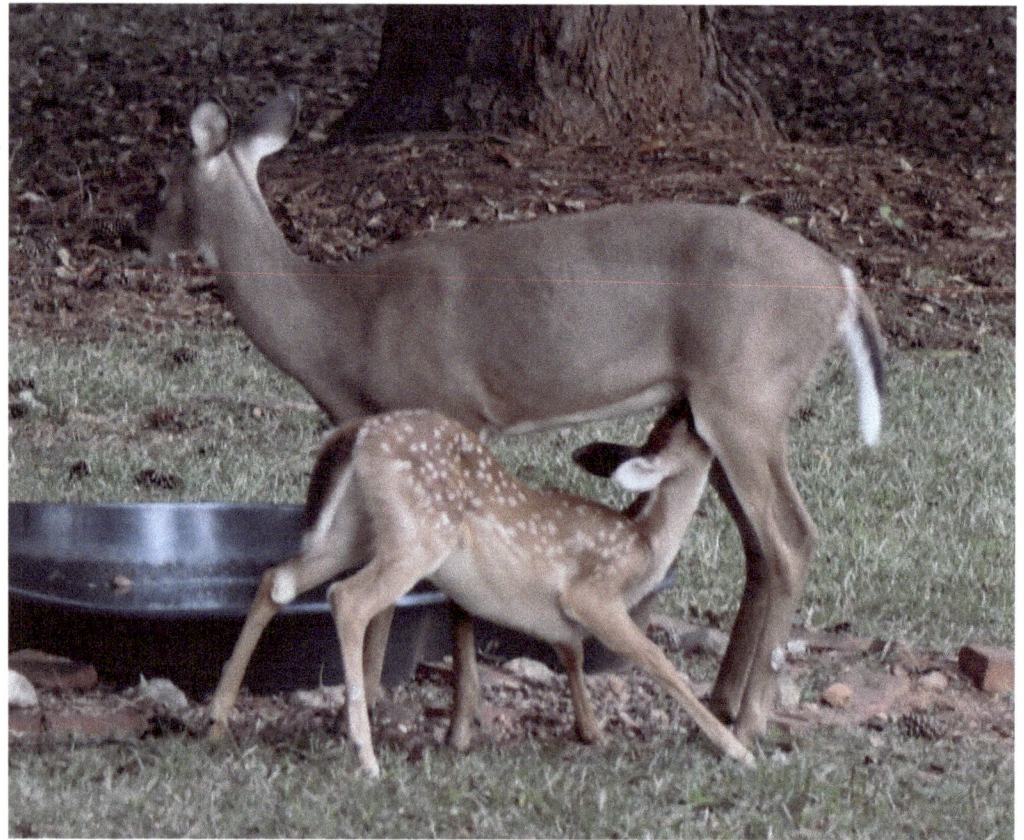

Sometimes, a doe will adopt an orphan. Here, I think both fawns are hers, but this is the only time I saw two fawns nurse at the same time. So this sequence was another wonderful surprise for me. Both fawns nursed for several minutes. The nearer fawn nursed with it eyes closed. These are only a few of the pictures in the series. Note in the last one, she almost chokes one of the babies with her hind leg wrapped around its neck.

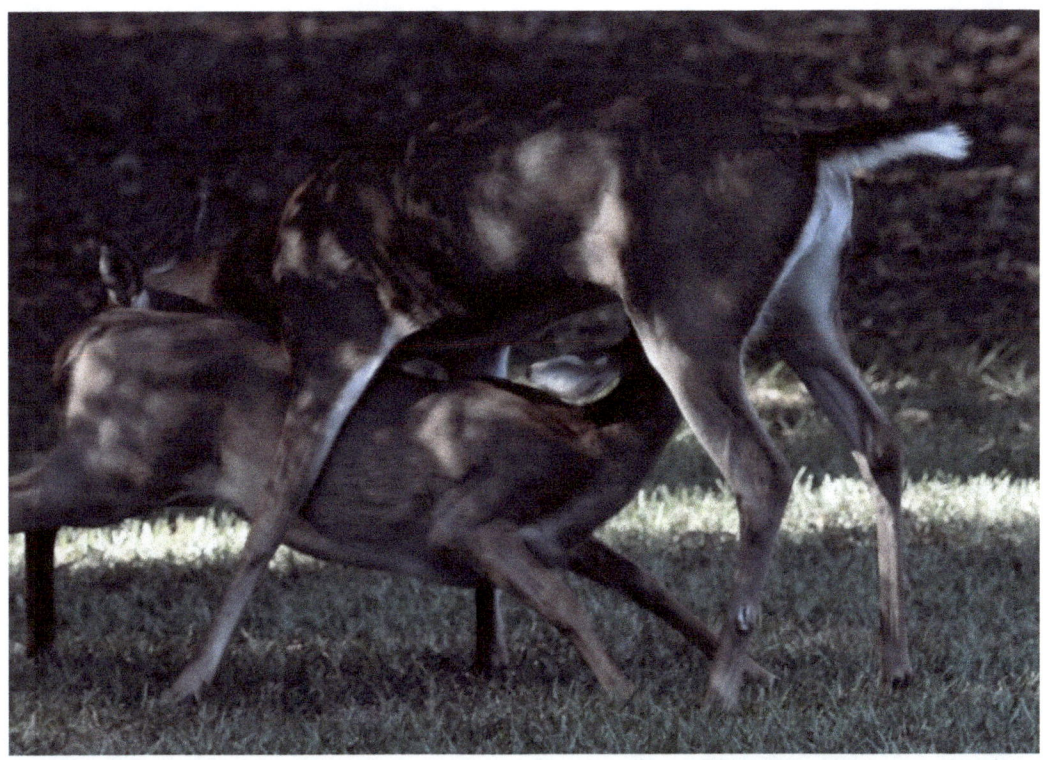

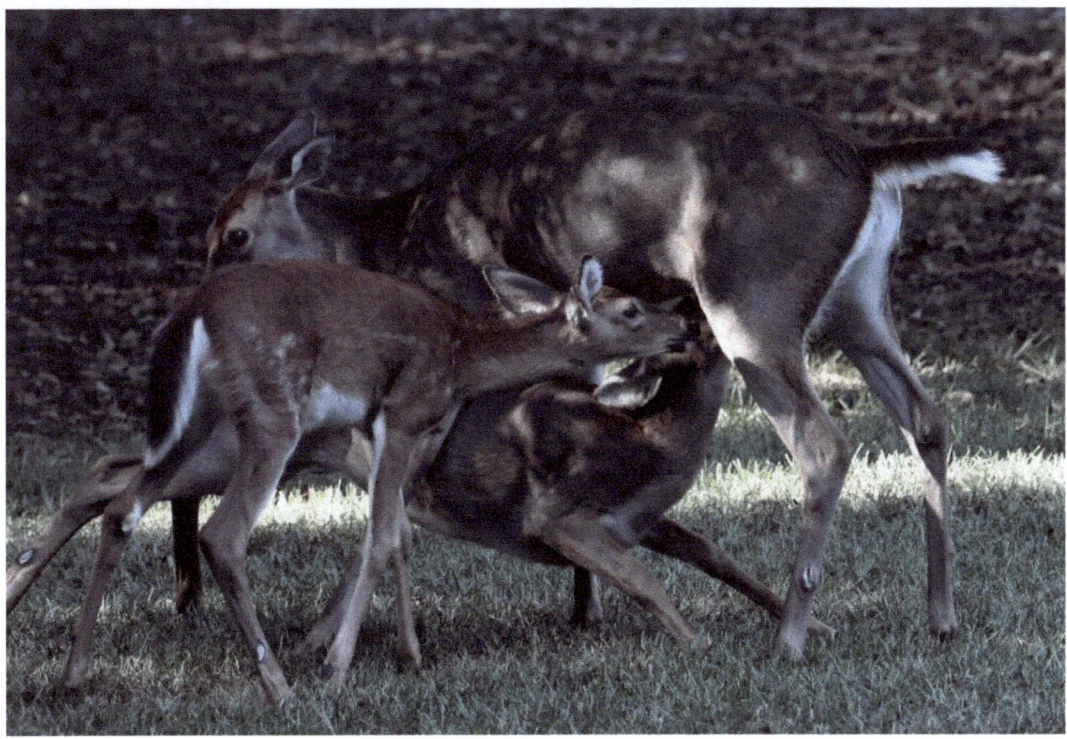

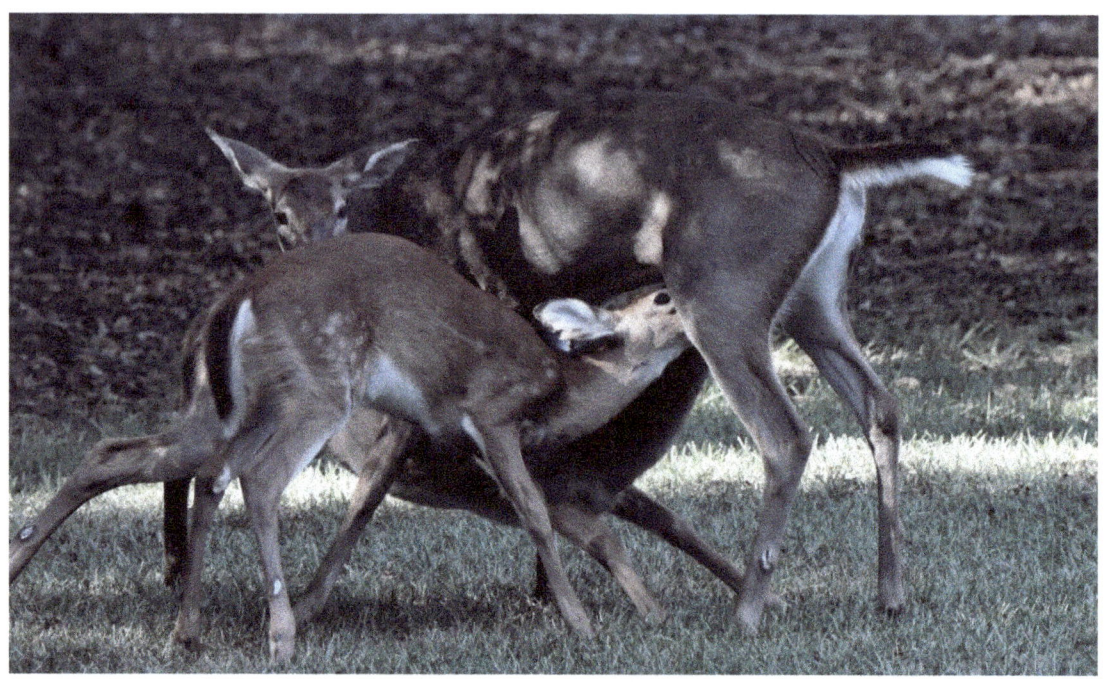

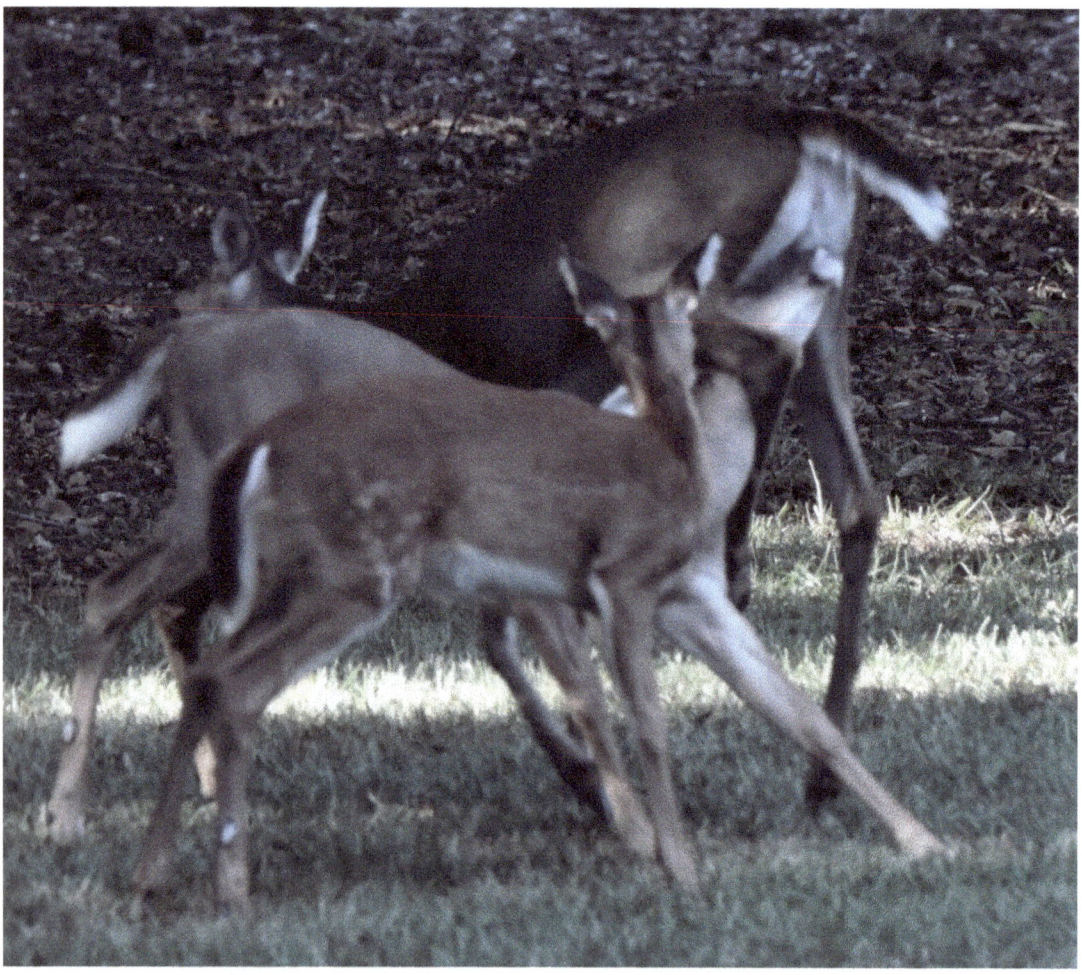

A common belief is that the doe leads her fawn into hiding and leaves it there. However, from what I've seen over the years, the fawn leaves the mother and hides. The fawn is odorless for some time after birth. If the mother led the baby into hiding, the doe would leave her scent at the site, which would be counterproductive. I've seen fawns come across my fields and hide, with no other deer in the distance.

LITTLE MISS ENTHUSIASM

I don't know that this fawn is a doe, but she was a bundle of energy and enthusiasm. When nursing, she wagged her tail. She ran from one side of the woods to the hayfields and out of sight, then roared back. No way could my camera freeze her activity. Some pictures of her are not high in quality but for me they are high in her enthusiasm.

She would hound another deer until she got what she wanted. She nagged until she convinced the other to join her in a race through the woods.

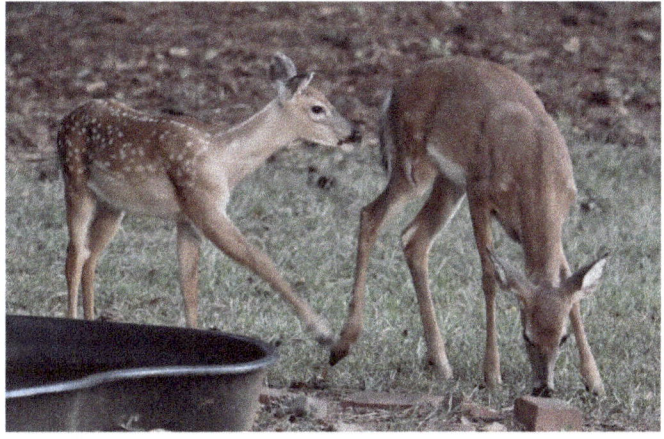

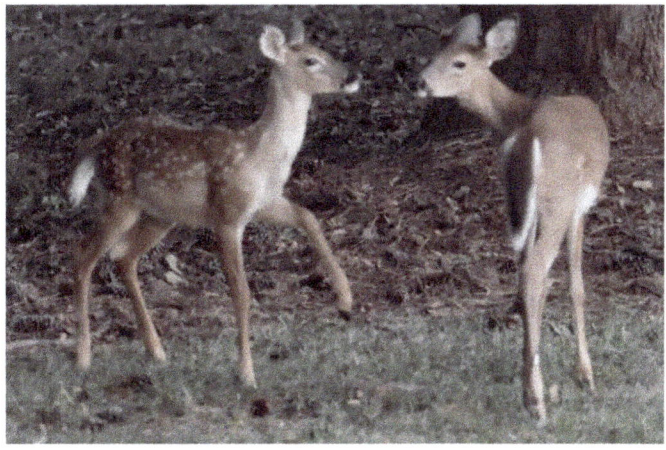

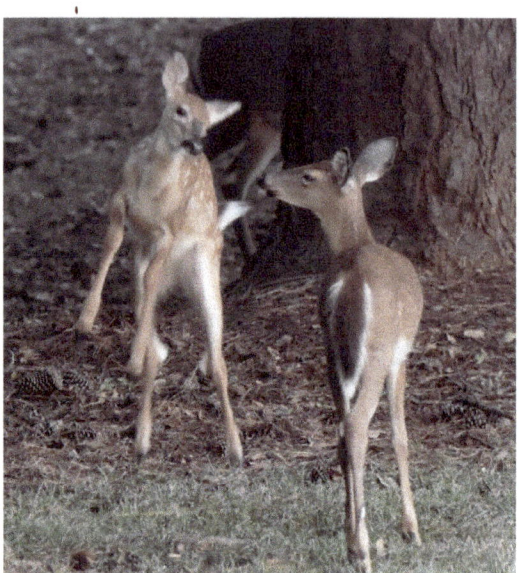

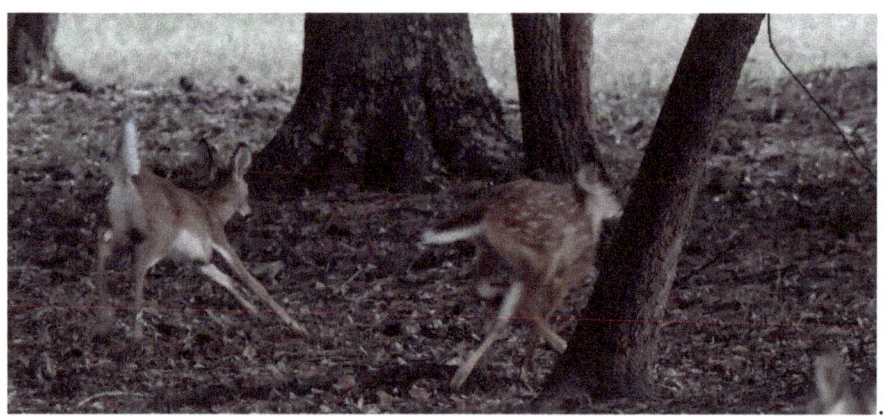

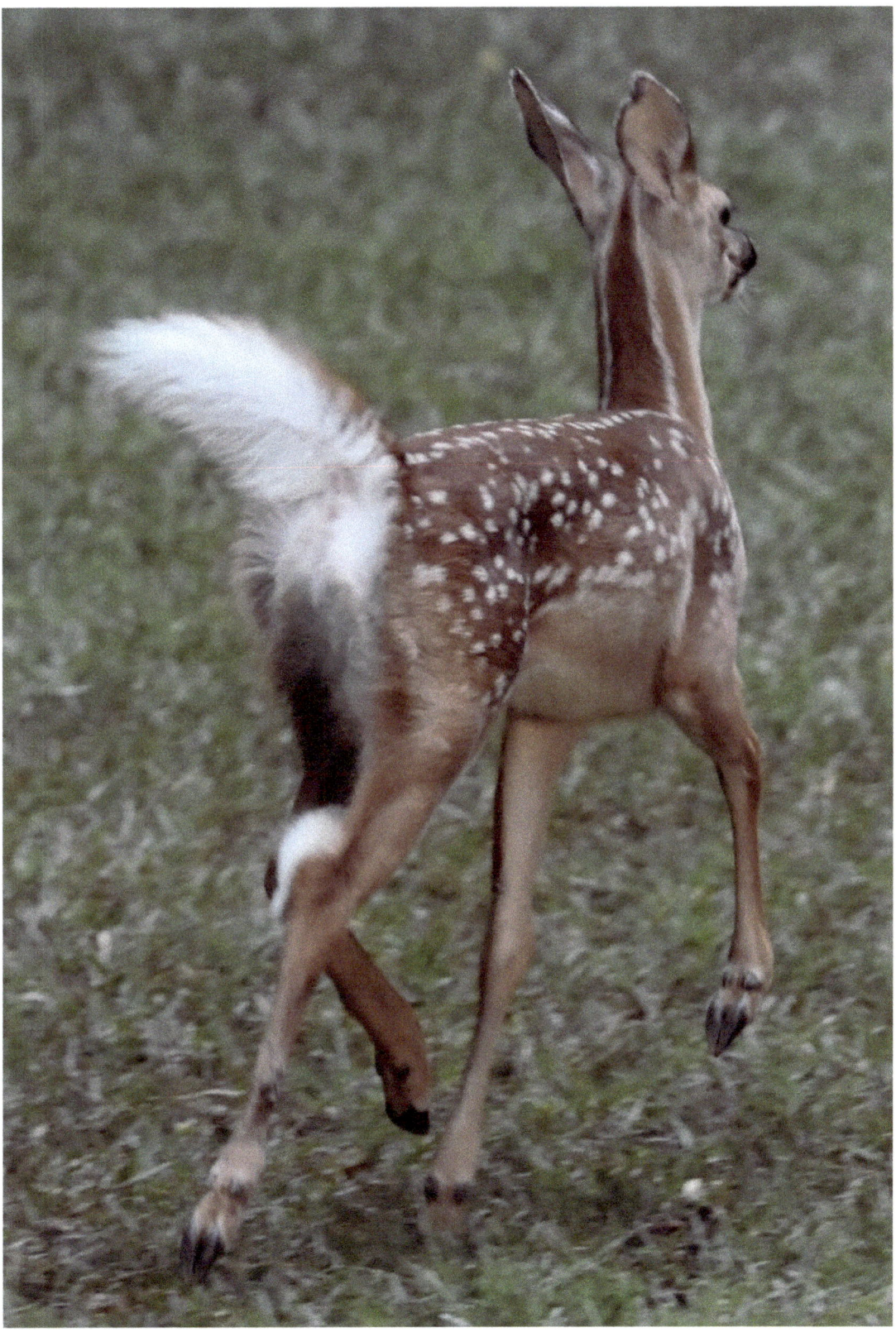

She never cared if no one else wanted to run. She just ran for the pleasure of living. She did stroll into the yard once in a while for me to get some special pictures.

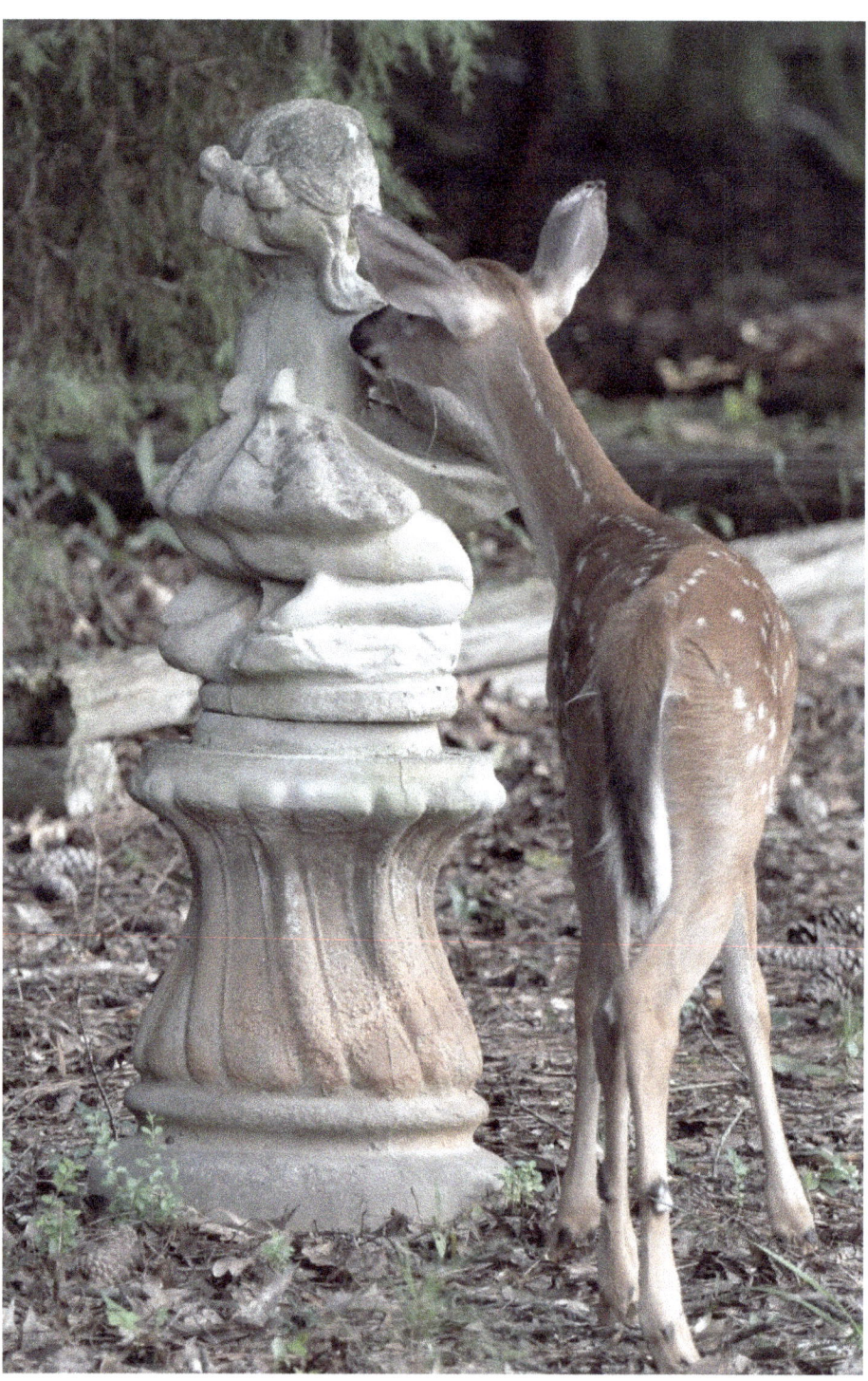

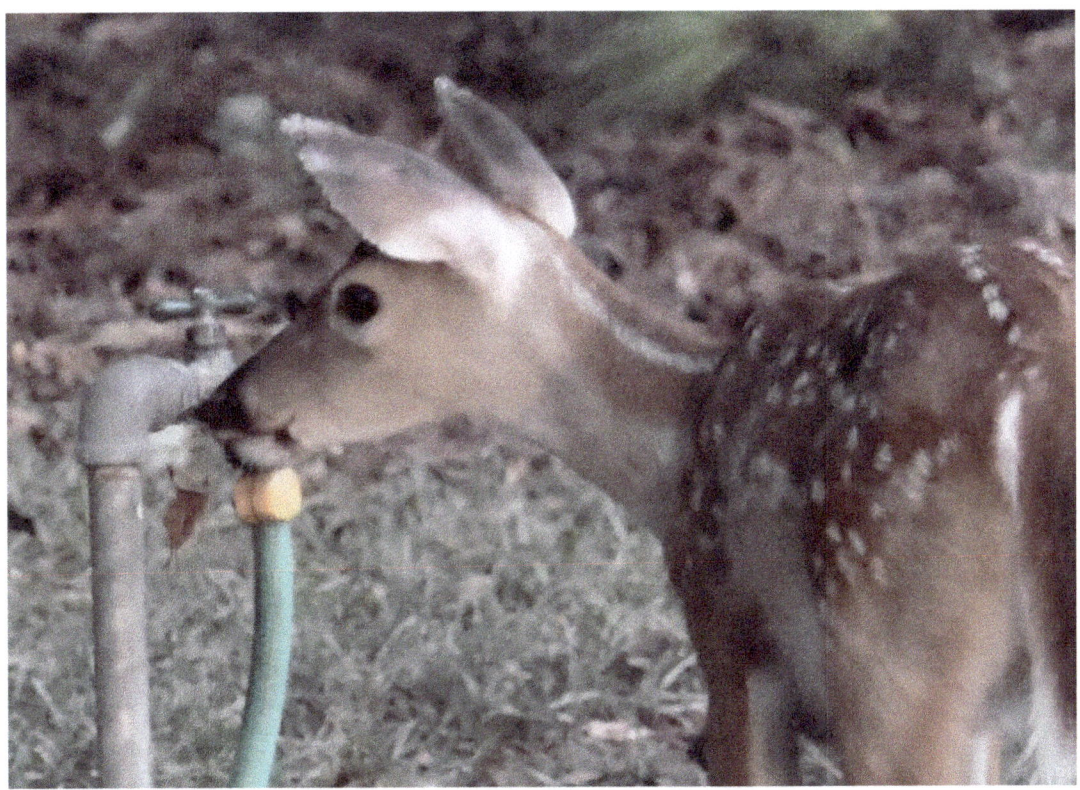

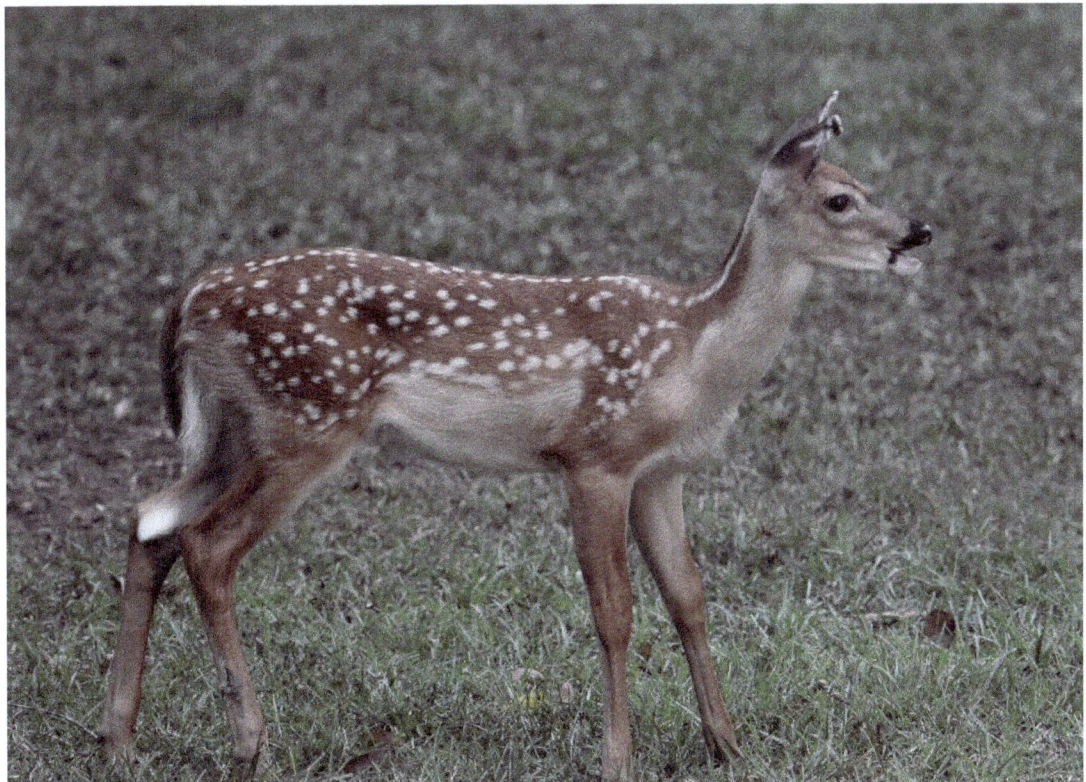

She is not bleating, but is panting from the heat. I could see her chest heave.

She didn't mind approaching any deer in the area to ask for some milk.

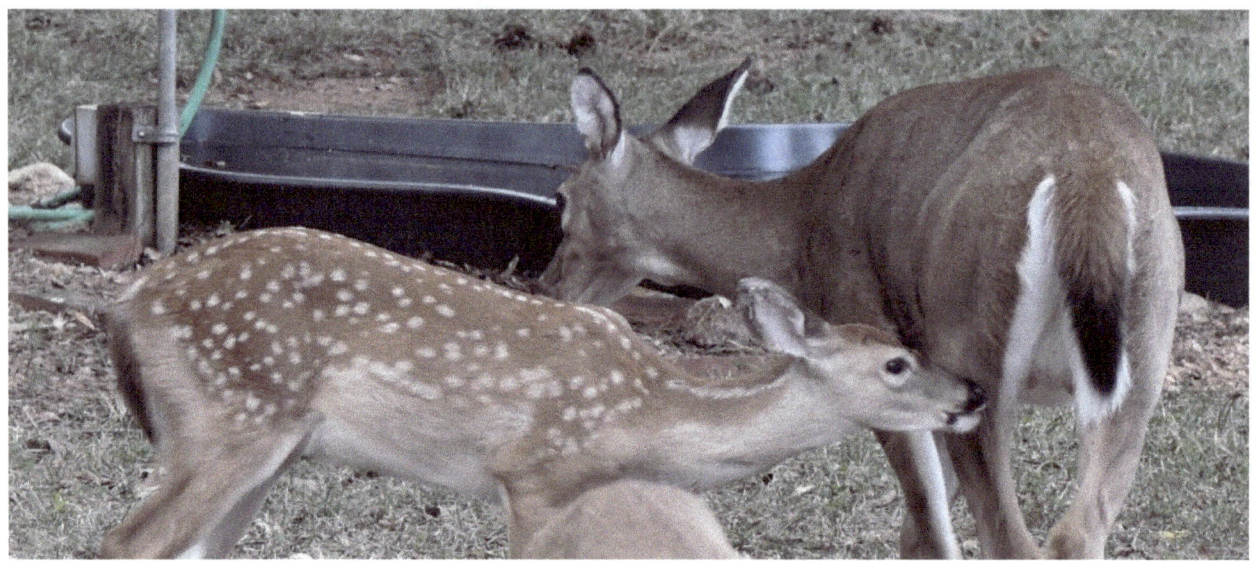

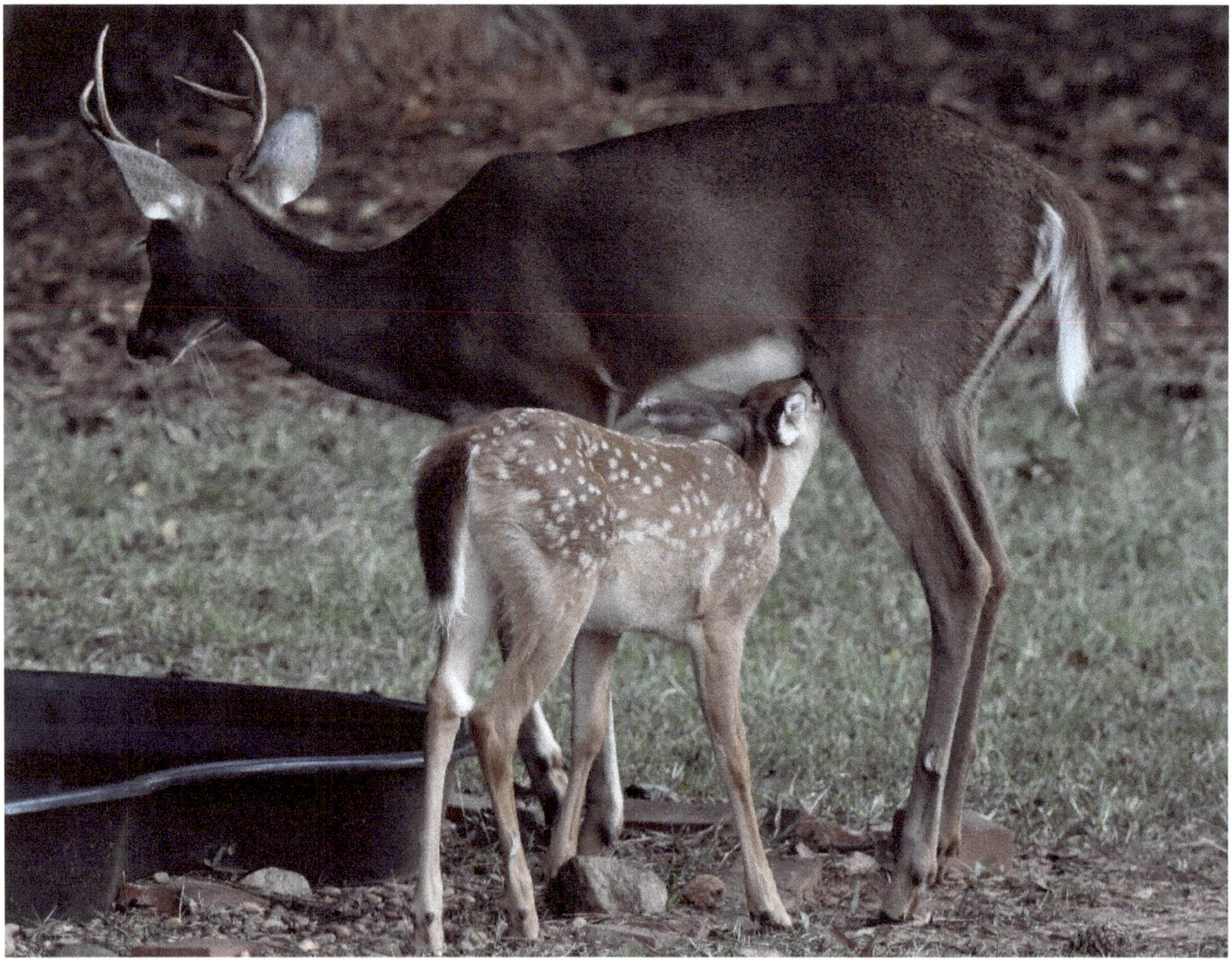

I can only wonder which was the more surprised.

Other fawns

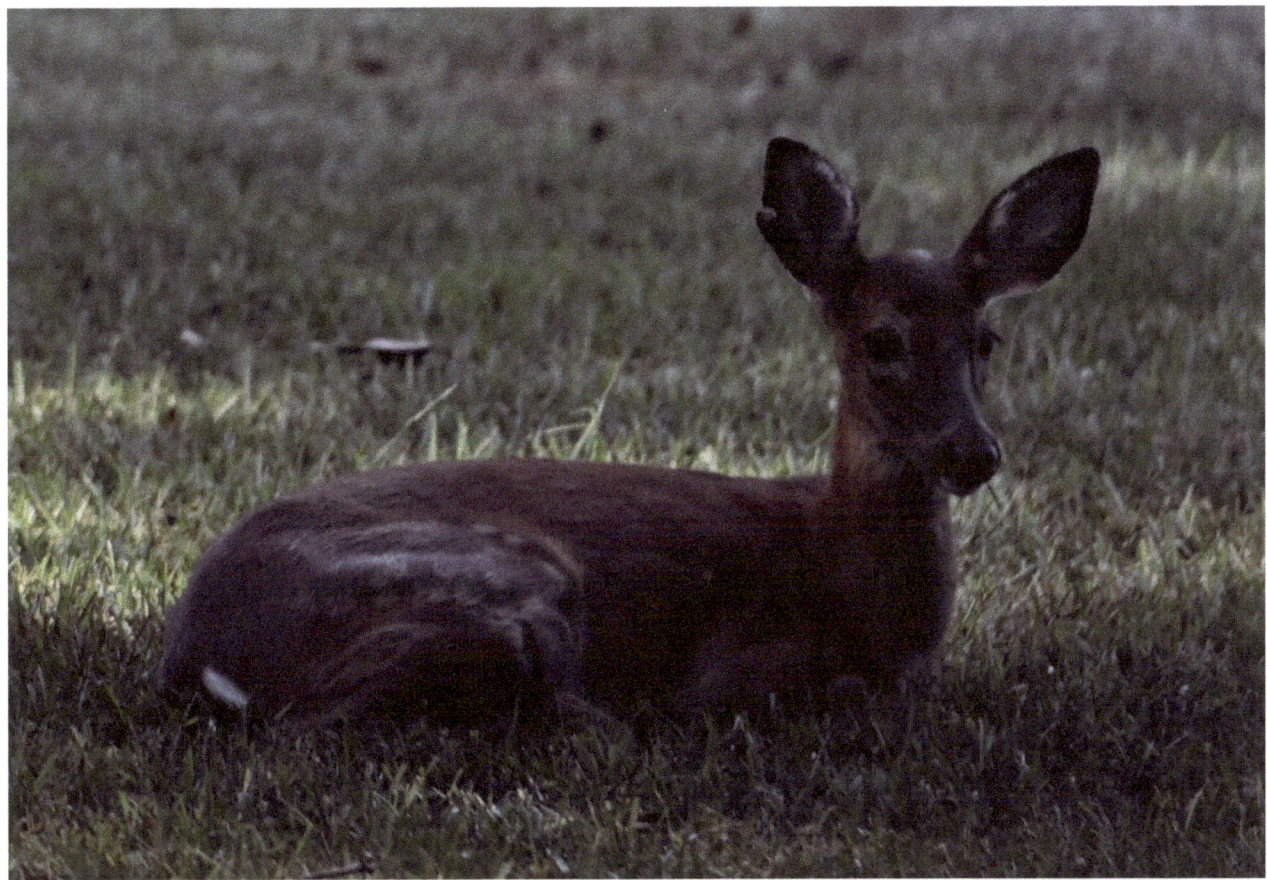

Note the slash on the fawn's hip. Probably a result of getting in the way of one of the adults who didn't want any other deer encroaching on its place at the corn table. Here it is seeking relief from the unusually hot September afternoon.

Other fawns also took every opportunity for a milk break.

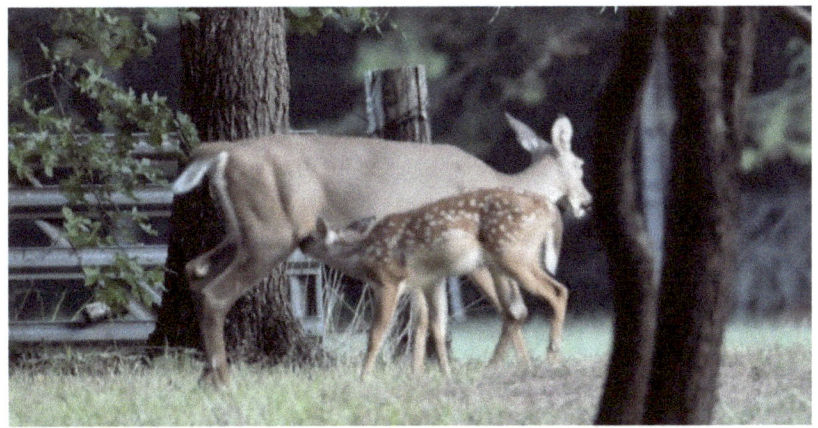

BATTLES OVER FOOD SUPPLIES

Does challenged all others for the spot they wanted at the table. Not just does, but bucks and sometimes even fawns. Often one or the other would rear up. Adults ran does and bucks and fawns off. Older fawns did not hesitate to challenge the smaller fawns. Other deer usually ignored the disputes. Another dozen or more are not shown here.

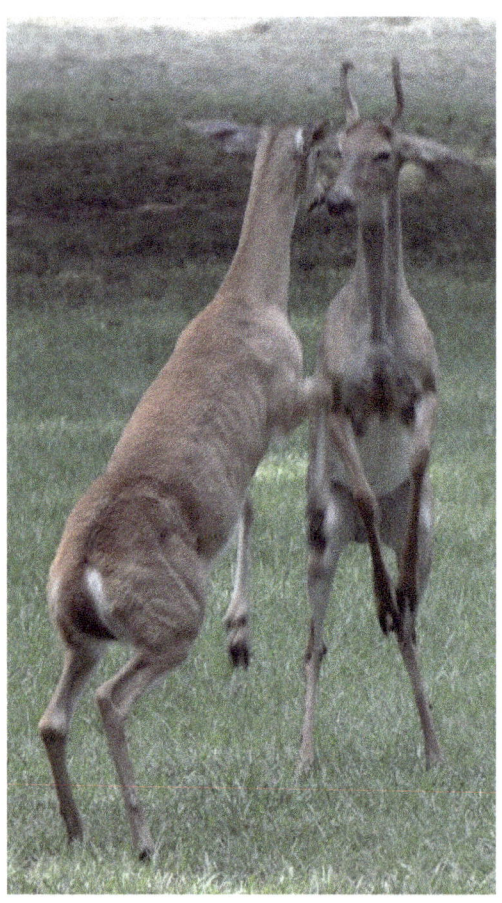 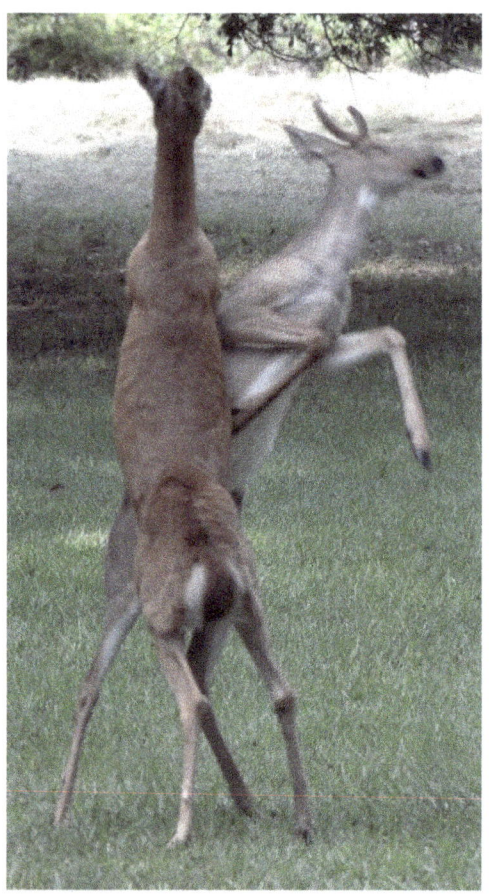

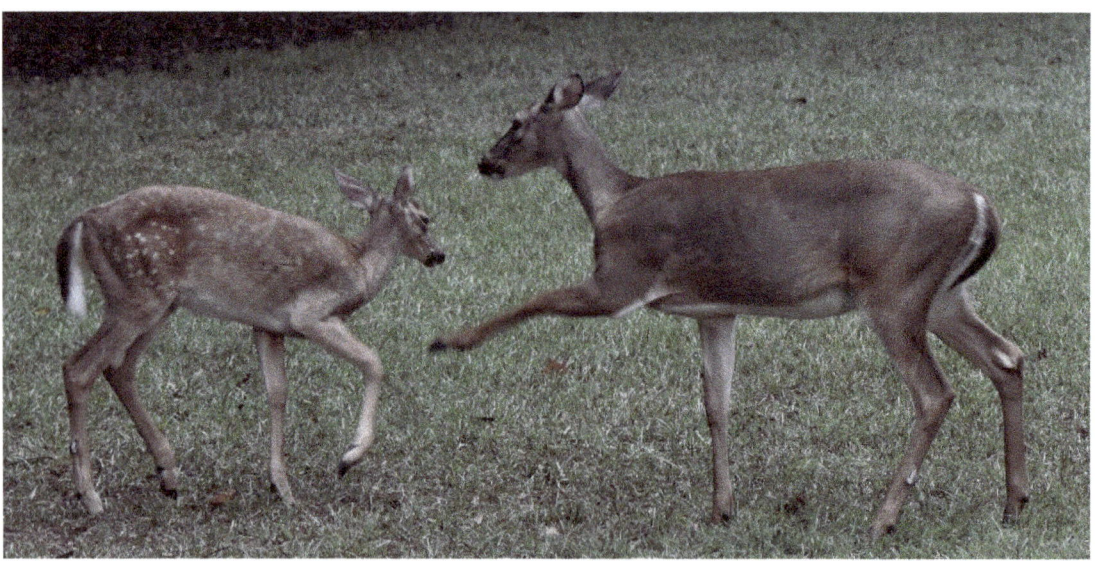

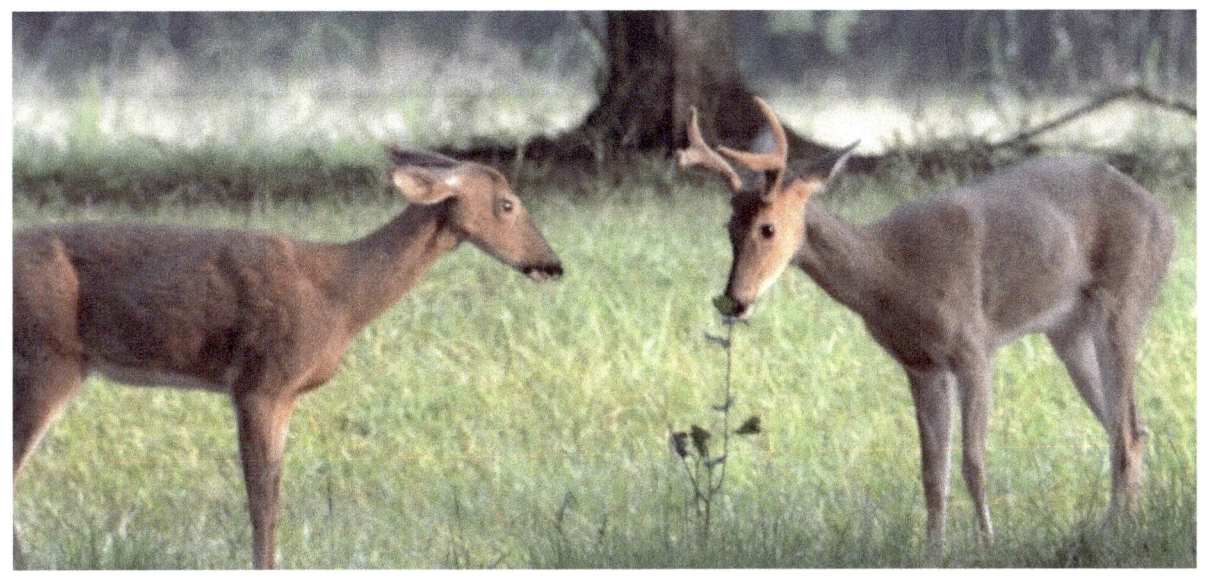

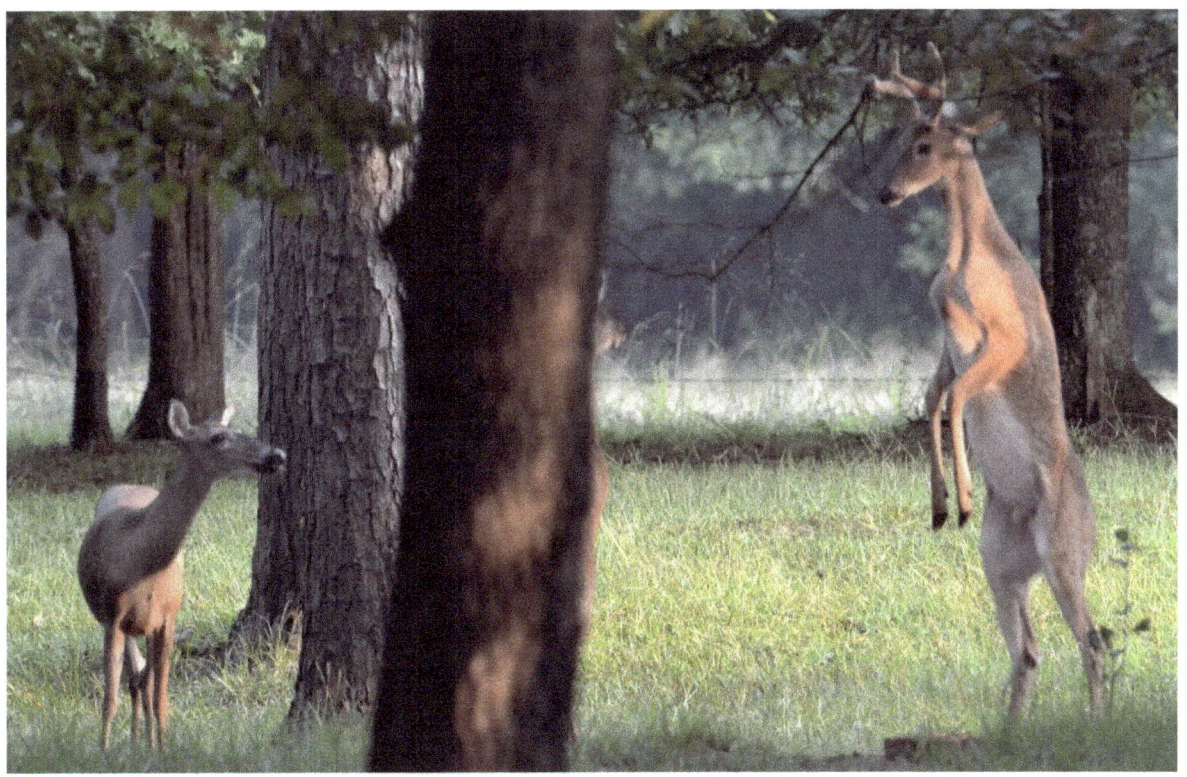

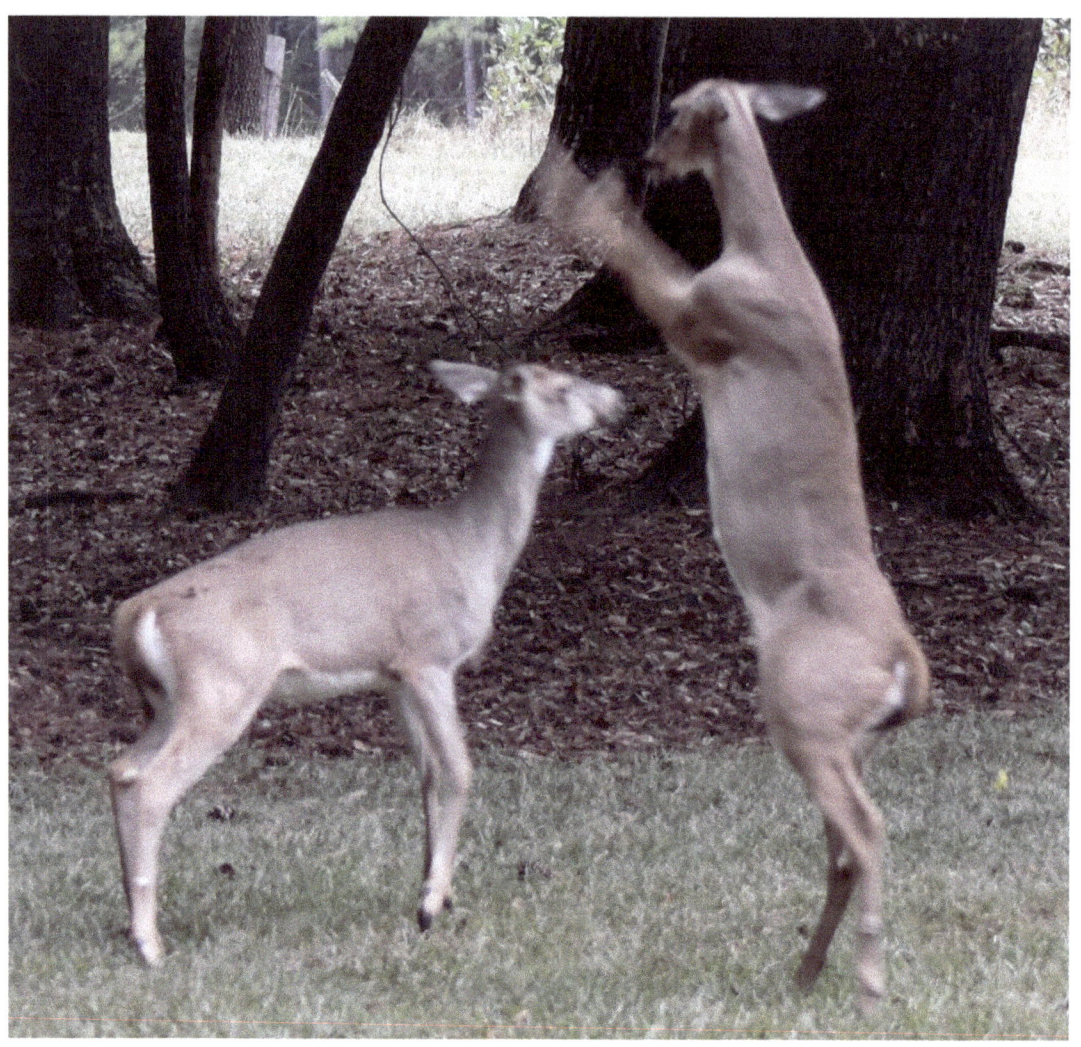

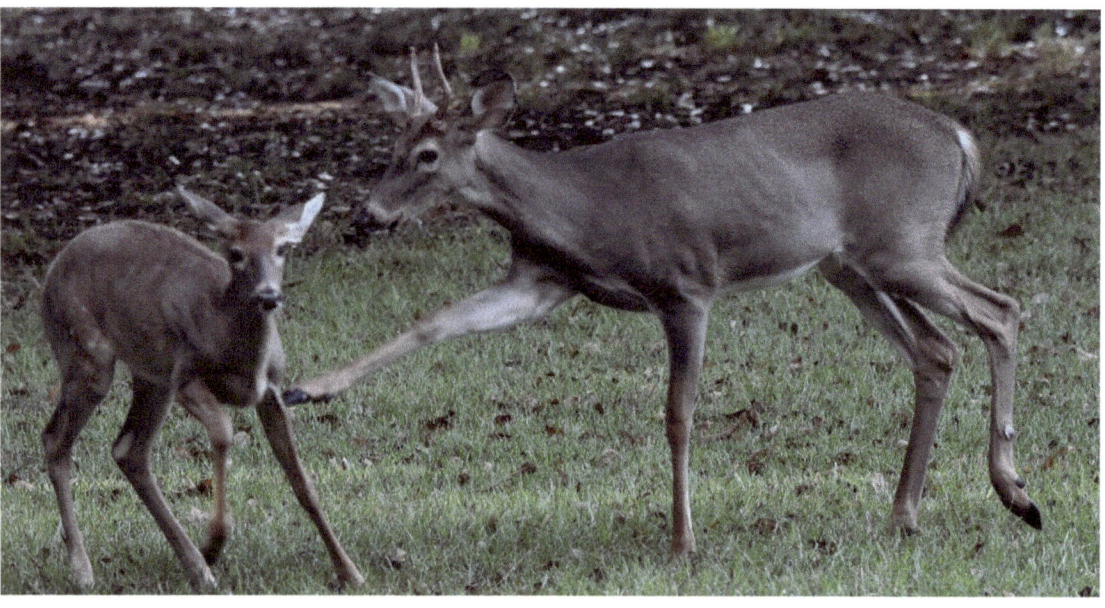

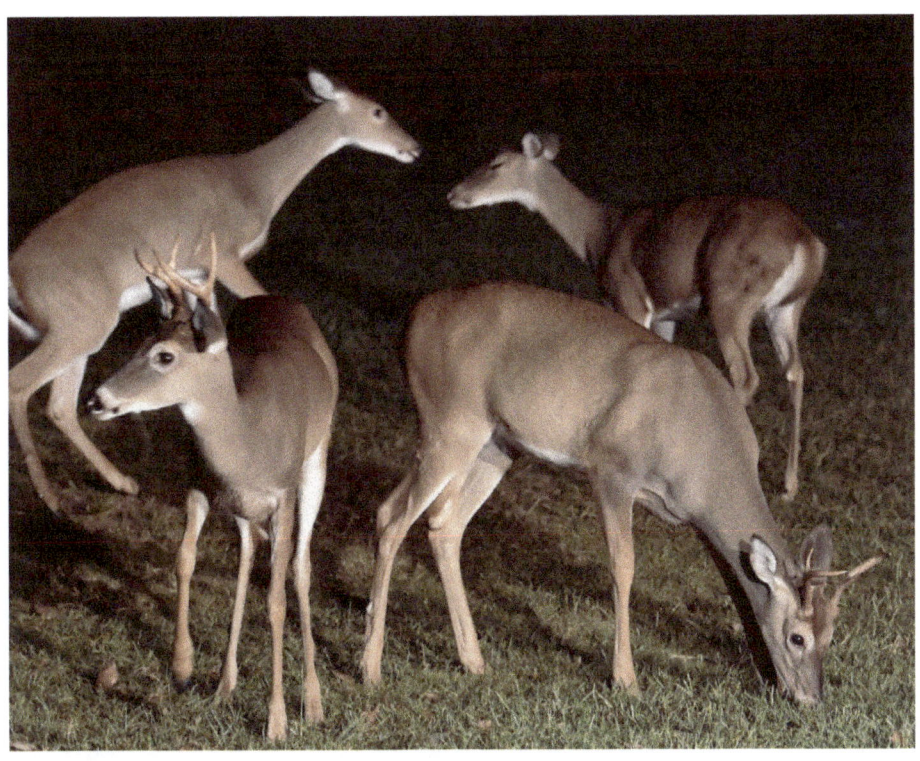

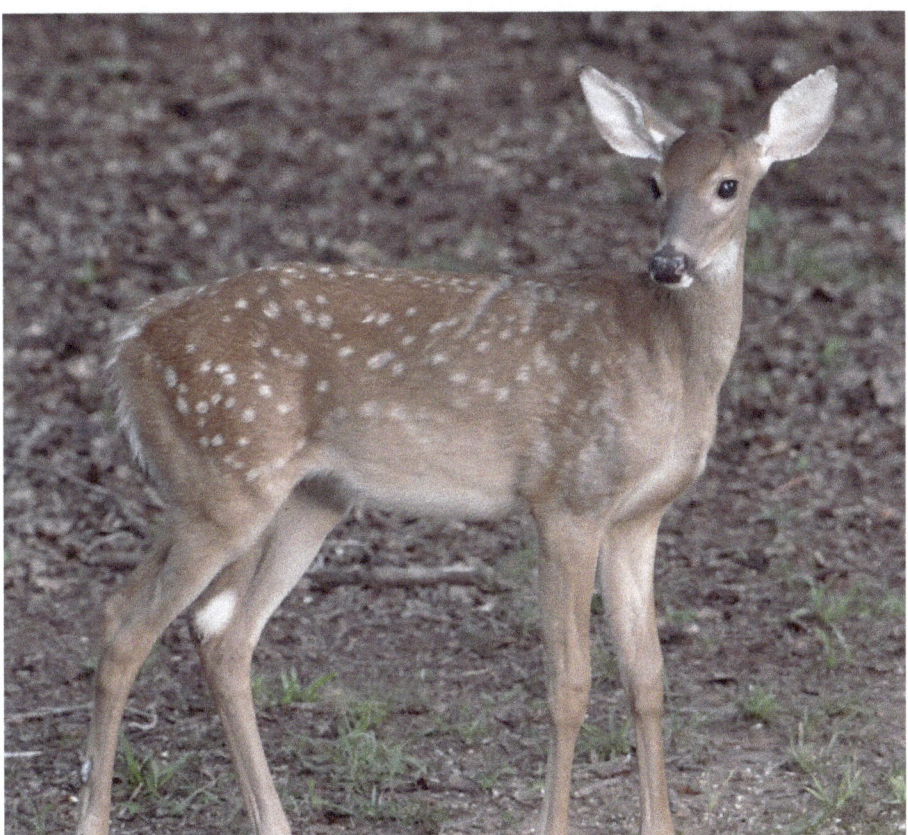

She took a slash across her back as someone ran her away from the food.

THE HAWK

The red-shouldered hawk was a delightful surprise. I had often seen hawks often flying over the hayfields, and when my neighbor harvested hay he saw hawks chasing field mice everywhere. But I had never had one this close. It came within only a few yards of my window.

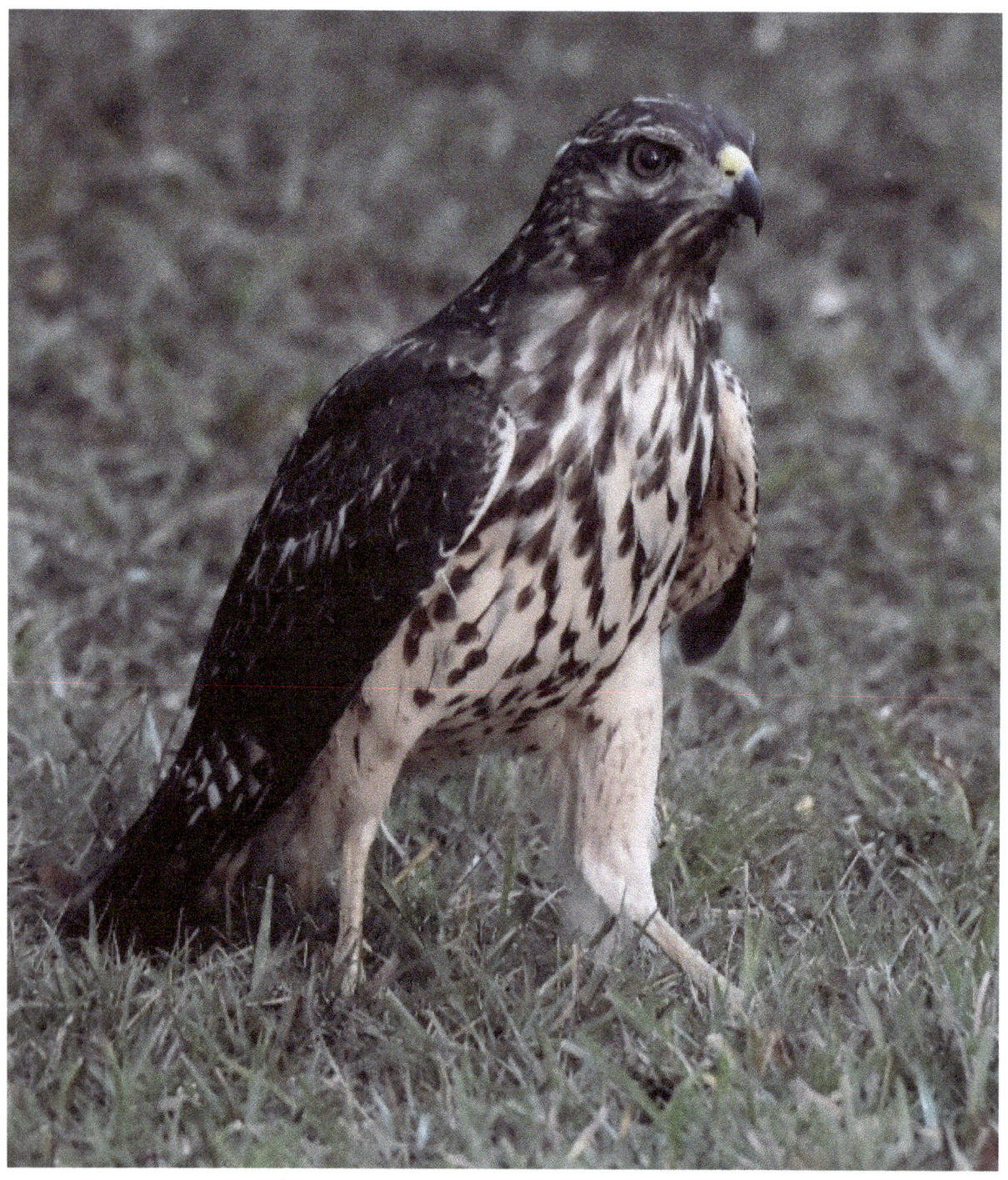

When he dipped his head, I thought he was eating corn, but instead, as I discovered when I greatly enlarged and reviewed the pictures, he grabbed an insect (or maybe it's a spider).

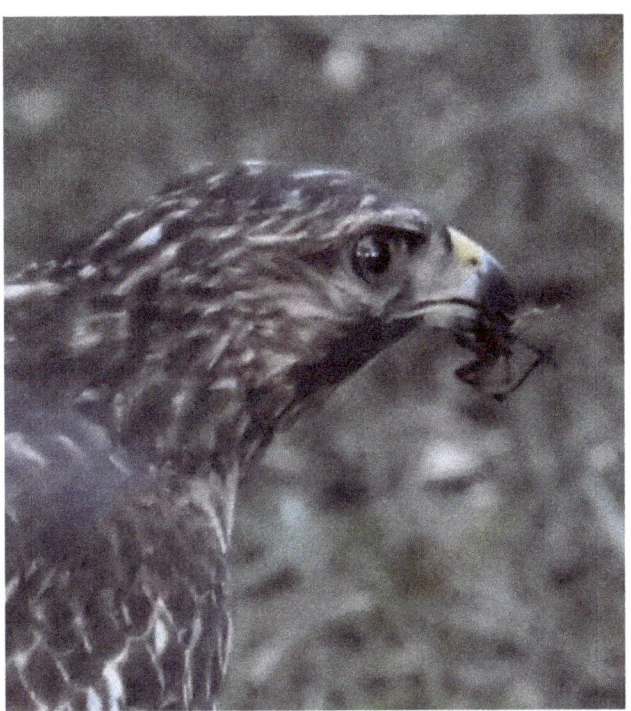

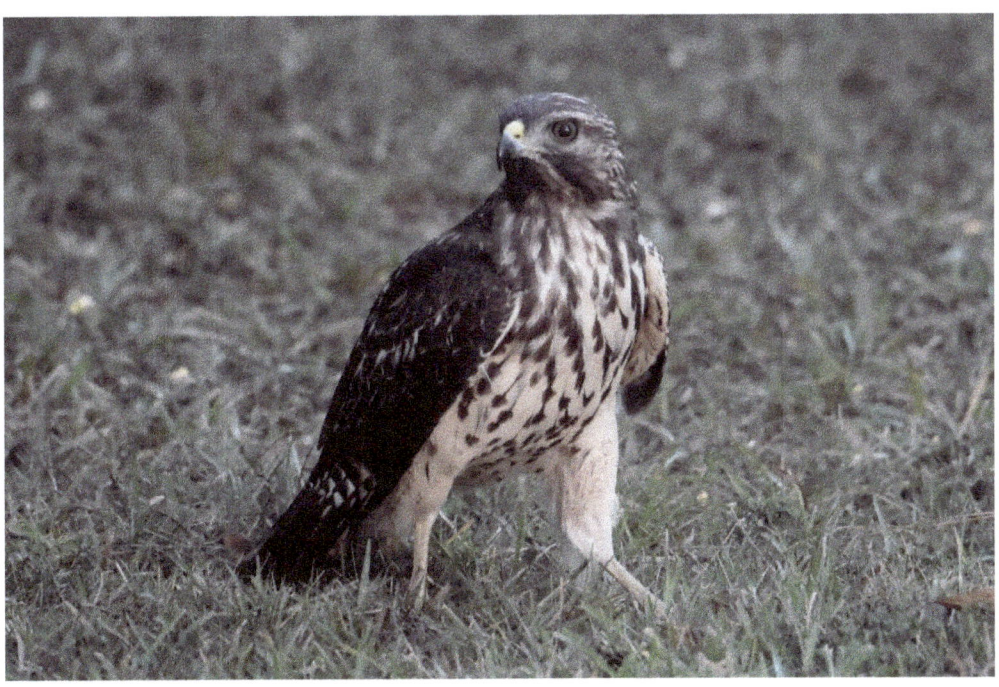

SQUIRRELS

Squirrels are often hated by city folks but are a source of wonder for the country boy who begins his hunting life seeking what the city folks call the bushy-tail rat. In the three weeks I watched the wildlife, I learned a lot about the secret life of these critters.

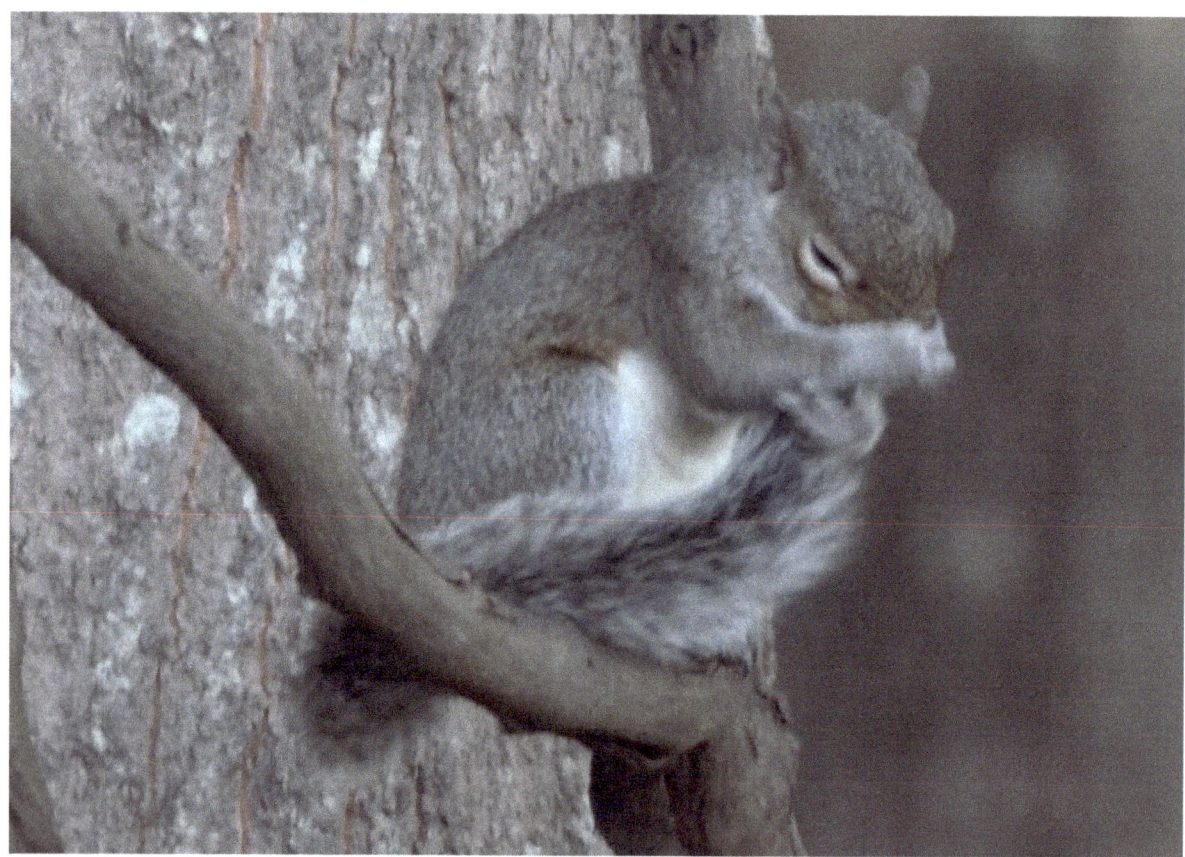

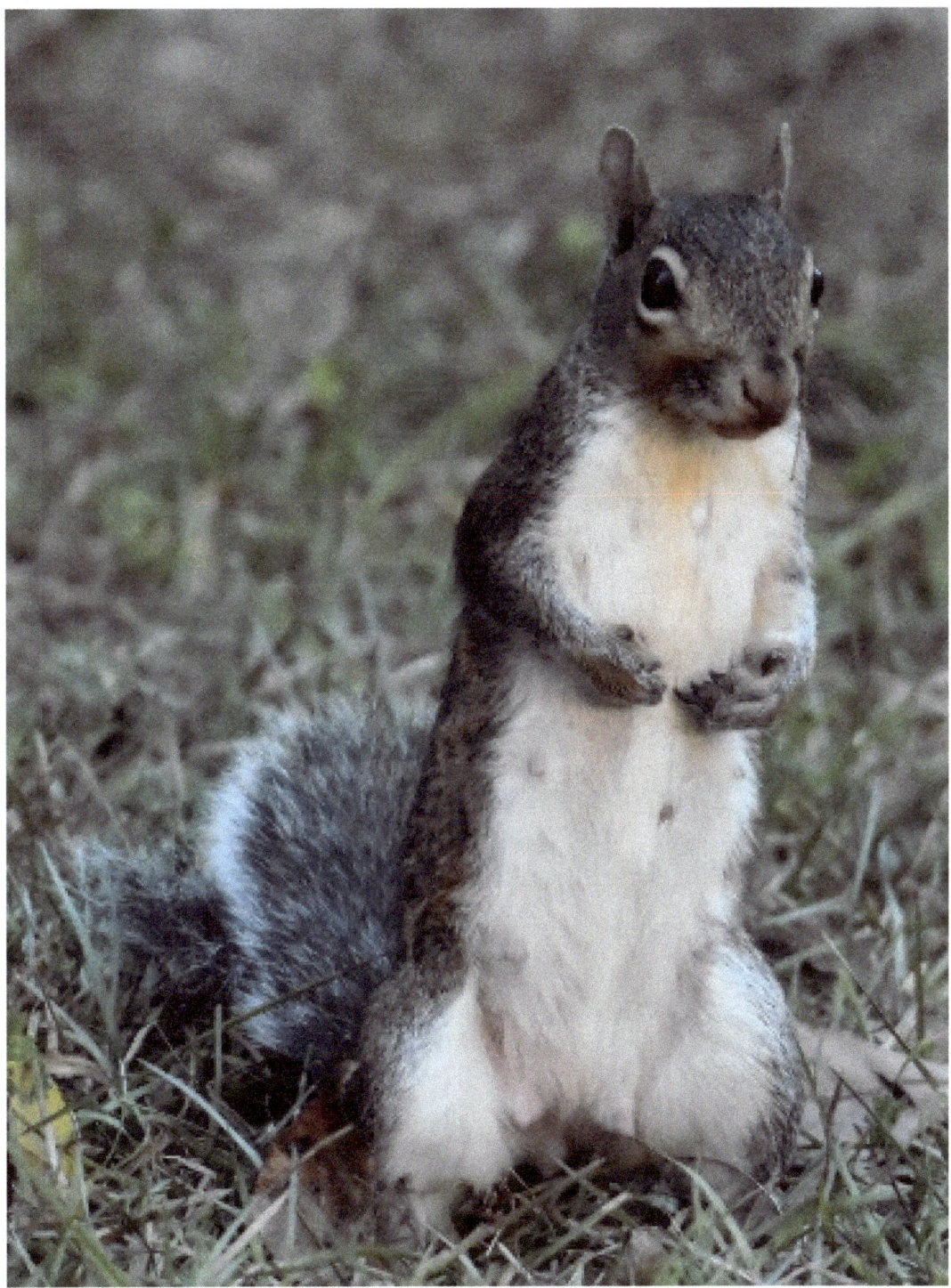

A mama stood and stared back at my window as if to show off her self-esteem.

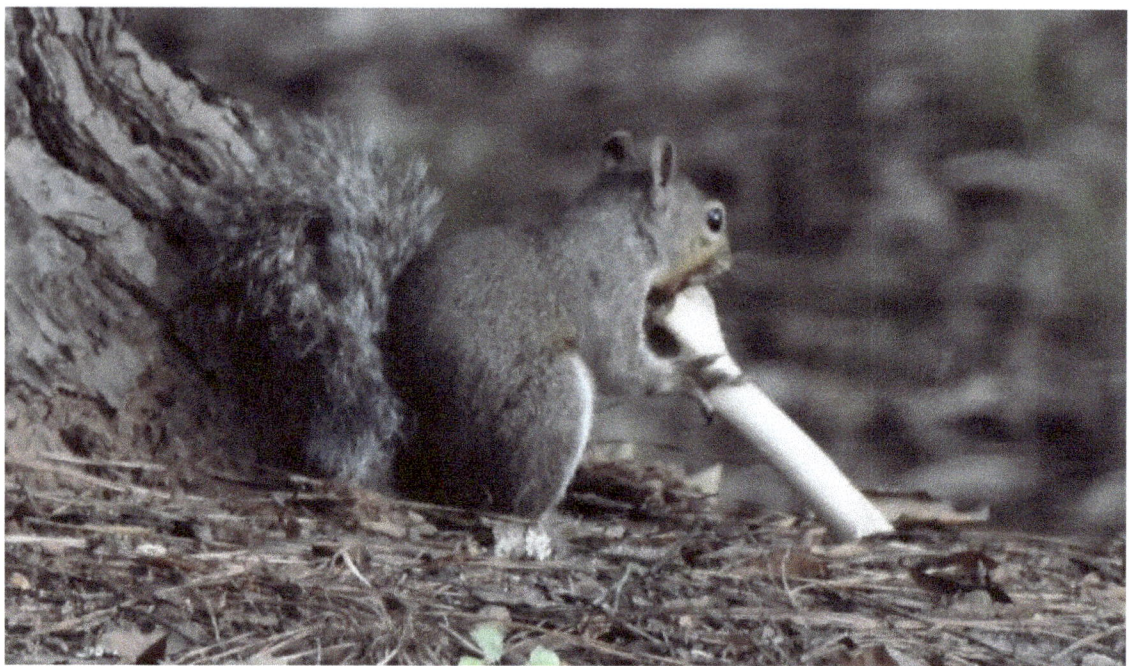

One treated himself for low levels of calcium by chewing a bone.

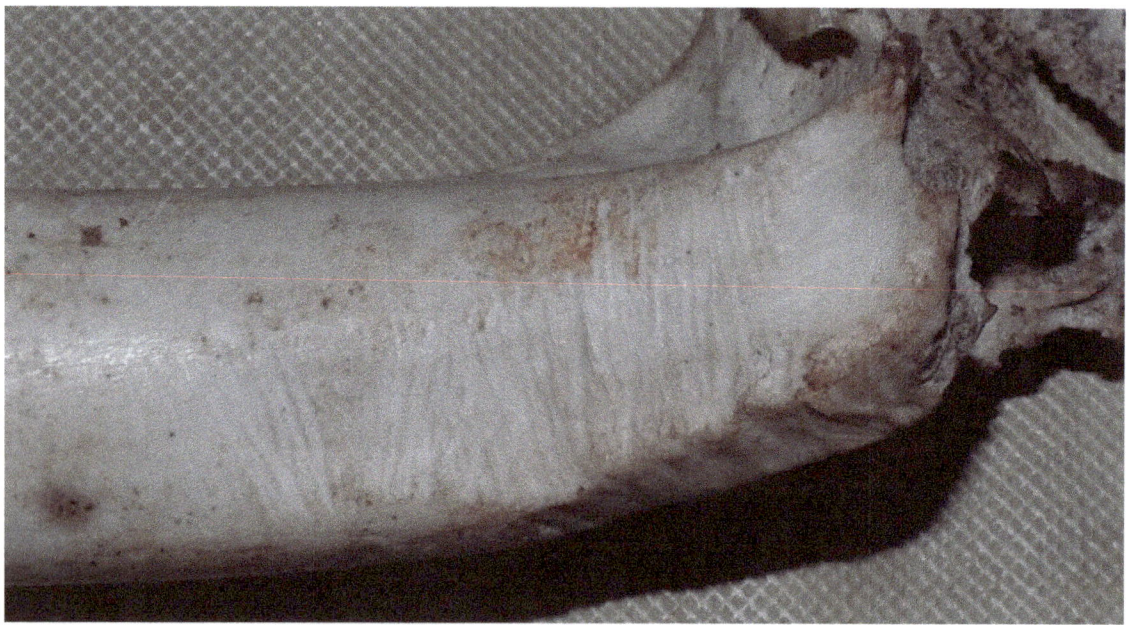

Tooth marks are easily visible. I have found numerous shed antlers that have been chewed.
But this is my first sighting of a chewing episode.

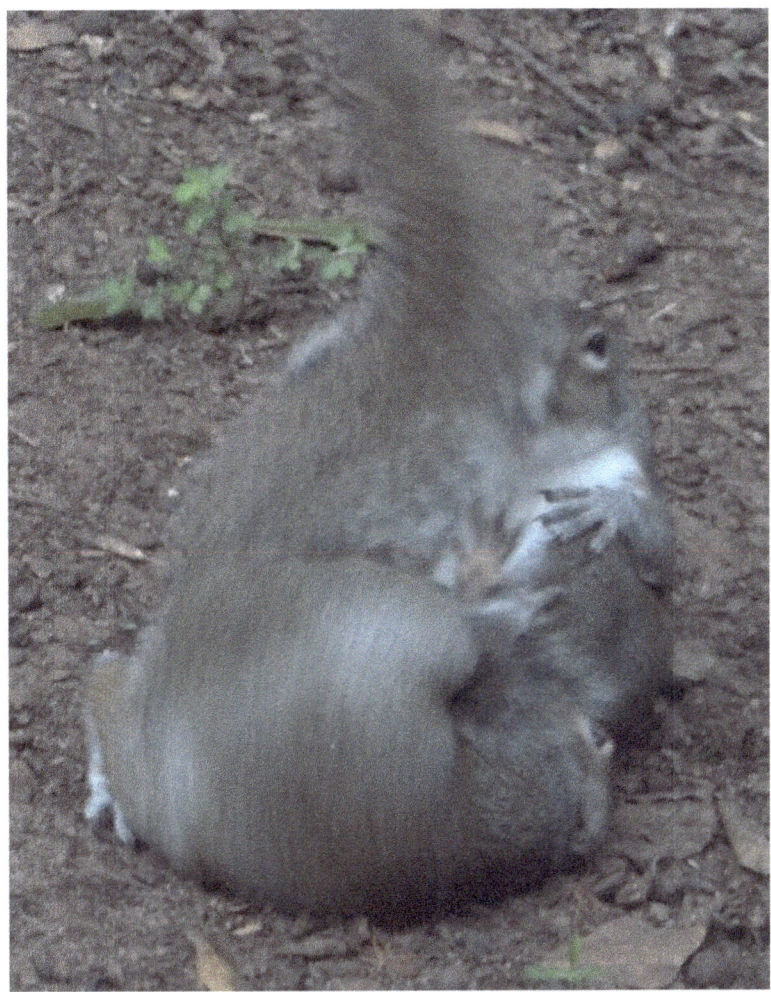

Just as deer engage in pushing battles, so squirrels tumble in fights or play.

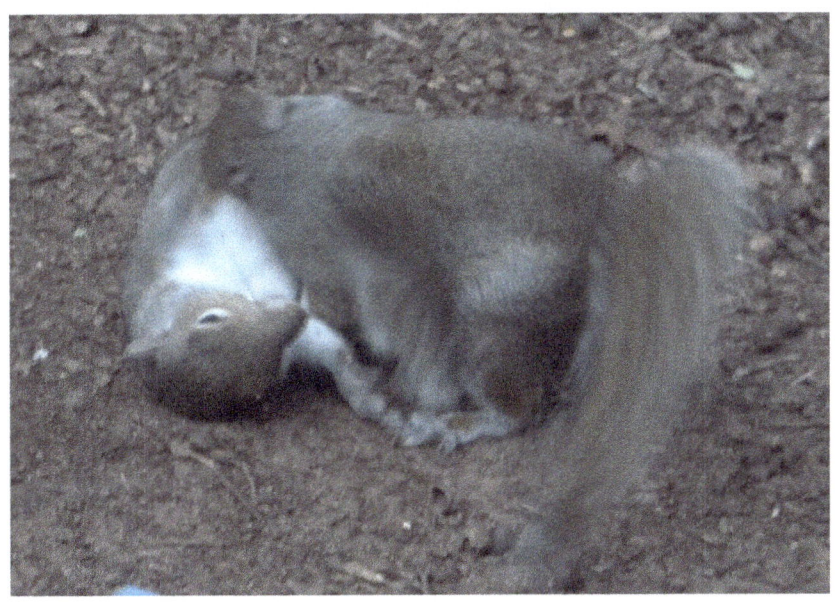

Sad for me, however, was to photograph what looked like injuries from a battle. But the injuries were not battle-inflicted—they were *warbles* caused by bot flies. (Hunters often call warbles *wolves* and will not eat an infected squirrel. The warbles do not affect the meat, however, and it is safe to eat the squirrel.) The fly's life cycle is weird: The female captures a mosquito or other biting insect and lays her eggs on the insect. When that insect bites a warm-blooded animal, the eggs react to the temperature change and hatch. The larvae burrow under the skin. The larvae remain inside the host for five to twelve weeks, then emerge and drop to the soil to continue the life cycle as pupae.

The animals survive unless the open wound becomes infected. It is *yuck* for the squirrels.

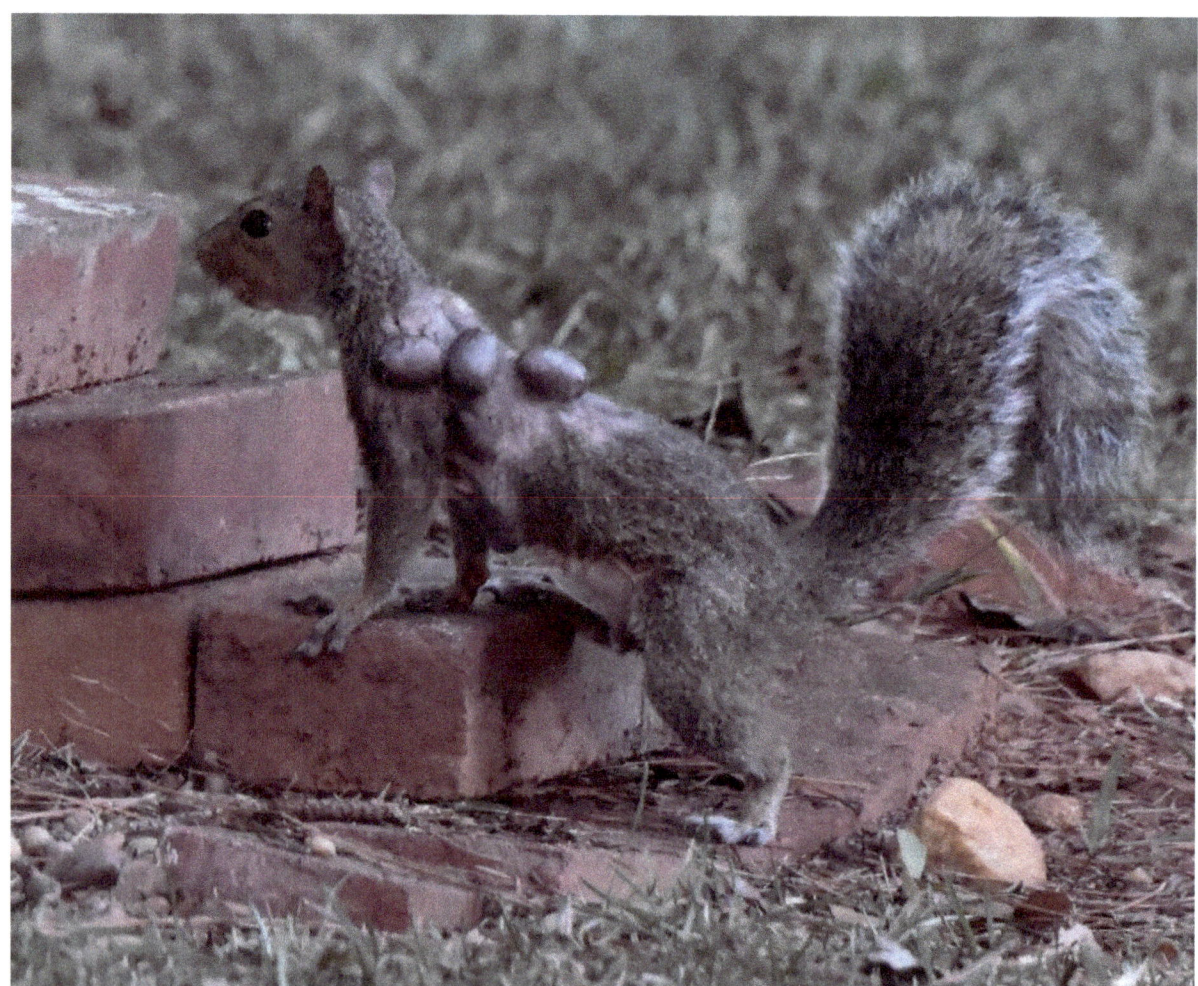

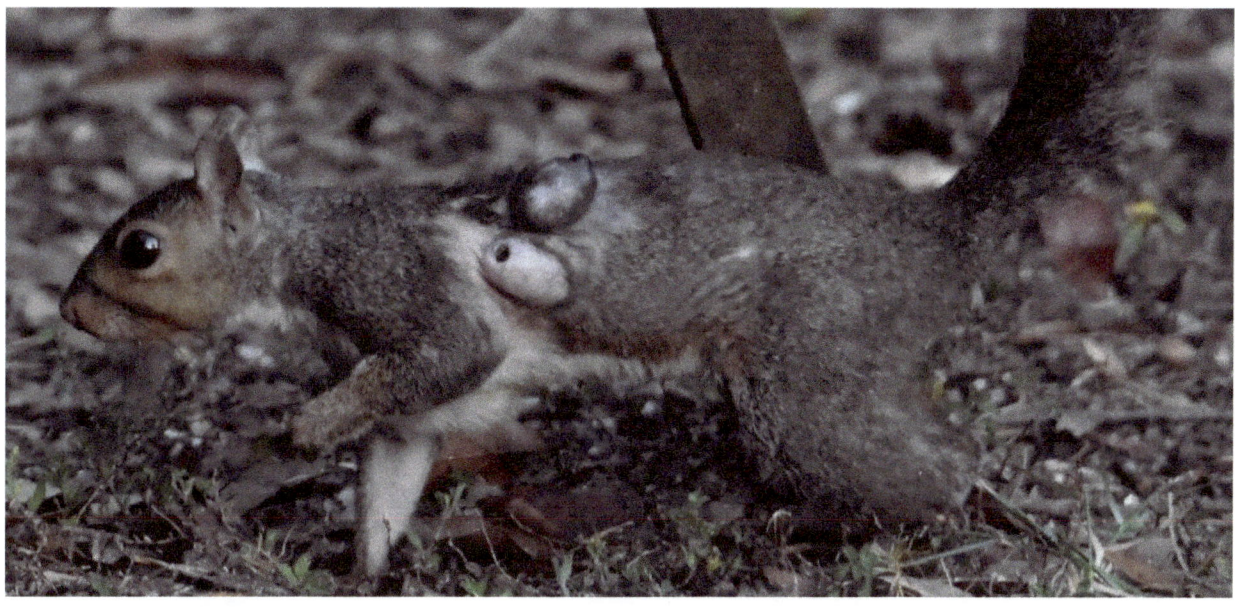

Squirrels apparently have the same olfactory sexual connections that other animals do. This female discovered the site where I had seen another squirrel urinate and she sniffed, rolled and slid over the spot.

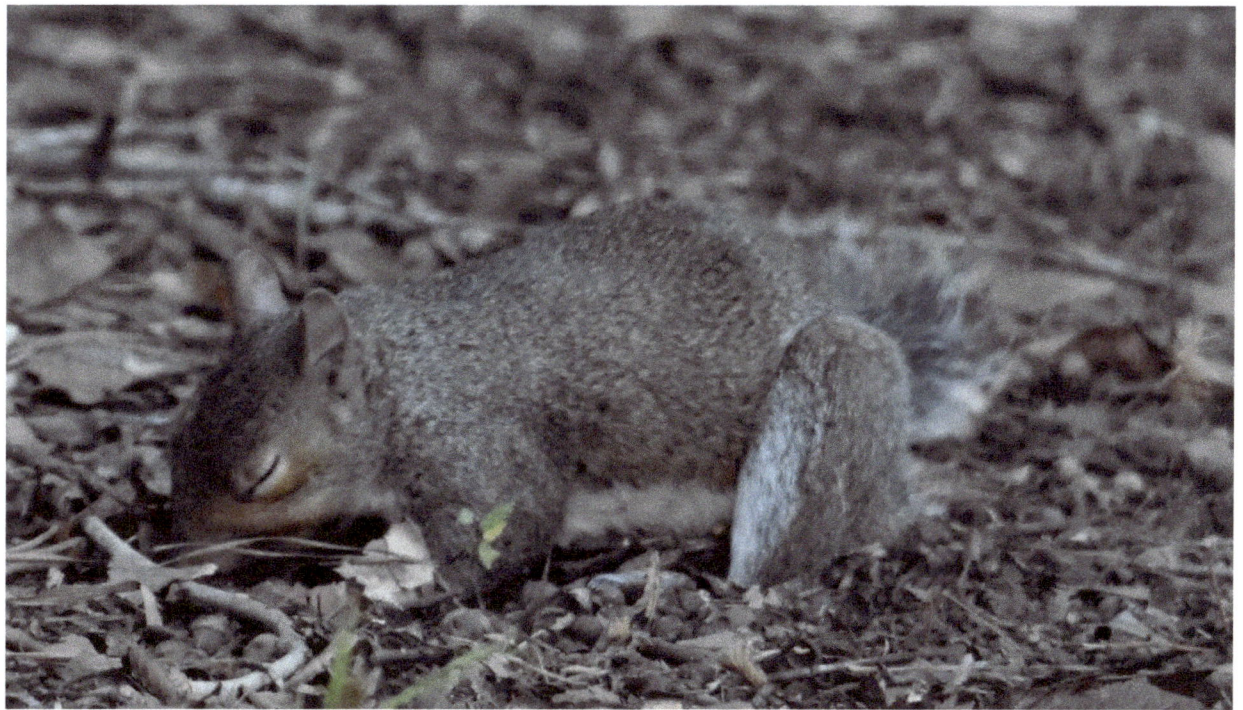

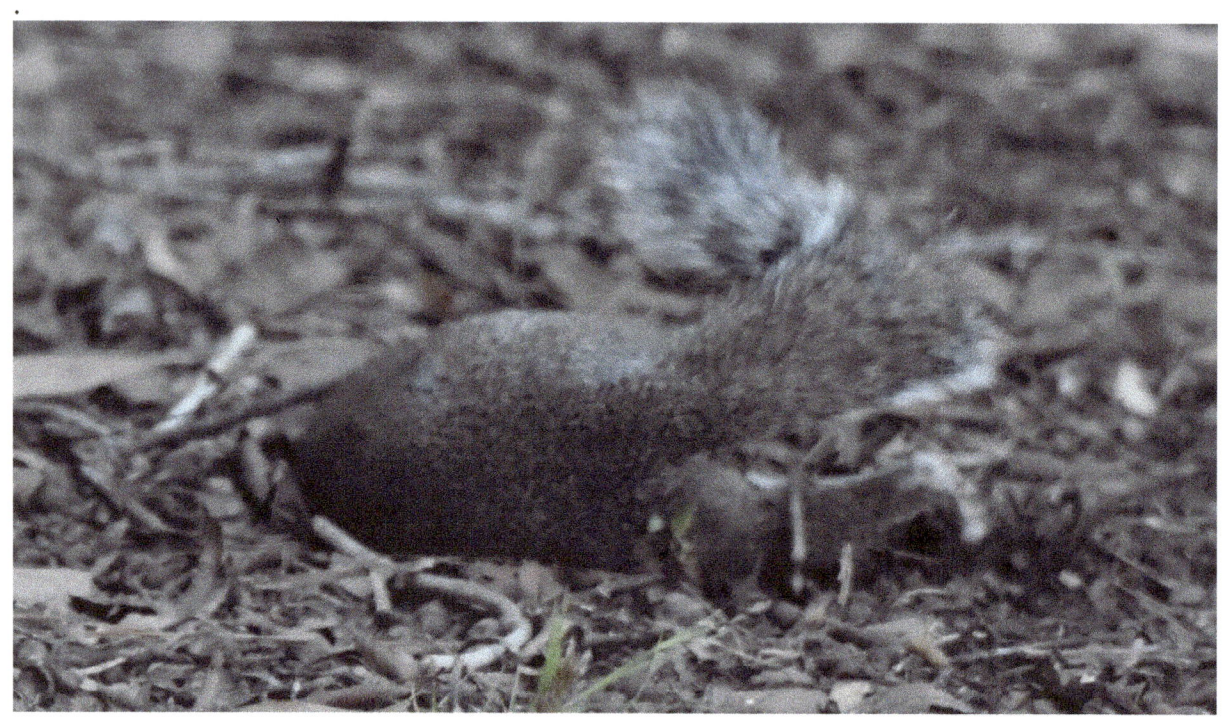

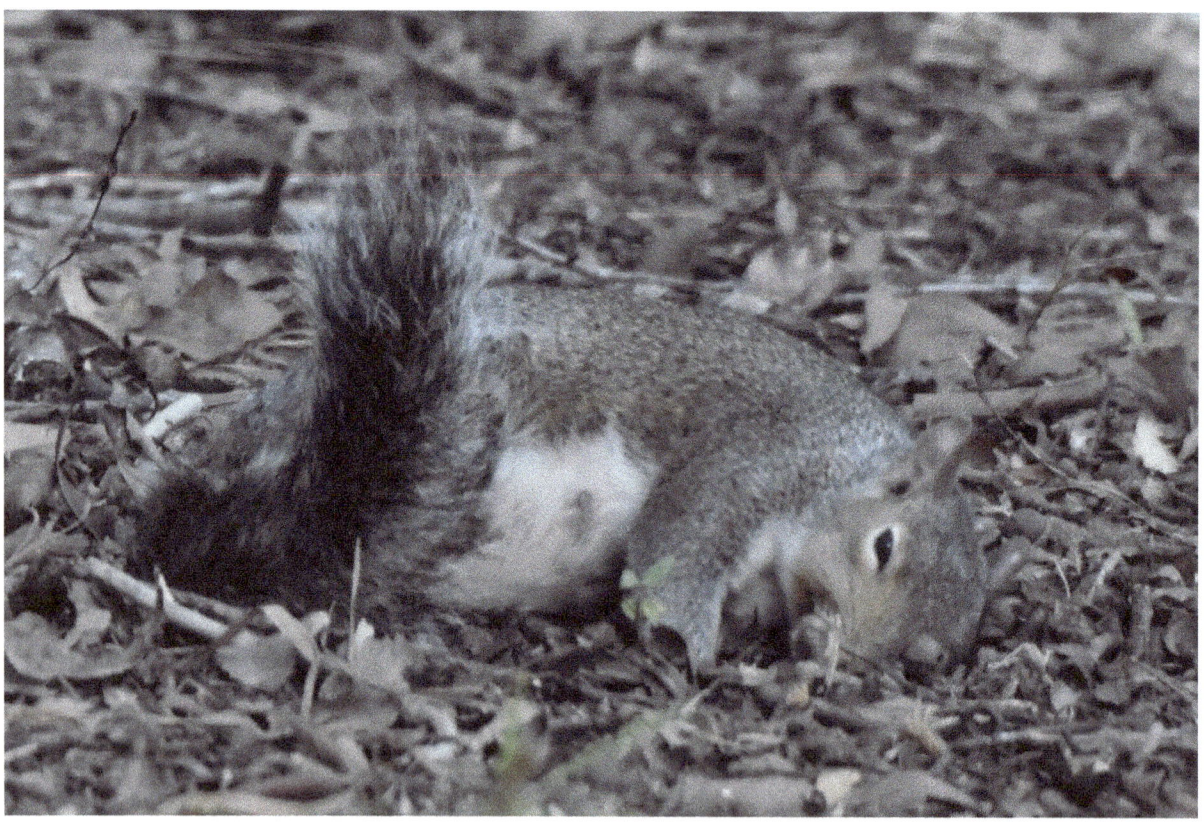

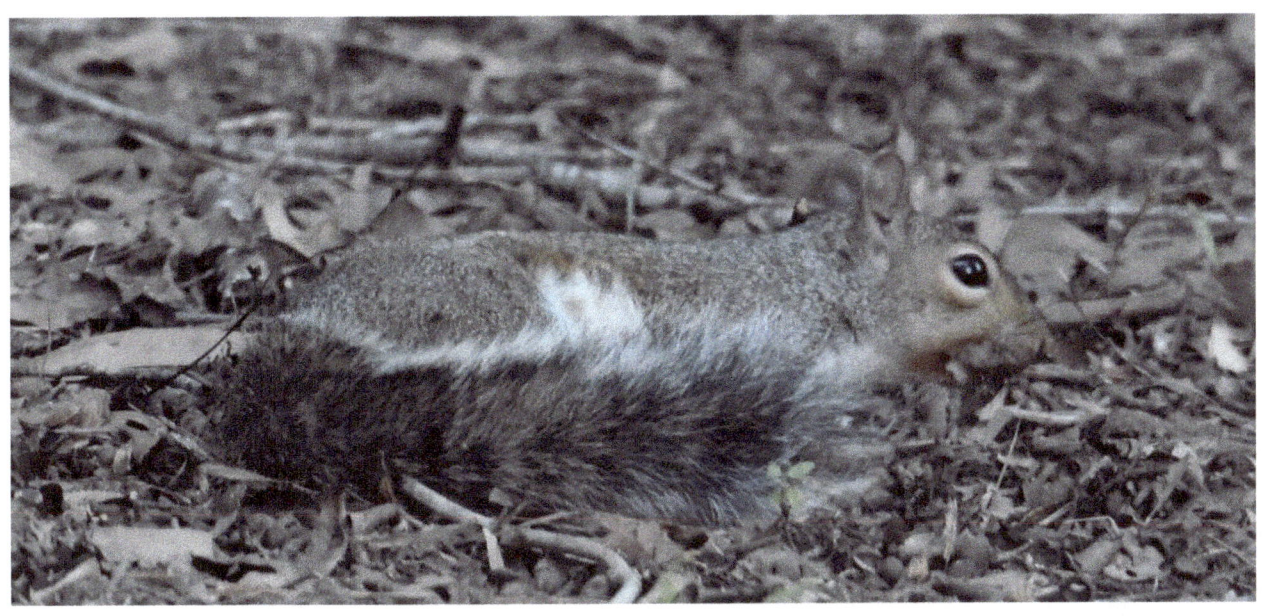

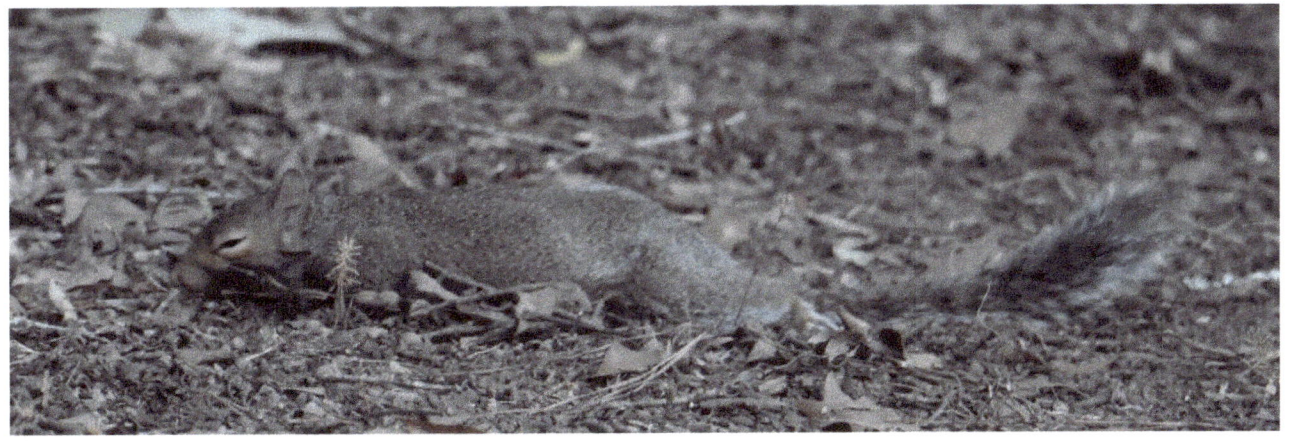

WILD TURKEYS
Georgia's Second Big Game Animal

The male turkey is perhaps the most beautiful bird in Georgia. His colors change as he moves from sun to shadow or as he turns. This iridescence is almost impossible to capture with a camera.

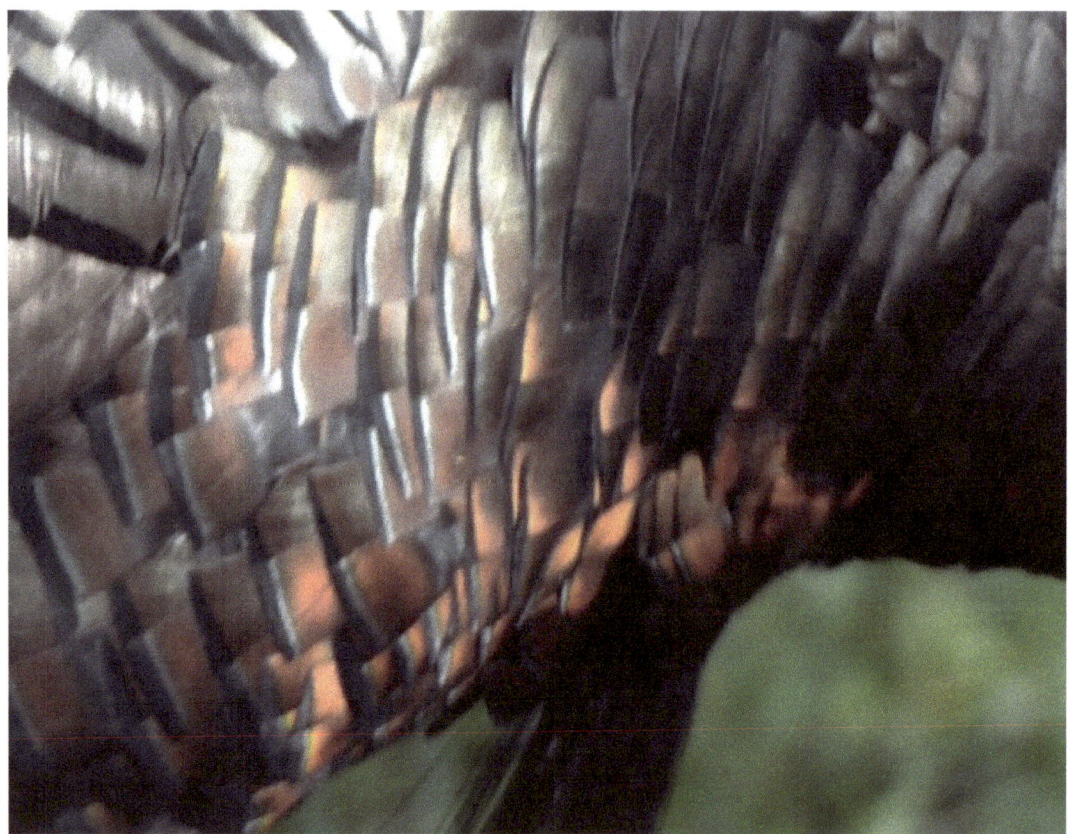

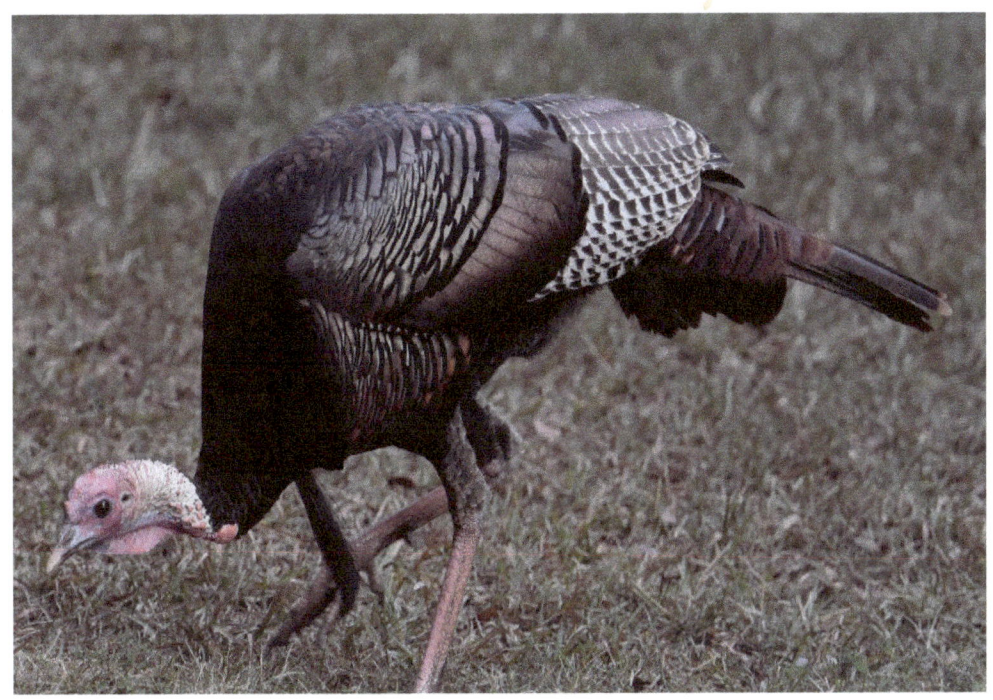

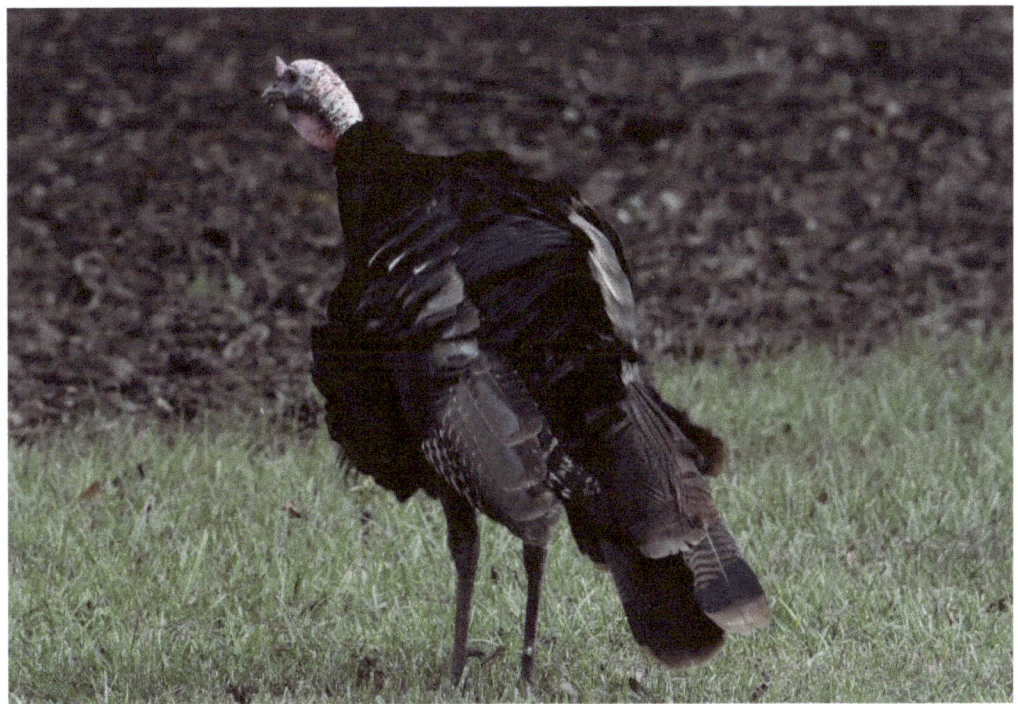

All color disappears when the bird fluffs up to shake off the rain.

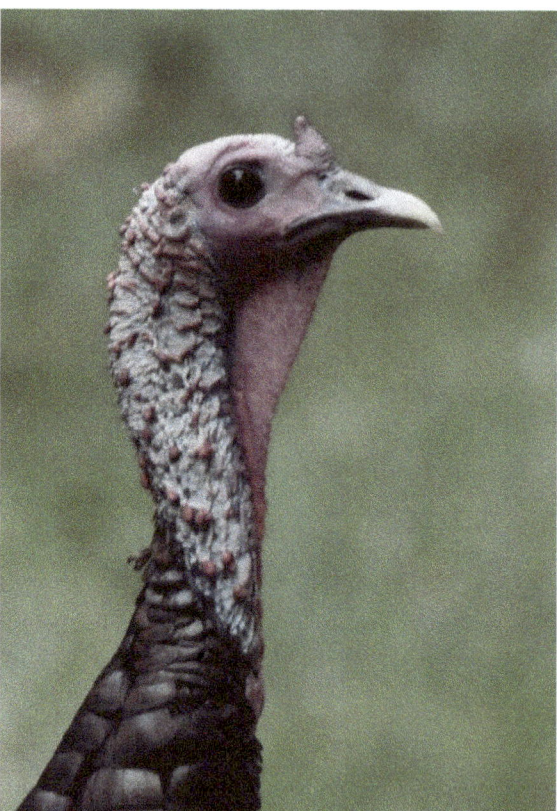

**Turkey hunters say that a gobbler's eyesight is so acute he can see you blink
at a distance of one hundred yards.**

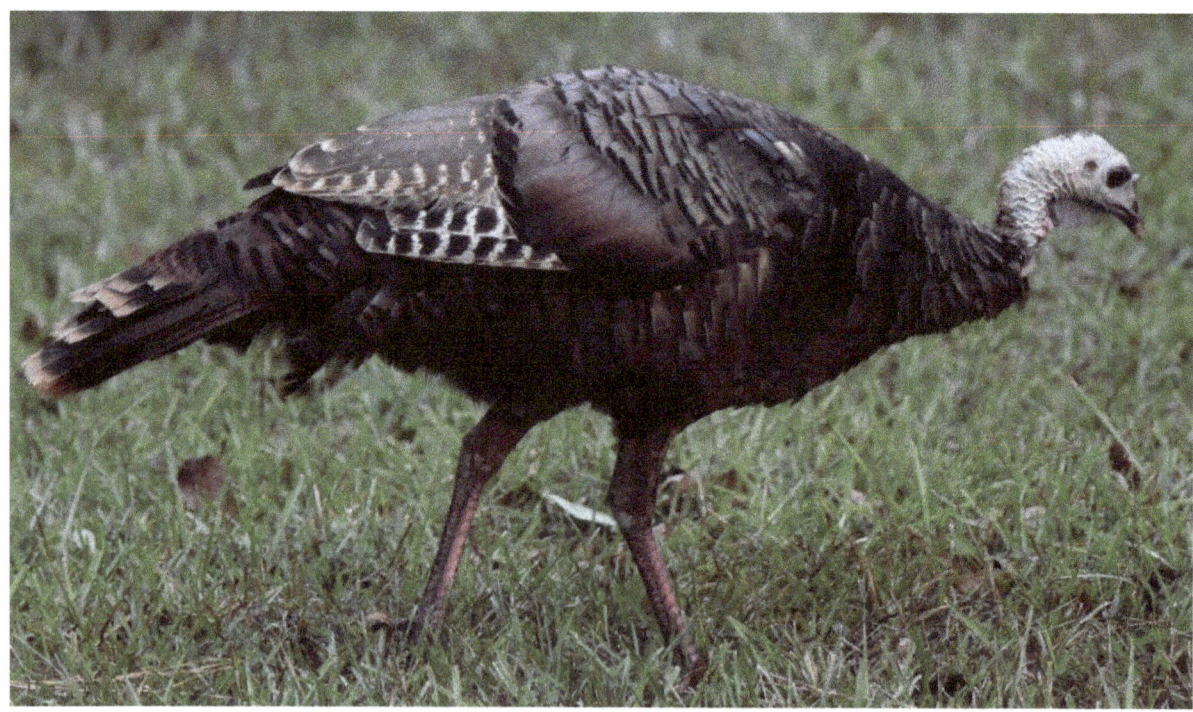

**Hens also shimmer, but not as vividly as the toms.
Like all female birds, they need to be hard to see when on nests.**

A tom can take flight before you can even lift your shotgun. And if you can get the firearm to your shoulder, you don't have his head (your target) in view. All you can see is a flurry of feathers.

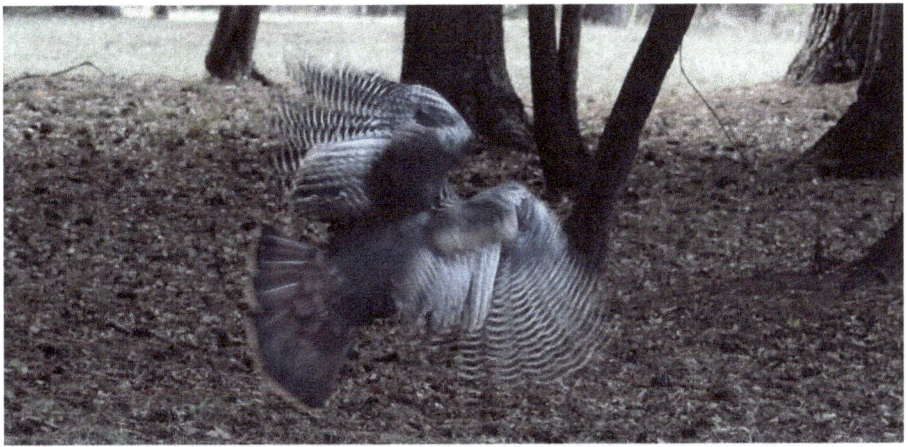

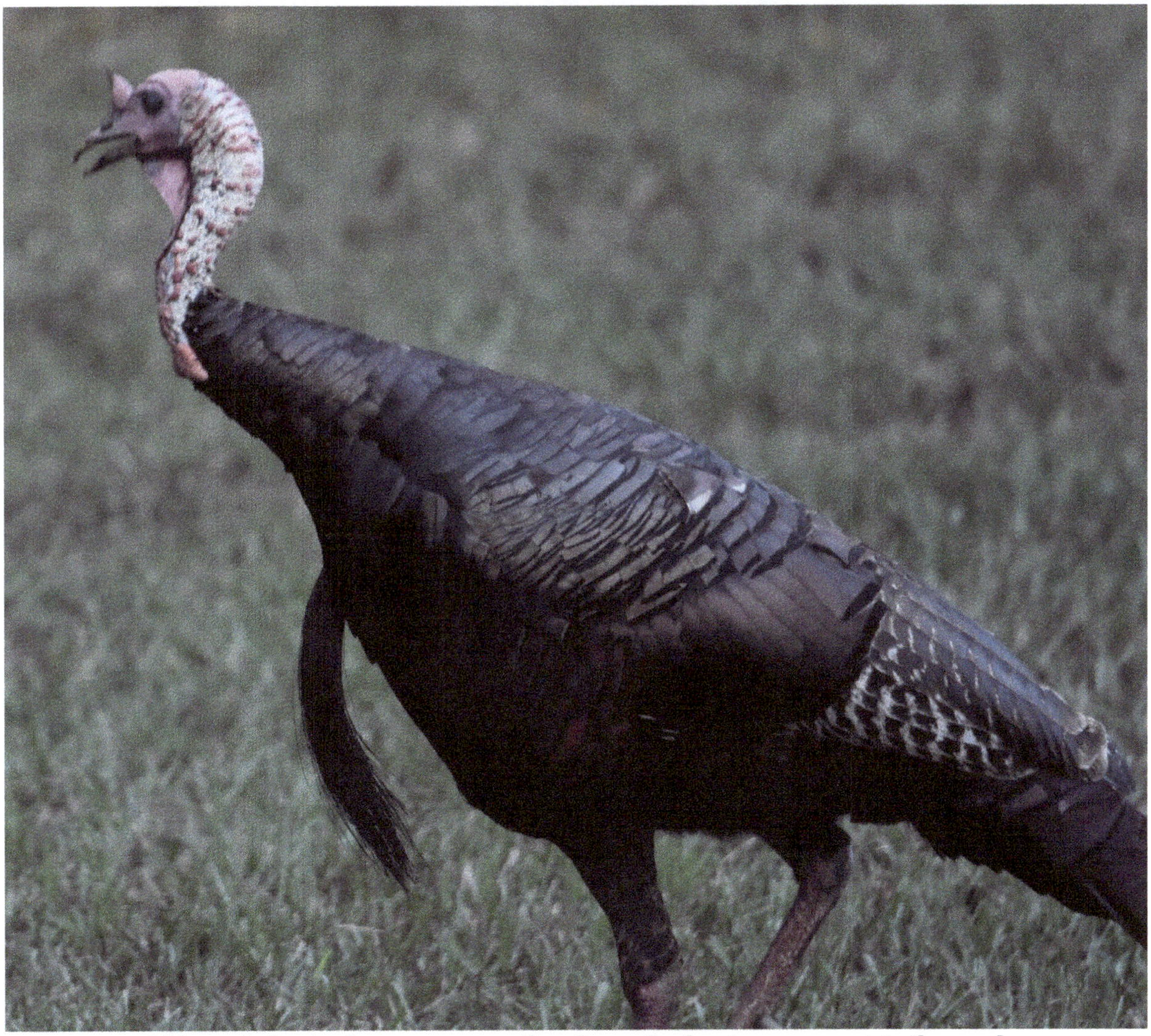

Although the turkeys were panting from the heat, none went to the pool.

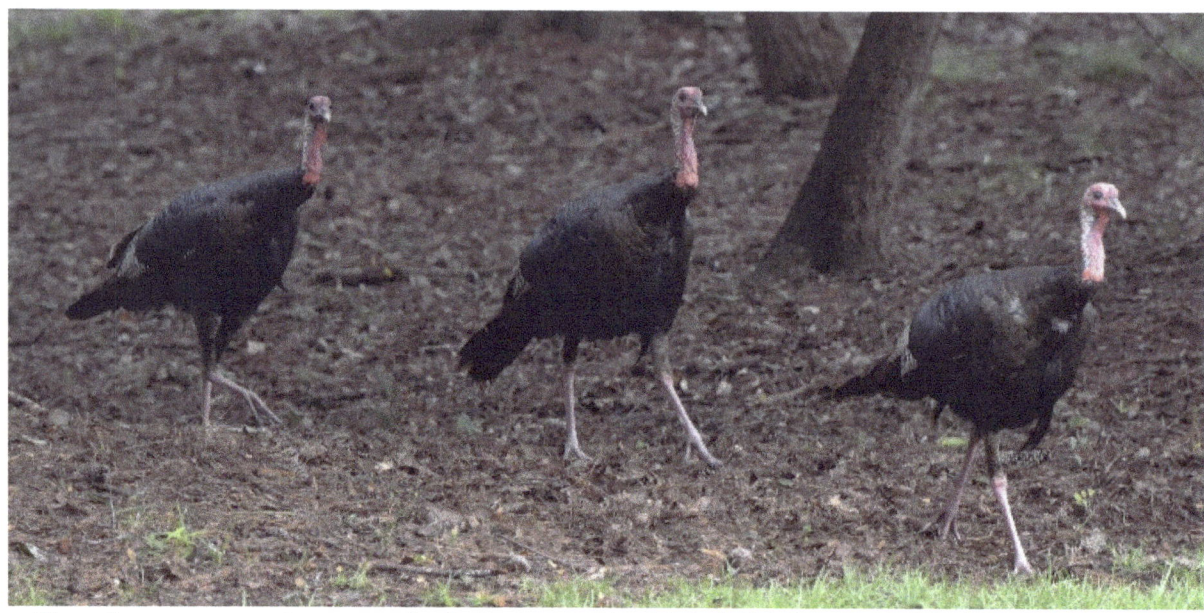

Since I can never get my own ducks in a row, the birds helped me out this fall. They always traveled in a line when they entered the yard. The dominant tom leads.

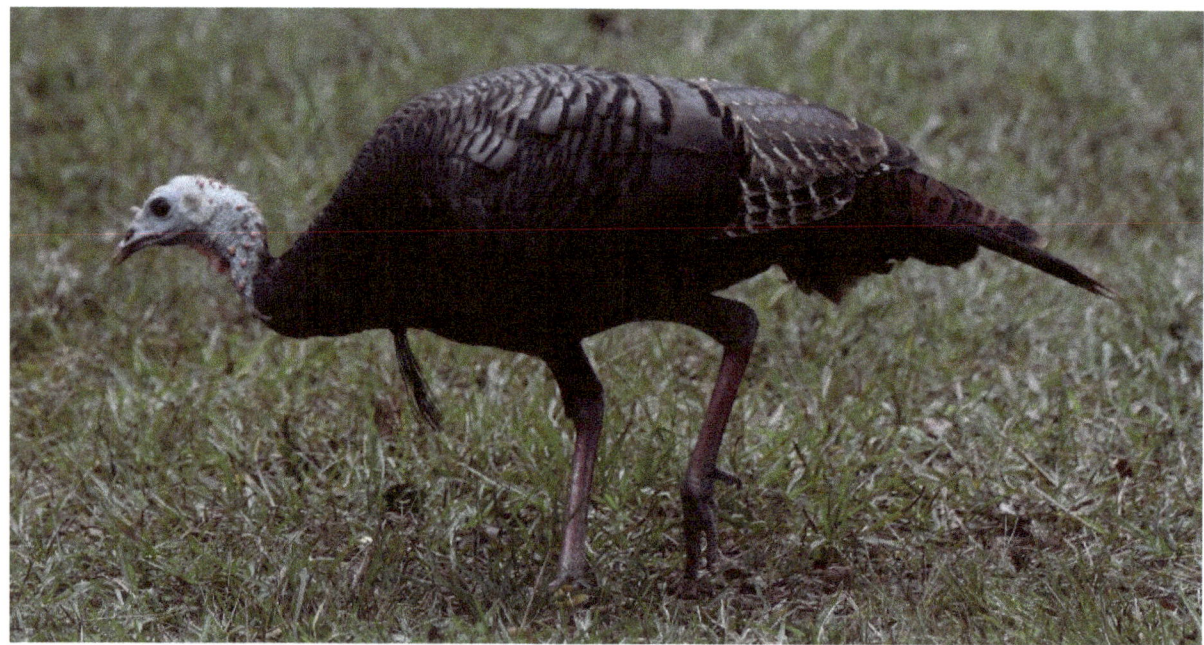

This hen should never be mistaken for a tom in spite of her beard. Hers is thin and wispy and she has no spurs on her legs. What looks like a spur on her near leg is a toe.

The doe-hen ballet

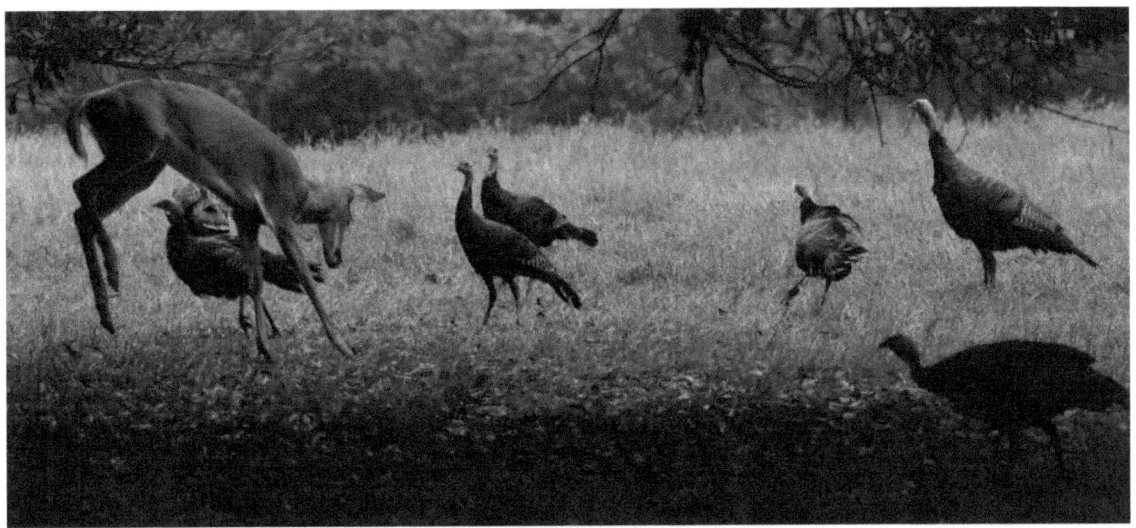

**Hens and toms also seem to enjoy life more than just food and courtship.
And the doe seems to enjoy the dance with the hens.**

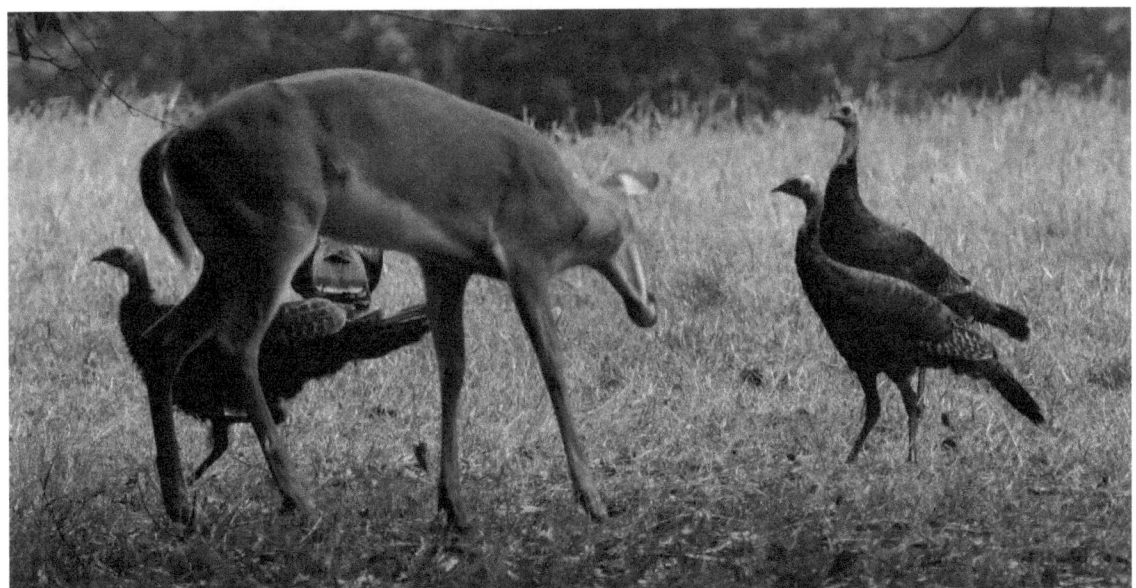

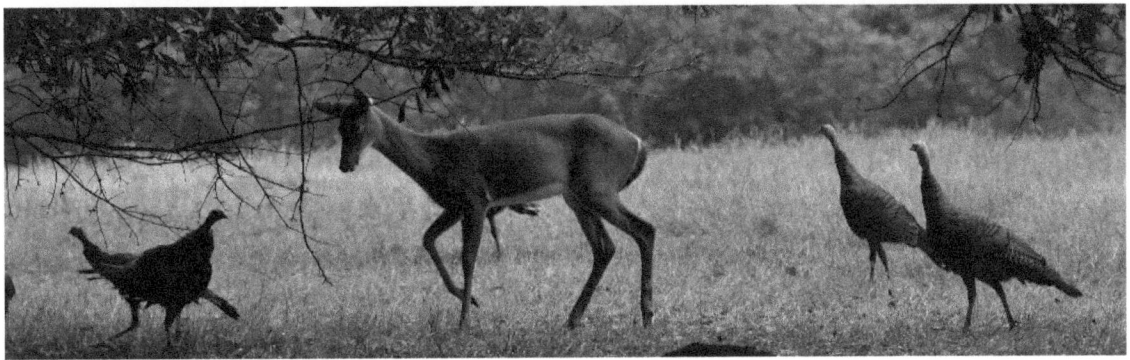

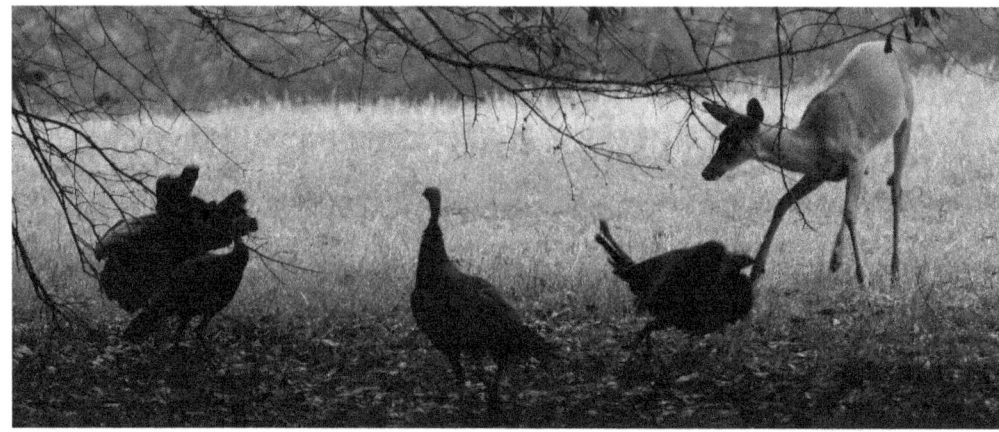

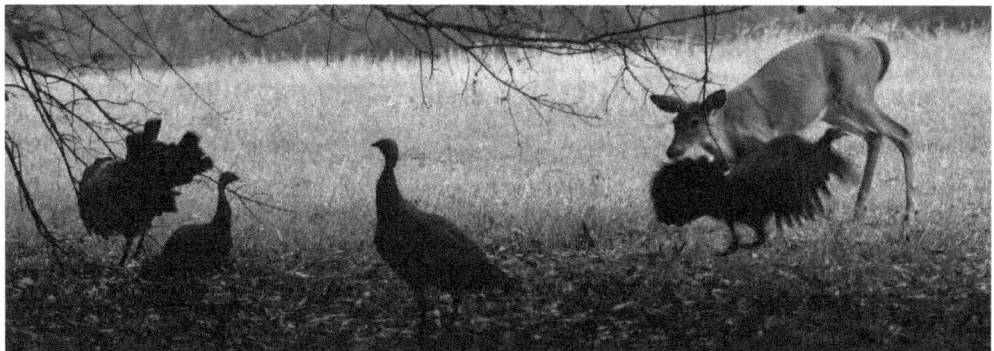

A few of the birds took to the trees. But the dance continued.

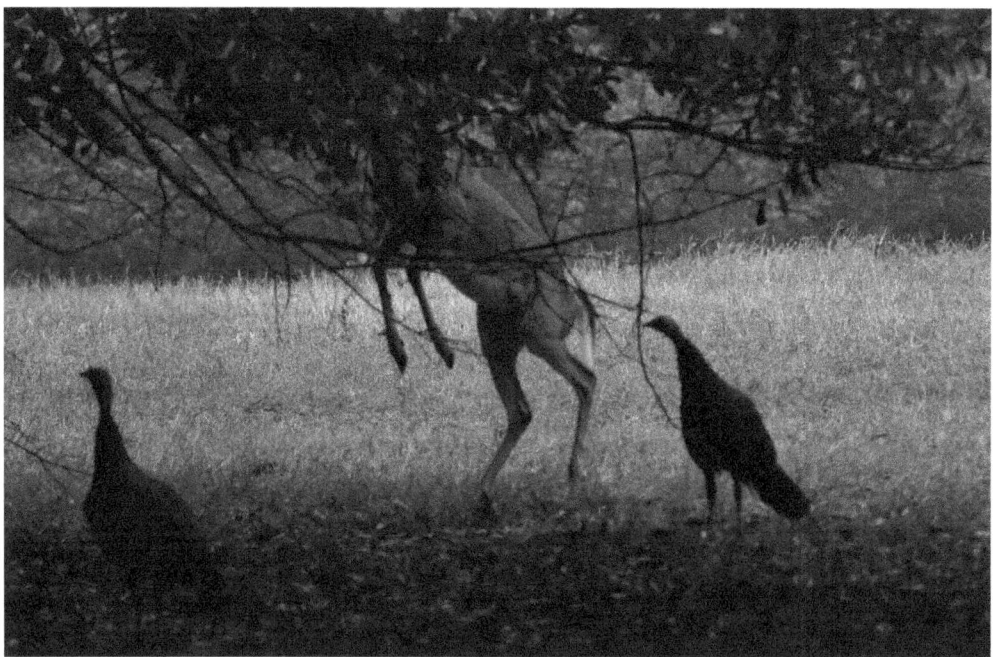

**She bunny-hopped forward several steps while reared up, as if to get a closer look
at the birds that flew up.**

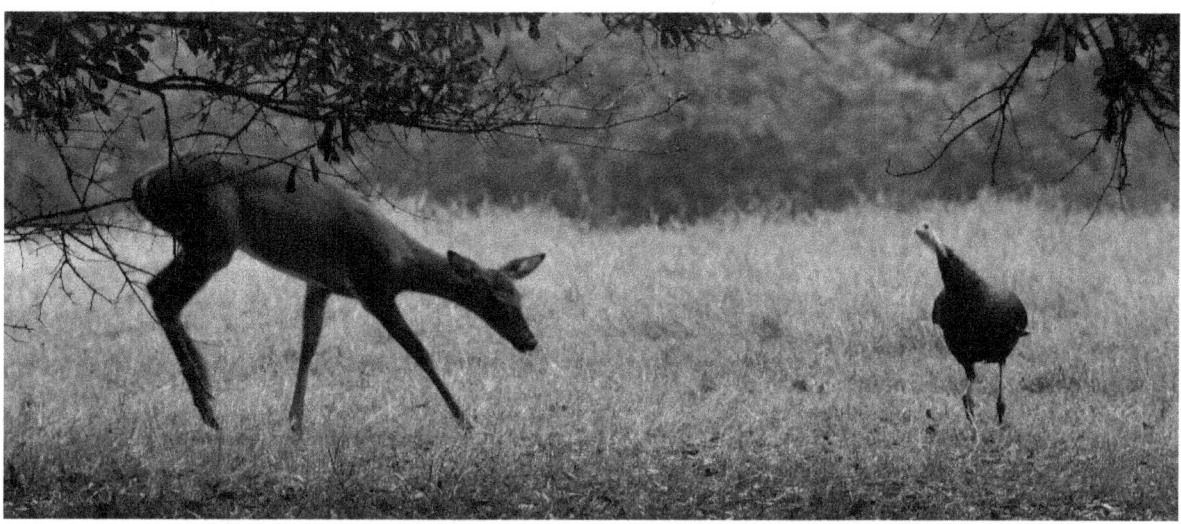

She immediately returned to her game, which ran on for about fifteen minutes. At one point, a buck stood in half-hidden in the trees to watch.

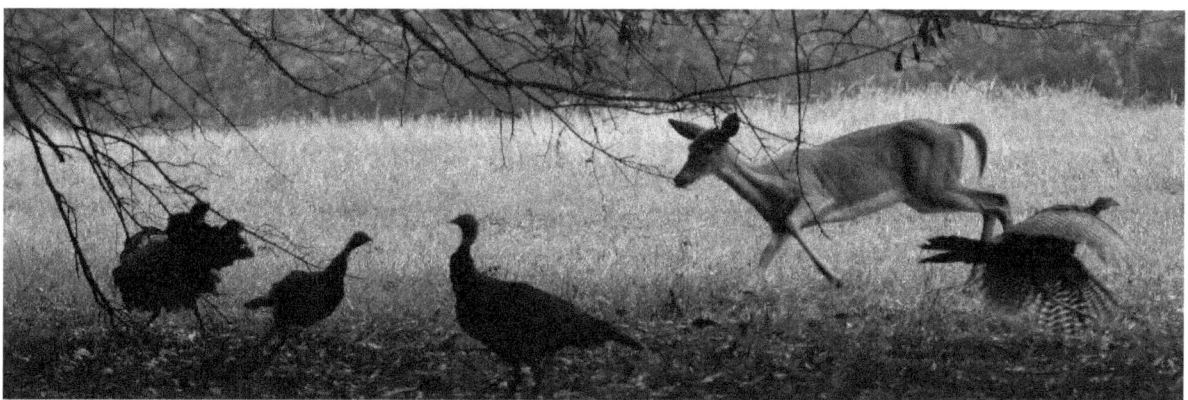

The Turkey Trot

Three toms played a game of chasing one around the other. This trio repeated the game almost daily, usually out of camera range but visible through brush or behind trees.

The oldest dominant tom stood in the center, and the youngest fled the middle-aged one. As the dance continued, the speed increased and the dominant one fluffed up his feathers. Also, note his snood has enlarged as it usually does in the spring mating season, and his wattles are going from blue to red. Early in September, these toms' heads were as blue as those of the hens. The September heat may have affected their hormones, because, out of camera range, I later saw the two older toms strutting.

I call this dance the *turkey trot.*

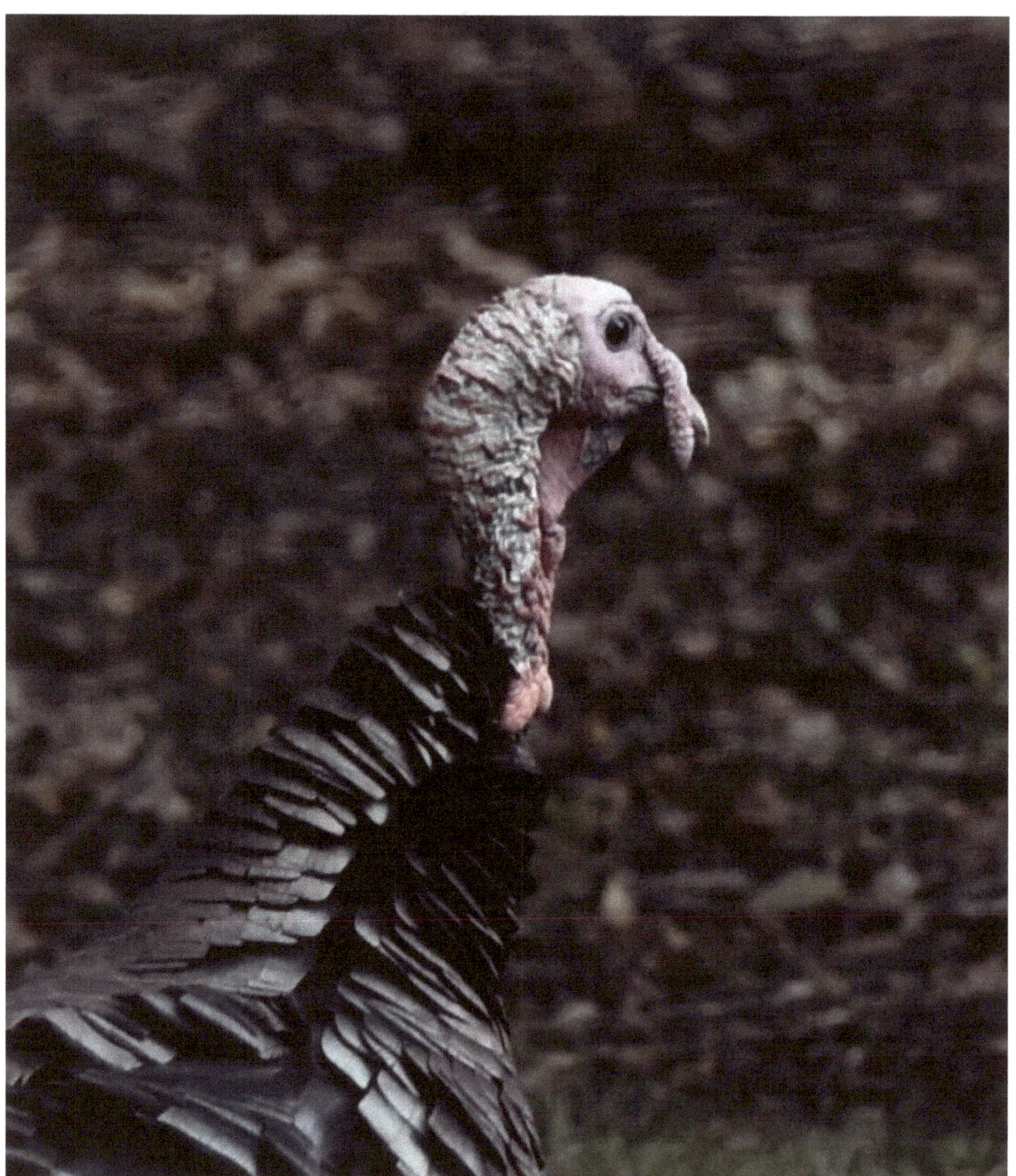

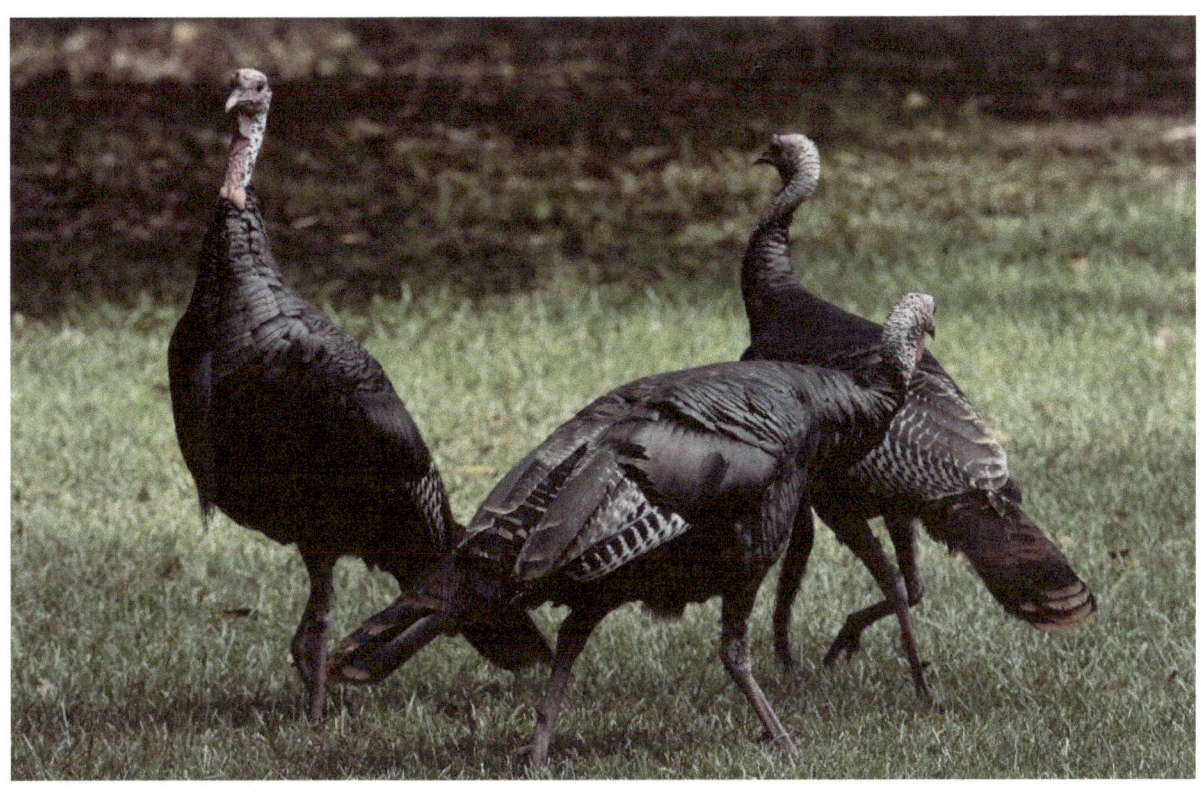

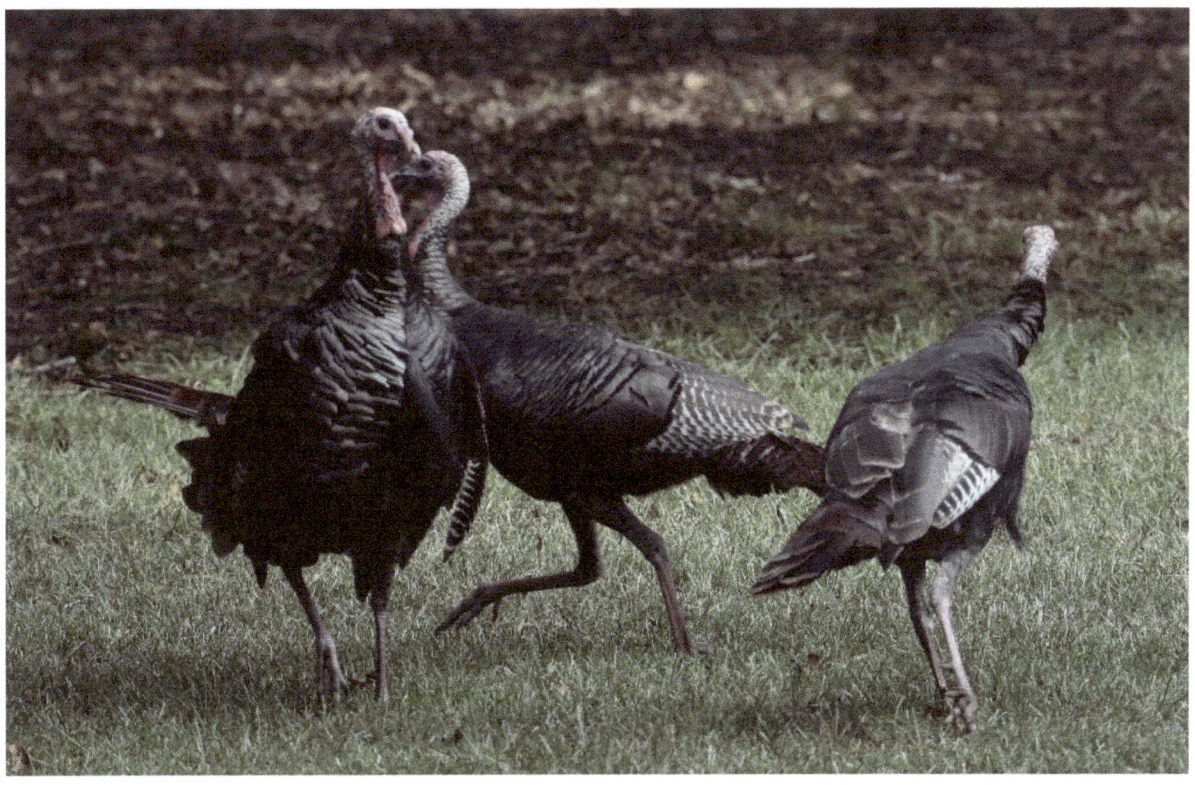

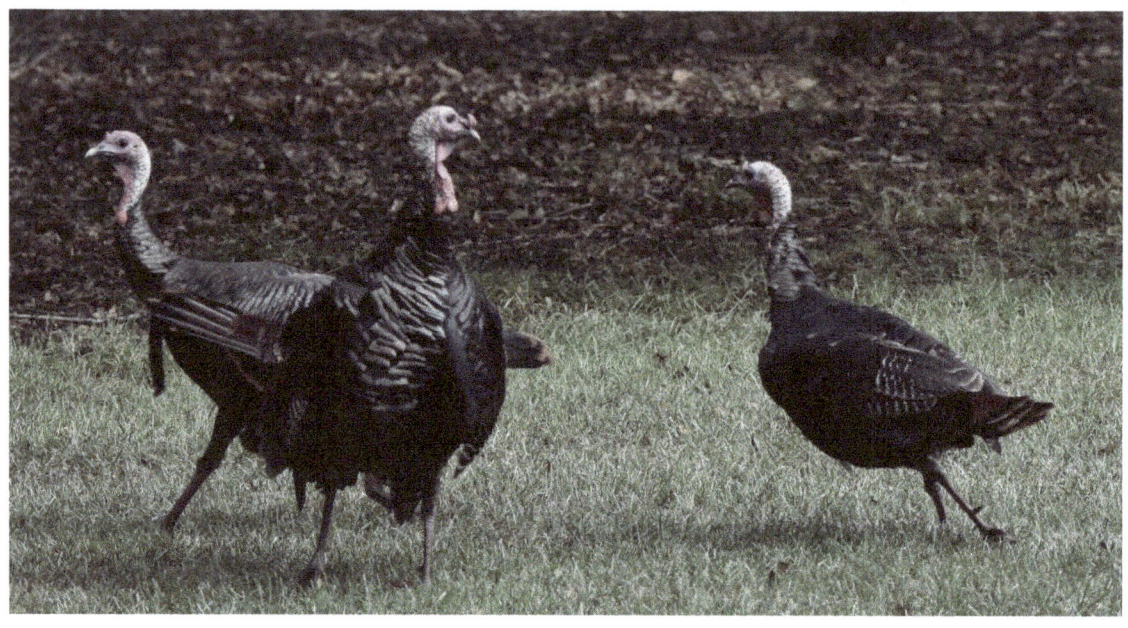

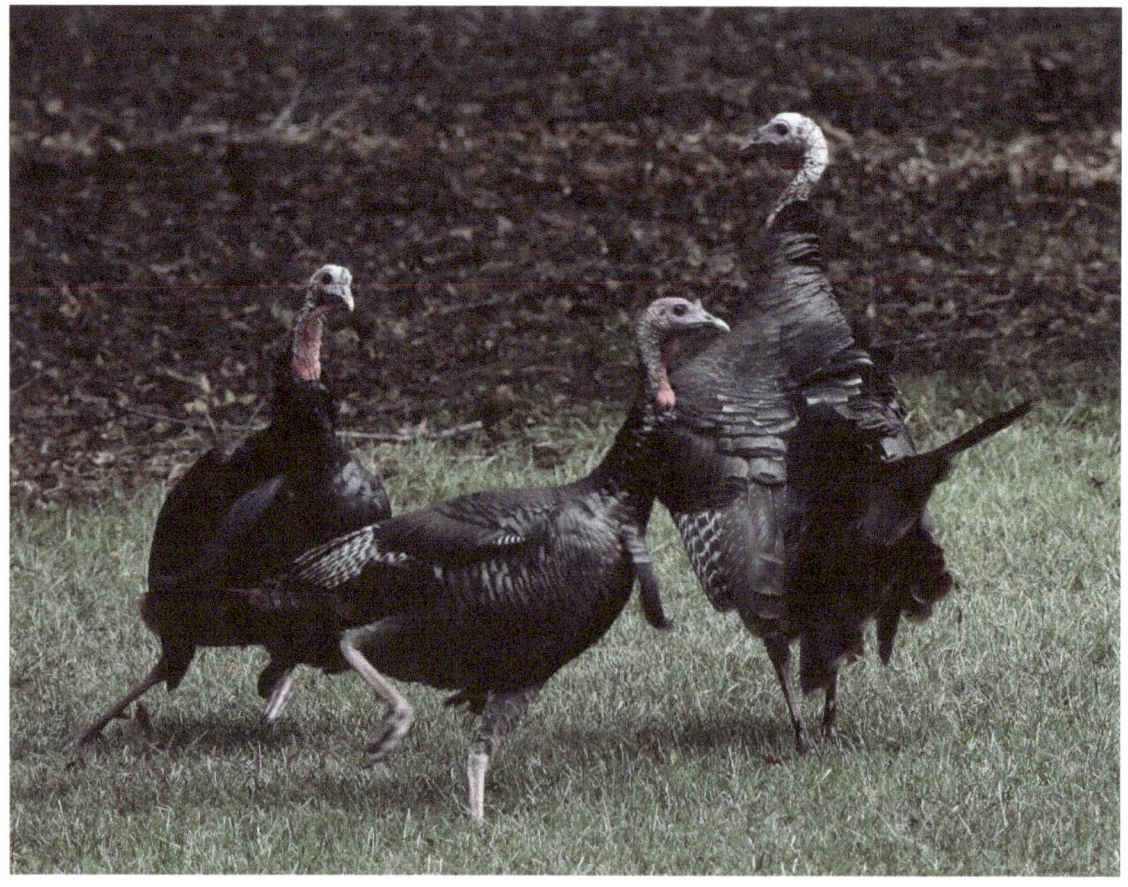

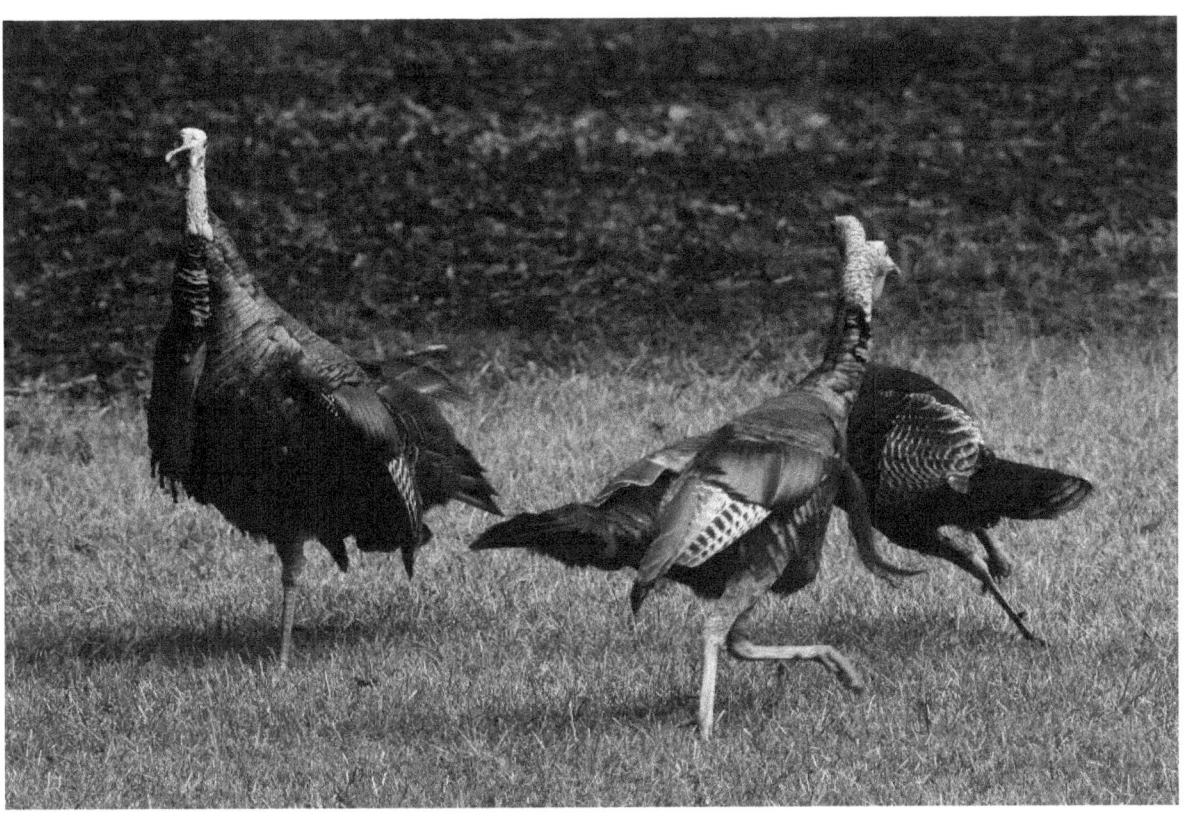

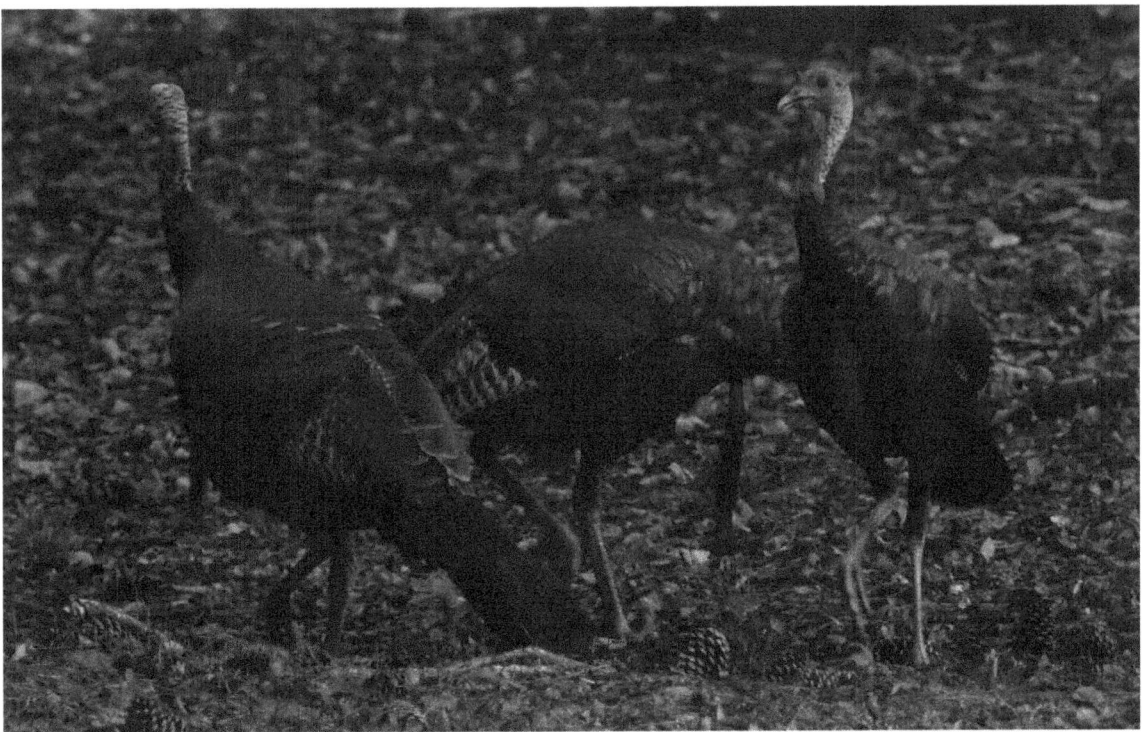

The gobblers moved to the shadows of the woods and continued their dance. The slow beginning moved behind trees as it also turned into a running circle.

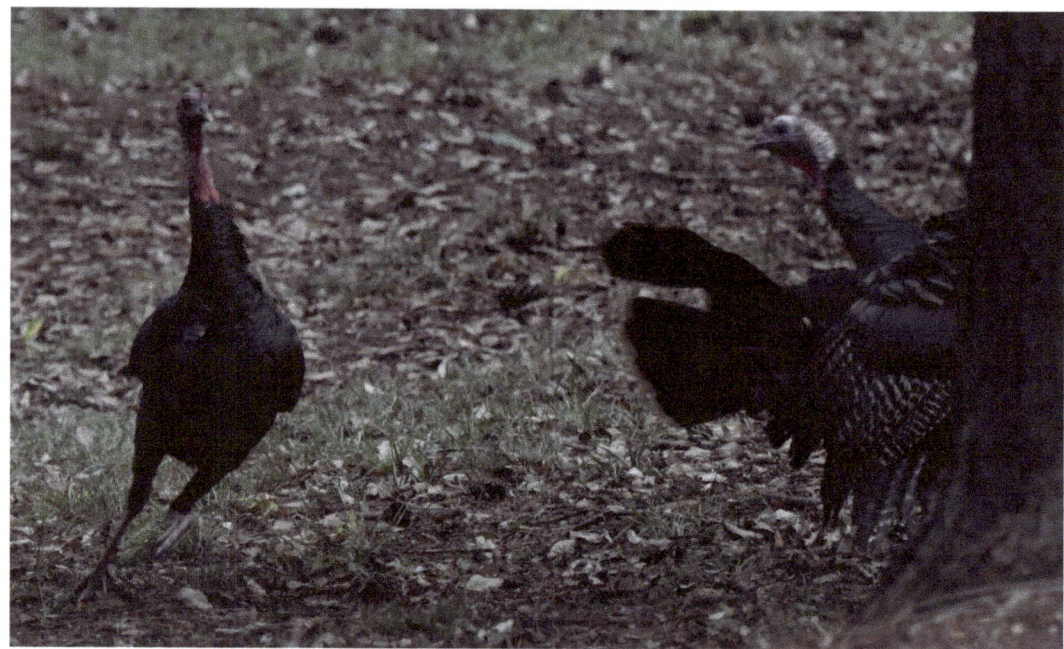

The dancing will continue into the spring. The birds moved into the distant field where I watched through binoculars. The two older toms strutted.

SOME FUN SHOTS

No book about Georgia's wildlife is complete without a picture of a possum. Unfortunately, my yard visitor never came close enough for a decent portrait. All I have in color is this night-time image of him scrounging under the persimmon tree.

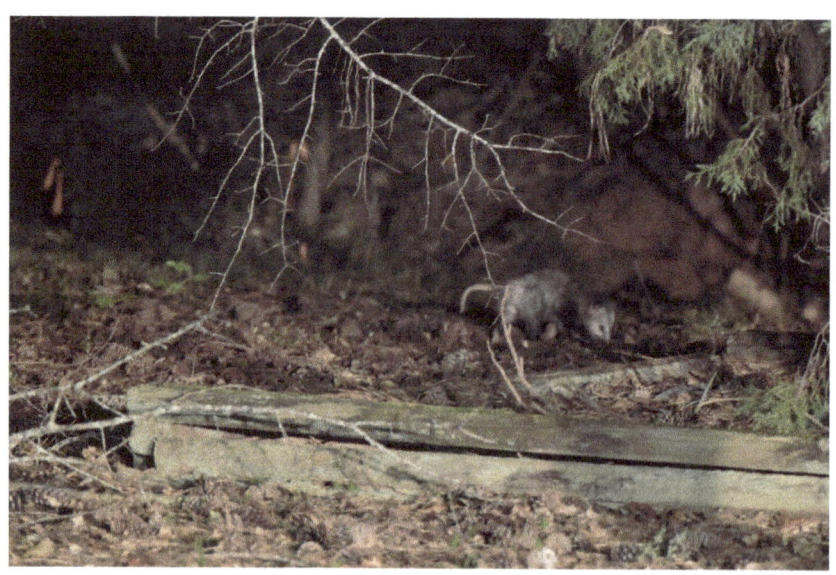

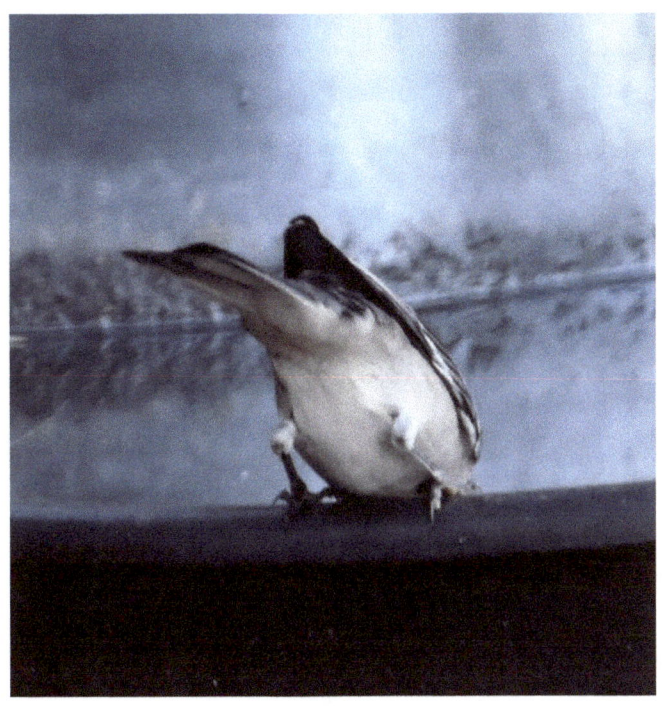

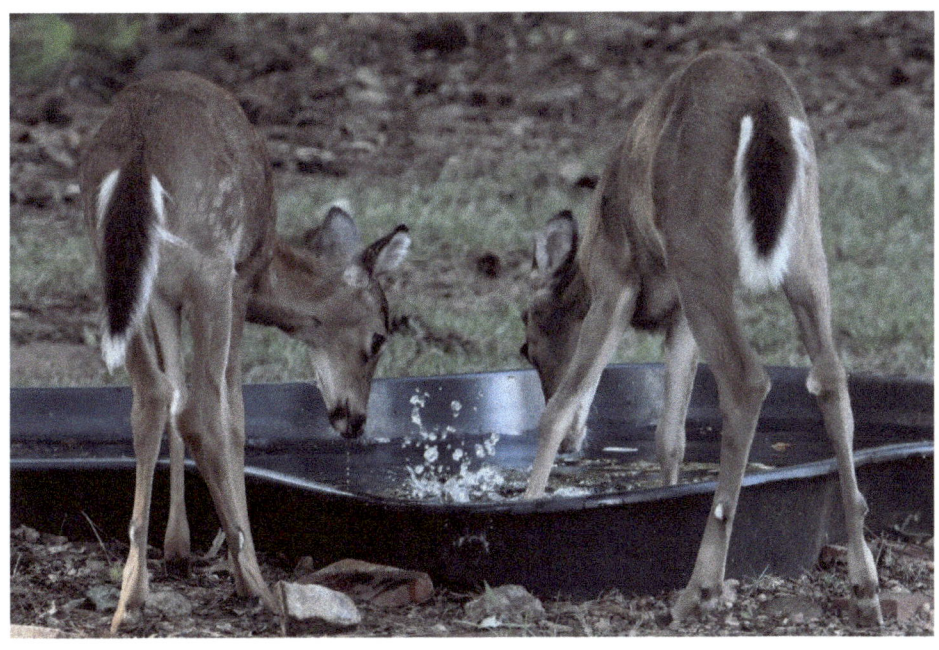

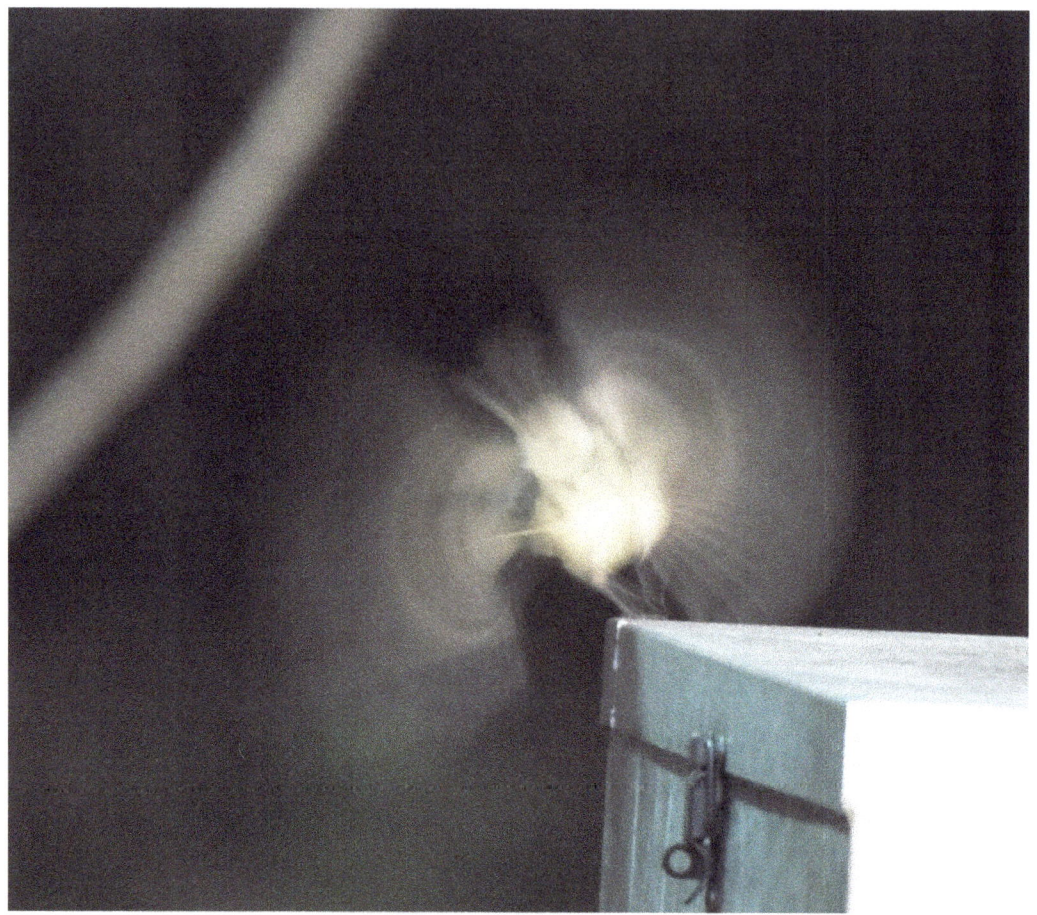

A songbird took flight from the top of the feeder.

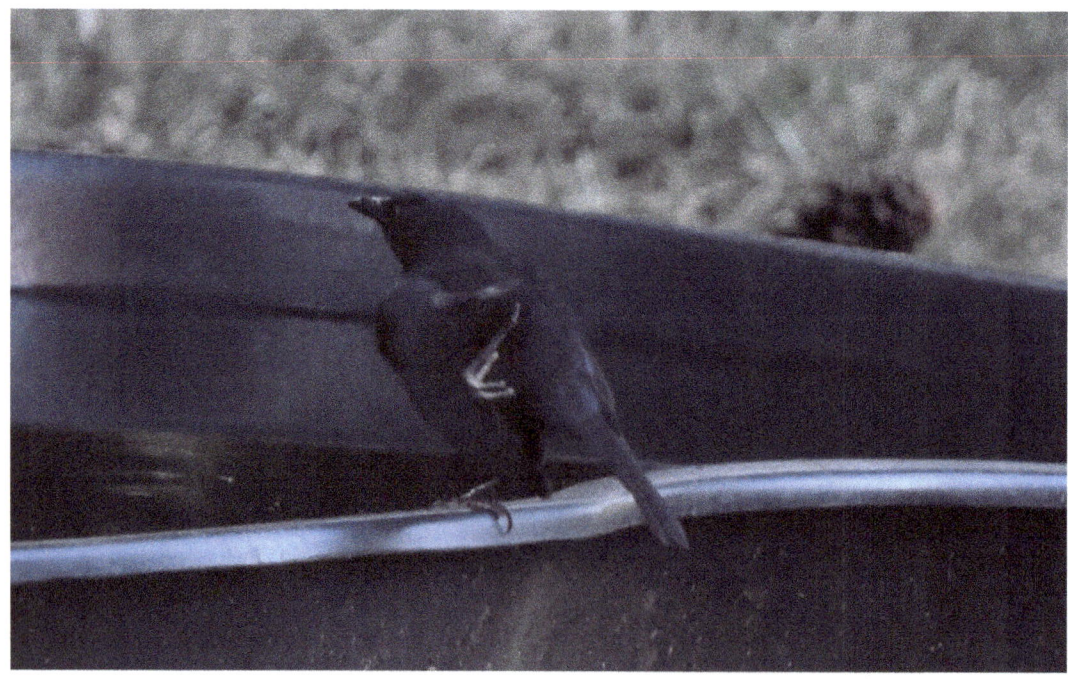

Persimmon Paradise is home to many persimmon trees out of sight of my kitchen window, so I set up a trail camera to overlook one of the trees. It became host to numerous animals, many of whom climbed. The gray fox can climb trees, but I hear tell the red fox cannot.

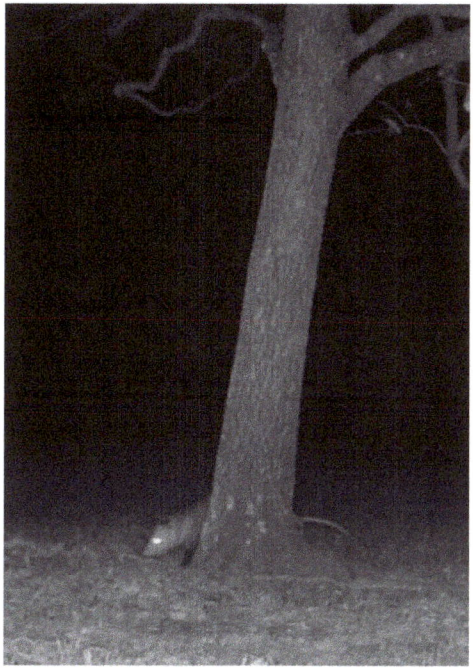
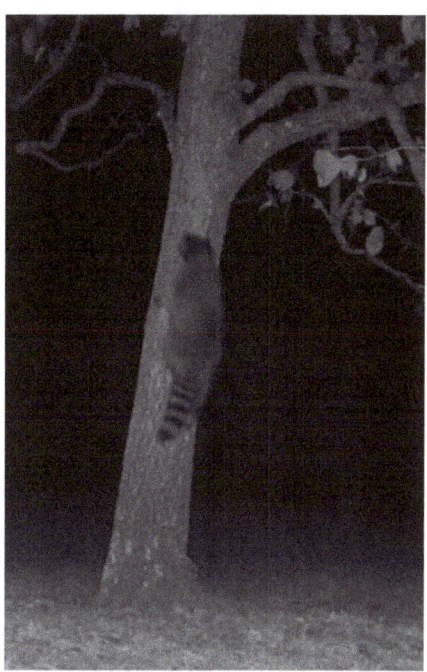

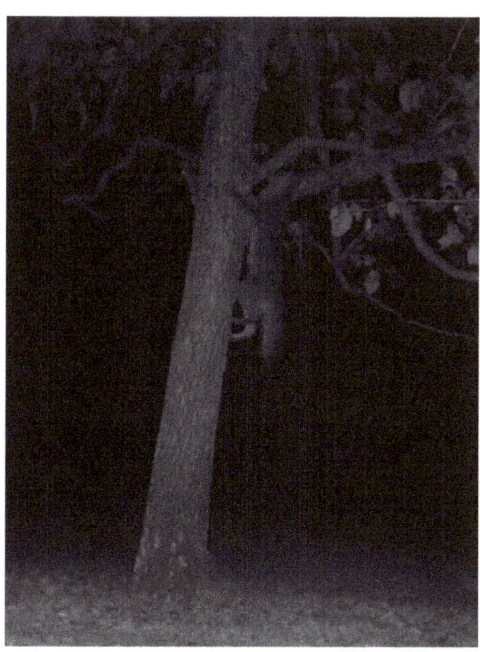
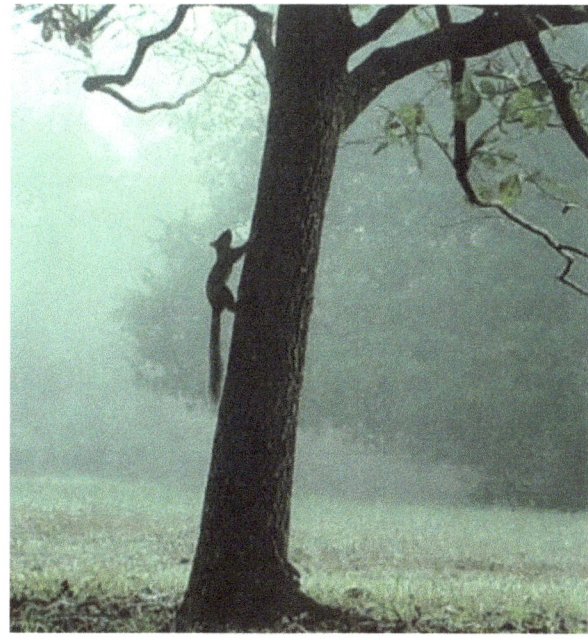

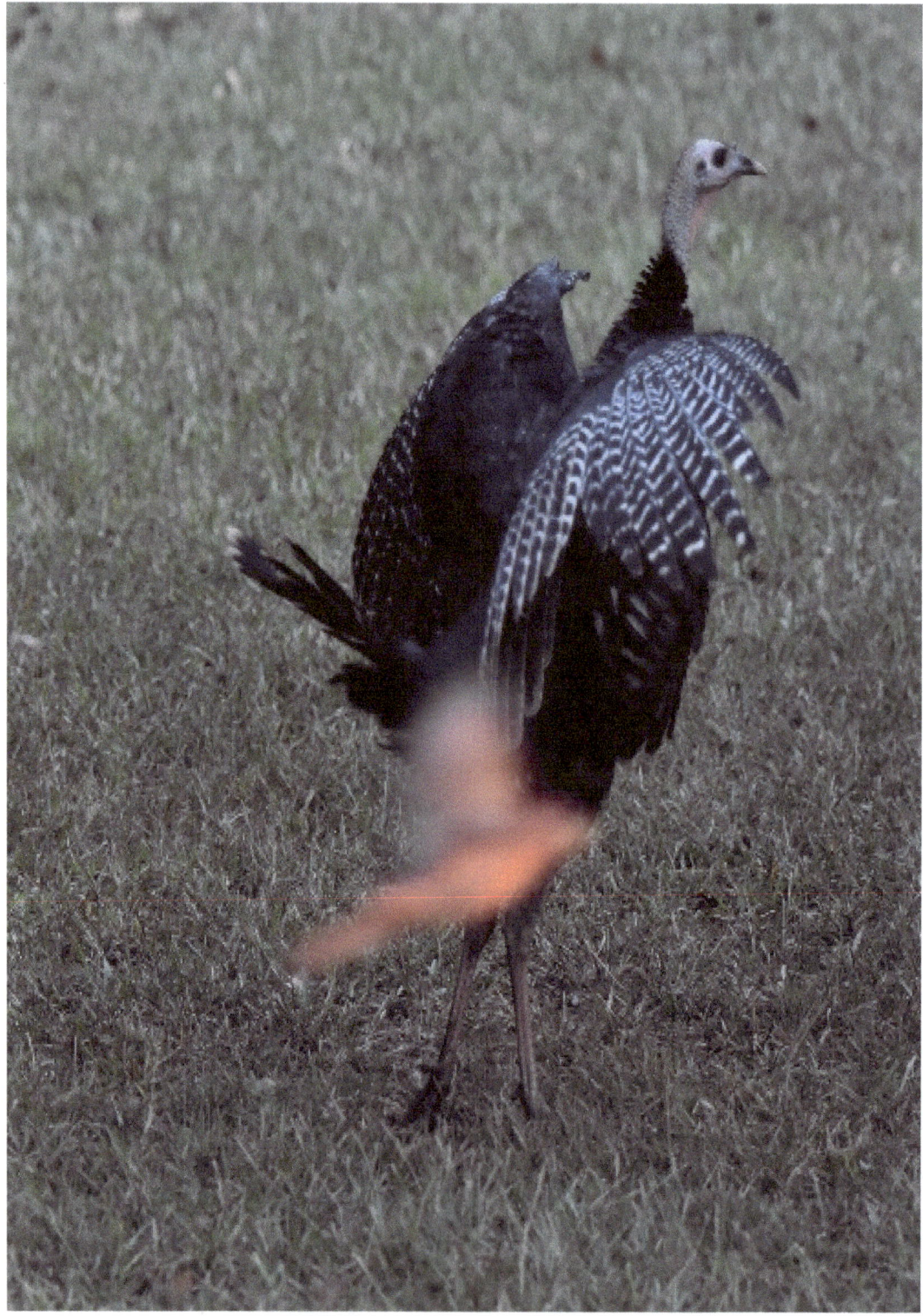

Birds can run interference and ruin an otherwise good picture.

THAT'S ALL, FOLKS. Autumn and persimmons have also run away.

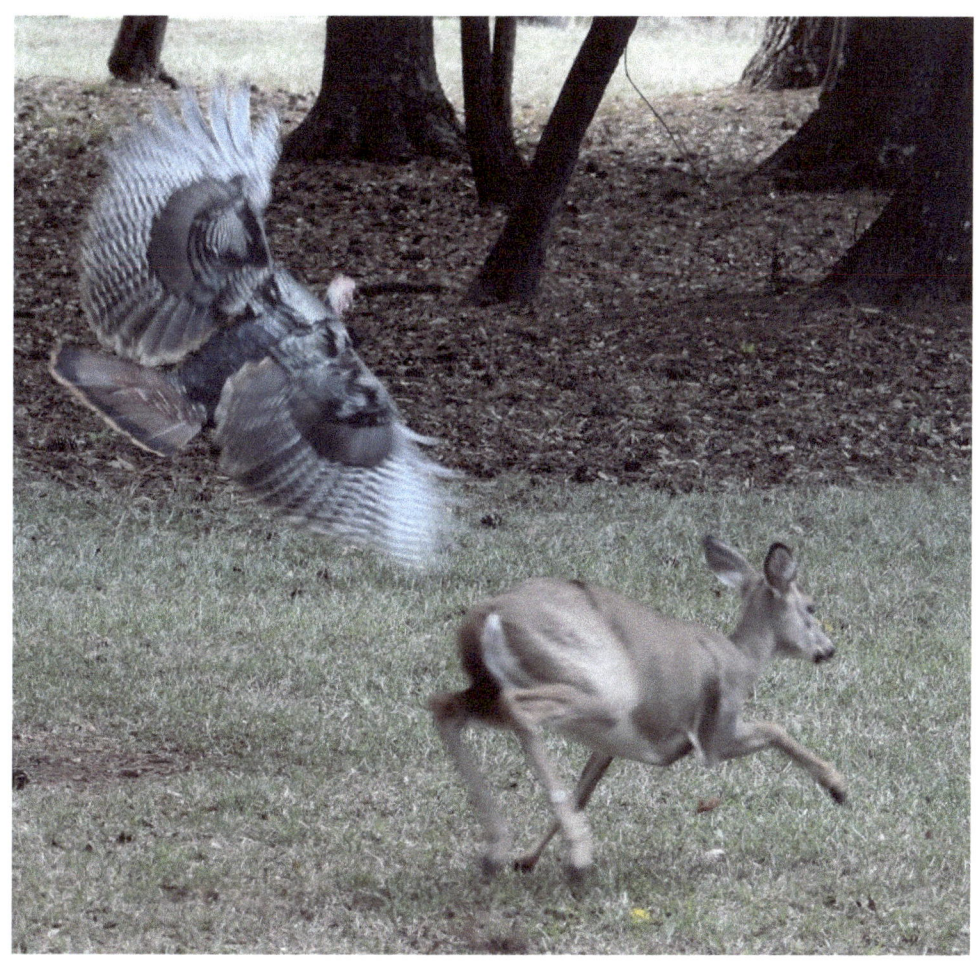

www.ingramcontent.com/pod-product-compliance
Lightning Source LLC
Chambersburg PA
CBHW052141170526
45159CB00017B/3134